ID0933735

Master Traders

Founded in 1807, John Wiley & Sons is the oldest independent publishing company in the United States. With offices in North America, Europe, Australia, and Asia, Wiley is globally committed to developing and marketing print and electronic products and services for our customers' professional and personal knowledge and understanding.

The Wiley Trading series features books by traders who have survived the market's ever changing temperament and have prospered—some by reinventing systems, others by getting back to basics. Whether a novice trader, professional, or somewhere in-between, these books will provide the advice and strategies needed to prosper today and well into the future.

For a list of available titles, visit our web site at www.WileyFinance.com.

Master Traders

**Strategies for
Superior Returns
from Today's
Top Traders**

FARI HAMZEI

WILEY

John Wiley & Sons, Inc.

Published by John Wiley & Sons, Inc., Hoboken, New Jersey.
Published simultaneously in Canada.

For general information on our other products and services or for technical support,
please contact our Customer Care Department within the United States at (800) 762-2974,
outside the United States at (317) 572-3993 or fax (317) 572-4002.

Wiley also publishes its books in a variety of electronic formats. Some content that appears
in print may not be available in electronic books. For more information about Wiley
products, visit our web site at www.wiley.com.

Library of Congress Cataloging-in-Publication Data

Hamzei, Fari, 1957–
    Master traders : strategies for superior returns from today's top traders
/ [edited by] Fari Hamzei.
        p.   cm. — (Wiley trading series)
    Includes index.
    ISBN-13: 978-0-471-79062-4 (cloth)
    ISBN-10: 0-471-79062-1 (cloth)
    1. Speculation.   2. Stocks.   3. Investment analysis.   I. Title. II.
Series.
    HG6041.H275 2006
    332.64—dc22

                                                    2006014069

Printed in the United States of America.

10   9   8   7   6   5   4   3   2   1

In Memory of

Heshmat Afshar-Bakeshlou,
Grandmother dearest
1911–1997

Khadijeh Elahi-Taleghani,
beloved Mother
1931–1998

Patrick B. Crisafulli,
dear friend
1918–2006

Contents

Foreword

A former boss and mentor once said to me that investing is a "business of probabilities, not certainties." Success, therefore, results from one's effort to measure the probability of a certain outcome while accepting the lack of inevitability.

Fancy words perhaps, but much easier said than done. For how can one possibly know all of the inputs needed to make logical estimates? And, in light of the ongoing geopolitical tensions, as well as the unpredictability of interest rates and economic trends, can an investor reasonably hope for anything more than a lucky call now and then? Maybe not, especially when the market's daily volatility shakes, rattles, and rolls one's very confidence. And maybe not, when the media attaches a sense of urgency to every data point, and gives the investor more twists and turns than his favorite chiropractor. In the end, does one really have sufficient control to elevate the probability of success?

The answer is an unequivocal yes, although one would be brazen and less than forthright in minimizing the effort involved in achieving success. Yet, enough people have mastered the daily twists and turns and have developed sufficient financial success to suggest that luck is not a pivotal factor.

Master Traders: Strategies for Superior Returns from Today's Top Traders is a comprehensive and sweeping look at how various individuals continuously master and overcome the emotionalism of every trading day. While not a daily journal, this wonderfully illuminating book succinctly describes the methodologies that have enabled the writers to translate probability into profitability.

Master Traders is not meant to be a how-to book. Rather, each chapter is more of a tutorial that shares with the reader various regimens that have enabled the traders and market analysts who have written these chapters to develop significant degrees of control over their investment destinies. At the same time it is a concession that there are many ways to skin a cat—that the uniqueness and individuality of every trader will probably be the most important factor in gauging the utility of any methodology.

When Fari Hamzei, the eloquent leader of the *Master Traders* effort, asked me to write this Foreword, I fretted and feared that the tone of the book would be didactic and condescending ("do it this way, or else"). I'm pleased to see that the tone and ambiance of *Master Traders* is far from patronizing. Rather, it is more an exhortation—an urging to develop game plans and to practice money management as means of improving the probability of profitability. Methodology and risk control are the common themes in each chapter of *Master Traders*, a beautiful book that, I hope, inculcates in everyone that you really do have a significant degree of control over your future in trading.

Steve Shobin
Vice Chairman
Americap Advisers, LLC

Preface

When I started my investing/trading career some 26 years ago, my passion was being a member of the team that would build the next generation of U.S. Navy air superiority fighter jet and U.S. Air Force advanced strategic bomber—not the stock market. I was the manager of the Operations Analysis Department of Northrop Corporation's Aircraft Division in Hawthorne, California. My only exposure to the stock market in those days was academic, based on my economics and finance courses at Princeton. Then one day, as I was having lunch at my desk, everything changed.

One of my colleagues rushed back from lunch, stopped at my desk and told me that the stock market had just "crashed," and it had "something to do with precious metals." What I would soon learn was that the Hunt Brothers had been forced to liquidate their massive silver positions, which created a domino effect in other markets. It was March 27, 1980, and the Dow Jones Industrial Average put in an intraday low of 729.95 on huge volume.

Being an avid capitalist and a believer in the U.S. economy and the strength of the U.S. financial markets, I wondered if this was an opportune time to hunt for some bargains in the stock market. I called my dear friend and Princeton's Cottage Club mate, Gil Caffray, who was then working at the NYSE specialist firm, Conklin, Cahill & Co. As Gil picked up the line, in the midst of tremendous trading activity for his clients, I asked him point-blank, "Is this a good time to buy?"

"We have a big drop in the market on massive volume," he explained. "This appears to be an important low in the market. So, yes, it is a good time to get in."

"What do I buy?" I asked him eagerly.

His explanation was simple and direct: "Buy America."

My goal was to help my parents build a nest egg. Gil's advice to "buy America" seemed like a great opportunity for them. The next day, I took my father to the Torrance, California, office of Merrill Lynch Pierce Fenner and Smith to open an account, and on the following Monday we started to "buy America." We bought Merrill Lynch, Eastman Kodak, IBM, Schering Plough, General Electric, and so forth. (I bought an equal number of shares for my parents' account; I knew nothing about beta-adjusted equal dollar amounts in those days.)

The ride the following four months was unreal as the market bounced back from that low. I felt like the smartest monkey on earth, blindly throwing darts at the *Wall Street Journal's* quote pages; any stock that we bought went up. When the stock averages hit a plateau, our broker suggested that we start selling calls as a way of generating additional income. The only downside, he explained, was that the stock could get "called away," and as he advised, "No one ever gets poor taking a profit."

My new task was to learn everything I could about call options. I contacted the Northrop library and asked for research on stock options to be pulled for me. That's when I discovered the work of Robert Merton, Fisher Black, and Myron Scholes (of the Black-Scholes model fame). Now I was an official investor—granted, on behalf of my parents—buying securities and writing call options. Two years later, working as a strategic planner in the Advanced Systems Division of Northrop, a fellow strategic planner, Meyer Alpert (an old-timer educated at "Harvard College," as it was known in his day) suggested that I beef up my financial education with a graduate level security analysis course at a local university. I decided to audit courses at the UCLA Anderson Graduate School of Management, where I met Professor Jack Shelton, who in 1967 had devised a corporate warrants pricing model. Options pricing theory owes much of its development to his work. Professor Shelton inspired me to go deeper in my research and trading of options, and as I worked with the Black-Scholes model, the concept of market implied volatility intrigued me from the onset.

At this time, technical analysis was gaining popularity, thanks in part to Dr. Marty Zweig, the inventor of the Simple Put/Call ratio. Armed with my original Apple II Computer and programming donated by my younger brother, Kory, I began studying things such as divergences of the advance/decline line versus key market indexes, and how to use this information for intermediate market timing. Then came the October 1987 crash. Fortunately, I had sidelined myself after partially cashing out on the previous August peak. I had left Northrop in 1983 and now was an entrepreneur involved in two technology-based companies, including as president of a high-tech text messaging company, and had become active in real estate–backed exotic mortgage securities.

In October 1990, with oil hitting a peak price of $40 a barrel (equivalent to $86 per barrel in 2006 dollars), I was working out of my office in Century City, next to the Northrop corporate headquarters overlooking the Los Angeles Country Club. This was just prior to the first Gulf War, and I was trading my own money using XMI options. To continue my financial education—now as a trader and an investor—I enrolled in a very popular derivatives course taught at UCLA by the visiting Professor Edward Thorp of the University of California at Irvine. Back in 1973, Professor Thorp, the author of the bestsellers *Beat the Dealer* (New York: Blaisdell/Random House, 1962) and *Beat the Market* (New York: Random House, 1967), had derived and published extensions to the Black-Scholes model allowing stock option contracts on stocks paying a finite series of dividends and having European-style exercise features to be properly priced.

As I relate in Chapter 7, I was looking at the same indicators as everyone else. This was most unnerving to me. I always seek to have an edge, whether I am playing a friendly game of squash or investing/trading in equities and derivatives. This led me, in November 1998, to develop the first generation of Dollar-Weighted Put/Call Ratio code, which in time would become the centerpiece of Hamzei Analytics. The following year, I beta-tested my system with the help of a fellow index trader who was a portfolio manager at Prudential Securities in Pasadena, California. On April 4, 2000—the day the NASDAQ Composite dropped more than 630 points on an intraday basis—the software program experienced its baptism by fire.

Now, fast-forward to today. I am the founder of Hamzei Analytics, LLC, with a stable of proprietary market sentiment indicators, and the proud host of a site that draws men and women of the trading community whom I admire and trust. Sharing information, market insight, and camaraderie makes our work at the trading screens immensely enjoyable and rewarding. In addition, Hamzei Analytics has the honor of being ranked by *Timer Digest*, and as of May 5, 2006, had tied for first place for stock market timing for the trailing 90 days, 180 days, and 52 weeks among approximately 150 market timers.

Most important, I have always enjoyed studying the work of highly competent people and their research on the markets. Indeed, I have been privileged to assemble a dream team for this book, *Master Traders*, with the active support and tireless encouragement of Gil Caffray and Steve Shobin, who helped shape and shepherd this outstanding lineup. Our publisher, John Wiley & Sons, immediately embraced this concept, and offered tremendous support (and understanding when traders sometimes sidestep deadlines . . .) to bring this project to fruition.

The real stars of this show are the individual contributors, professional traders and analysts covering many disciplines who undertook masterful dissertations on the market. Without their willingness to give of their time, talent, experience, and wisdom, and their commitment, passion, and attention to detail, this book would not have been possible. Amid turbulent times in our financial markets, they wrote chapters that inspire and inform—which is nothing less than a Herculean accomplishment.

I wish to recognize them individually and collectively here:

- Frank Barbera, co-manager of the Caruso Fund, which trades precious metals, stocks, and currencies, whose technical work in gold and silver stocks is considered among the best in the industry.
- Greg Collins, chief operating officer and portfolio manager of Tuttle Asset Management.
- Timothy Corliss, partner and director of trading at Sierra Global Management, a fund that invests primarily in European derivatives.
- Jeff deGraaf, chief technical analyst at Lehman Brothers, and a perennially top-ranked technical analyst on Wall Street.
- Phil Erlanger, president of Phil Erlanger Research, and twice president of Market Technician Association, as well as former senior technical analyst for Fidelity Management.
- Alex Jacobson, vice president of education at the International Securities Exchange (ISE) and a former vice president of business development for the Chicago Board Options Exchange (CBOE).
- Dennis Leontyev, chief executive officer of Experity Group, LLC, a hedge fund company, where he is the portfolio manager for two market-neutral derivative hedge funds.
- David Miller, CEO and co-founder of Biotech Stock Research, LLC, publisher of *Biotech Monthly* and one of the few independent small-cap biotech research firms.
- Jon "Doctor J" Najarian, co-founder and partner of Najarian Capital; founder of InsideOptions.com, an online publisher of options and futures commentary; and a former CBOE designated primary market maker.
- Tim Ord, president, editor, and publisher of "The Ord Oracle," which reports on the S&P, NASDAQ, and gold issues, and frequently listed in the top 10 of market timers in the country.
- Steve Shobin, vice chairman of AmeriCap Advisers, LLC, and former senior vice president of Lehman Brothers.
- Jeffrey Spotts, hedge fund manager at Prophecy Funds, a technically managed hedge fund catering to institutions, pensions, and family offices, and a recognized expert on technical analysis.
- Kai-Teh Tao, president of Asgard Management, LLC., an institutional money management firm that opportunistically invests utilizing proprietary fundamental research derived from its broad network of contacts.

- Kevin Tuttle, president and chief equity strategist of Tuttle Asset Management, and co-founder of Church Street Capital, LLC, which runs a managed growth portfolio for high-net-worth clientele.

With my profound thanks and admiration for these contributors, I am honored to present *Master Traders* with the sincere wish that it educate, enlighten, and empower us all—regardless of our level or experience in trading. For the trader who stops learning is soon sidelined. Knowledge is power, especially when your hard-earned money is on the line.

All the best,

> Fari Hamzei
> Founder
> Hamzei Analytics, LLC

Acknowledgments

In honor of my mentors:

- At Farhad School: Mrs. Tooran Mirhadi.
- At Princeton University: Gil Caffray, Provost Neal Rudenstine, Dean Howard Menand, Professor Burton Malkiel, the late Professor Stuart Hunter, Professor Charles Issawi, Professor Fouad Ajami, Professor Bernard Lewis, and Astronaut Charles "Pete" Conrad.
- At Northrop Grumman Corporation: Dr. Donald A. Hicks, M.O. Hesse, Warren Klauer, James D. Willson, and Kent Kresa.
- At UCLA Anderson Graduate School of Management: Professor Jack Shelton, Professor Ed Thorp, Professor Bob Geske, and Professor Richard Roll.
- At Electronic Clearing House: Herbert Lucas, Carl Schafer, and Larry Thomas.

With highest esteem for their invaluable contributions to the financial markets: Professor Robert Whaley at Duke University Fuqua School of Business, and Professor John Hull at University of Toronto Rothman School of Management.

Saluting fellow traders: Brad Sullivan, Mike Heraty, Pete Stolcers, Sally Limantour, Geoffrey Garbucz, James DiGeorgia, Skip Shean, Arnon Kolerstein, Kris Monaco, Dan Zanger, Peter Schultz, Dave Baker, Stan Harley, Larry Katz, Barbara Star, Carl Swenlin, Sunny Harris, Peter Slaga, Margery Nelson, Charmaine Balian, Bijan Khezri, Dimitri Villard, Steve Salek, Omid Nikzad, Max Vafi, Kevin Haggerty, Jim Bittman, Miles Dunbar, Carl Rafiepour, Nestor Turczan, Bill Wong, Joseph Del Rivo, Marshall Fried, Greg McKay, Don Coyne, Helen Lepor, Sterling Nelson, Roberta Brown, John LaRocca, and Bruce Arnheim.

With greatest respect for the financial media: Bob Pisani, Mary Thompson, Tom Costello, Leslie Dodson Laroche, Alexis Glick, Scott Cohn, Julie Hyman, Aaron Task, Dan Fitzpatrick, Dan Colarusso, Jim Schmidt, Todd Harrison, and Kevin Wassong.

Recognizing my tireless dream team at Hamzei Analytics, LLC: Lawrence Studnicky, Lawrence Brown, Nancy Scott, Maya Sobolev, Matt Boyce, Jing Shao, Randy Ali, Tom Sawyer, Mark Staskus; and the senior technical staffs at eSignal (Jason Keck), TradeStation, and Townsend Analytics (Joe Goldberg and Jeremy Spanos).

Many thanks to friends and supporters: Elizabeth & Kevin Weiss, Don Seitz, Whitney Baldwin, Skip Walsh, Cathleen Hoza Lysak, Bo Torrey, Kim Torrey Kraus, John Bodel and Brian Morris (aka Bomo), Jack Herbert, Bill Hines, George Howell, Hamp Skelton, Catherine McCarthney Miller, Dennis Love, Scott Quackenbush, Bruce Quackenbush, Ella Cooper, Matthew Glinka, Jim Rutherford, Bob Turecamo, Chris Rulon-Miller, Bob Klein, Tom Leighton, Tom Page, Nancy Gengler, Nader Safai, Farhad Safai, Leah Lundquist, Richard Lundquist, Tricia Crisafulli, Joe Tulacz, Chuck Thompson, Marisa Arnold, Raphel Finelli, Darla Tuttle, Kevin Edgmon, Med Nikbin, Mitch Zarrabi, Lou Friedmann, Mike Felix, Kambiz Shokati, Ladan & Massoud Atefi, Mahsha Behzadi, Behzad Shahpar, Ramin Khajevi, Firooz Farmand, Parviz Ilbagian, Rob Sepasi, Sam Sepasi, David Afradi, Kash Mokhber, Amir Ansari, Bradley Benjamin, Vegis Nuri, and German Bitar.

With love to my family and those dearest to me: Dad, Ahmad, Hamid, Nahid, Kory, Pearl, Nader, Siamak, Ashley, Tess, and Julie Anne Carruthers.

And with special thanks to my Wiley editors: Kevin Commins, who espoused the vision for this book from inception, Emilie Herman, who tirelessly marched forward on the project while taking no prisoners, Laura Walsh, and Todd Tedesco.

And I seek forgiveness from those too numerous to mention here without whom I could not have embarked on this lifelong journey that led to this project.

INTRODUCTION

Trader Evolution and the Keys to Success

Greg Collins

I am not a master trader. Rather, I share—no doubt with all of you—a desire to learn more about what it takes to become a *more successful* trader. To that end, I've been fortunate enough to spend the last few years working and interacting with countless gifted professionals. As I worked with these "masters," I listened and learned. And, while there is no substitute for sitting in the bunker with great traders day after day, this book does contain helpful guidance that a number of astute professionals have agreed to share. Great traders follow no set of secret recipes; rather, they acknowledge that trading is as much art as science.

This book focuses on how the contributors achieve their own brand of master trading. None of them claims to have figured out the stock market in its entirety. What they have managed to find is a system that works for them. As you read their discussions of systems and strategies, you will sometimes be reviewing basics. But even master traders who have moved on to greater levels of sophistication understand the need to conquer the basics and progress beyond them. The contributors to this book are, first and foremost, students of the markets, willing to offer ideas and share a career-long commitment to learning.

If you had a 30-minute lesson with Ben Hogan, you would not spend it asking him what type of ball to hit or what kind of grips he kept on his clubs. Sure, you would want any tips he was willing to impart, but an issue of *Golf Digest* could tell you a variation on the same. No, what you'd *really* want to learn is how he found his greatness; what extra something allowed him to separate himself from the pack—what made him an artist among athletes; what made him a master.

Numerous books have been written by investment professionals, so let's begin with a discussion of how this book is unique. Sure, an analysis of the investments and strategies of Warren Buffett or George Soros would be a fascinating read—they are icons in the investment world. But the question remains, how directly applicable are their megabuck, market-moving strategies to most professionals? The focus of *this* book is on exposing practical methodologies with the hope that you can find an idea or two to actually incorporate into your daily routine or your thought process. It's the difference between watching a bass fishing tournament and learning how to catch dinner for yourself.

As a disclaimer, there are obviously many great traders out there, and we certainly do not claim to have included all of them. On some levels, the selection process was akin to an age-old barroom discussion: If you could assemble the ultimate baseball player by combining the talents of multiple baseball players from history, who would you incorporate? "Add Babe Ruth's power plus Lou Brock's speed plus Pete Rose's determination, and I'd say you've got the ultimate ball player," might be one response. A more relevant discussion, to better compare with the task at hand, is to ask the question, "Which athletes *from any sport* would you combine to make the ideal baseball player?" In this case, the answer might be, "the power of Jim Brown, the speed of Carl Lewis, and the determination of Lance Armstrong."

Obviously, such a task is subject to intense debate and there is no boilerplate right answer. Our quest is to better understand what separates truly gifted traders from the rest of the pack—a chore that centers on combining unique attributes from wide-ranging skill sets and perspectives. To further comprehend the notion of a master trader, I spoke to numerous professionals in the investment business, individuals ranging from rookie traders to billion-dollar managers. When I finished boiling down all the elements of a successful trader, I found that such traders exhibit, in varying forms and across numerous specialties, a number of key characteristics that I would like to share.

SELF-AWARENESS

Perhaps the most valuable exercise for anyone seeking to become a more successful trader is a simple but thorough self-evaluation. The importance of understanding your own strengths, weaknesses, habits, and biases cannot be overemphasized.

Another aspect of self-awareness centers around the contention that not all human beings are born to trade stocks. That statement is (at least in part) confirmed by some research on the human limbic system, which reveals that the human brain contains an amazingly complex set of wiring that does not equip all of us with the delicate balance between its left and right sides that is critical to trading successfully. Review the following checklist to help avoid some of the potential obstacles that trip up many traders, and ask yourself how many apply to you.

- *Set realistic goals.* Most traders talk about the balance between risk and reward but many do not practice what they preach in their actual trading decisions. Often, traders fail to align the risk/reward dynamic with a consideration for the appropriate time frame. Rome was not built in a day; neither is the accumulation of wealth.
- *Control emotions.* We've all known that emotions can become a trader's worst enemy. We cannot rid ourselves of emotions; we can only prepare for them and be aware of the impact they will have on our decision-making process. Successful traders keep tabs on their emotional capital as closely as they do their monetary capital. They have learned to harness those potentially damaging emotions and have turned them into motivating forces.
- *Adapt.* Human beings tend to seek confirmation of their existing views and to see only what they want to see. In many ways, traders should play the role of detective—what do the clues or evidence suggest? Keep an open mind and understand the perspective of traders who are on the opposite side of the trade. The market is a constantly changing system. Failing to adapt to market changes by falling in love with ideas, themes, or companies is a potentially harmful affair.
- *Do not force trades.* Patience and the ability to *not* trade are skills great traders understand. Too many traders make a mistake and attempt to recover by doing something outside the scope of their approach (such as overtrading) or forcing opportunities where they don't exist. These traders stray from their established strategies and employ hope. Hope is not an investment strategy.

HUMILITY

We've all heard the phrase, "Stay humble or the market will do it for you." Time and time again, arrogance and pride creep into the equation and cause major problems. If you've been a trader for any length of time, you've undoubtedly experienced both sides of the pendulum. It is important to realize that you're not as good as you think you are at your highest;

nor as bad as you believe when you are at your worst. In fact, some of the most self-deprecating individuals in this business are those who have achieved great results. No one walks on water. In order to work through tough times and maintain balance, consider the following aspects of humility.

- *Accept responsibility.* I've seen even the most experienced traders blame an action or inaction on the thoughts or advice of others. Take ownership of your decisions and be willing to live with the consequences.
- *Recognize cause and effect.* Often traders are rewarded (in the short run, anyway) despite a false premise, improper framing of a scenario, or unsubstantiated analysis. This positive reinforcement cements bad habits, skews perspective, and creates a false sense of accomplishment. Detach yourself, step back, and take an honest look at your activity and the underlying reasons for it. Comprehend the difference between cause and effect and randomness, between luck and skill, before patting yourself on the back.
- *Ask for help!* Humble people are not afraid to ask for help or admit they are wrong. Our society looks at these actions as weakness. There will always be people with more experience who can add insight and perspective to help keep the rest of us grounded. Be savvy enough to learn from the lessons others have already paid for—it could be the best investment you make.

STRATEGY AND FOCUS

Trading is a serious endeavor and must be treated as a business. The rise of technology, the development of hyper-liquid trading vehicles, and the ease of access to markets have unfortunately resulted in the misconception by some that trading is a video game—that they are traders simply because they can easily execute trades. The major focus of this book is on the unique methodologies utilized by the contributors. Those methodologies focus on the following:

- *Develop a blueprint.* A house is not built without a plan for creating a solid foundation to ensure its structural integrity. So, too, must a trader be grounded in his system. Without adequate plans, you've simply built the proverbial house of cards.
- *Think for yourself.* GMO Chairman Jeremy Grantham said, "If you are not prepared to be different, you will lose money." The process to-

ward differentiation begins with seeing what others don't. In other words, understand where the herd is most at risk.

- *Focus.* By focus, I am referring to a recognition of what the markets are focused on, not what you think they *should* be focused on. There is a tremendous difference. Hearing the market's message requires immense concentration and discipline.

CONSISTENCY

We cannot predict the future. We can only rely on a well-planned trading/investment approach that is based on preparation, a consistent application, and a constant effort to hone skills that will guide us on the path toward profitability. Growing up in Baltimore, I developed a special appreciation for former Orioles superstar Cal Ripken, Jr. In many ways, Ripken embodies the notion of consistency traders must seek to sustain success: immense preparation, a solid approach, and a desire to fight the fight—every day. Over time, the application of these key ideas will yield results.

- *Excellence is repeatable.* Good golfers know that mechanics—consistent putting, good swings, and solid contact with the ball—are the keys to low scores. Over the course of a round, we may get lucky on a few bad swings and end up with adequate results; but luck, like that of a gambler in Vegas, will turn. Only discipline and consistency provide results over time. Former Tiger Management executive Gil Caffray addressed this point by defining consistency as the "repeatability of excellence." What sets the master trader apart is the ability to execute his strategy over and over and over again.
- *Trading is a marathon, not a sprint.* Perhaps Americas Cup Skipper Dennis Conner captured this characteristic best: "My goal in sailing isn't to be brilliant or flashy in individual races, just to be consistent over the long run." Skilled traders understand that results are a function of not simply a few great trades but rather a lifetime of good trades.

RISK MANAGEMENT

There are no certainties in trading. Trading is a game of understanding the delicate balance between the right amount of risk and reward. Successful traders understand both sides of the equation, just as trauma surgeons do: Sometimes it is necessary to cut off a hand to save the rest of the body.

- *Protect capital.* You can't win from the sidelines, so the key is obviously to stay in the game. Determining how much capital a trader is willing to risk on any one idea or trade is crucial to success. Oftentimes, traders fail to take *appropriate* risk, subjecting the portfolio to greater risks when they shouldn't and failing to take enough risk precisely when they should. Remember, swinging for the fence also increases the risk of striking out.
- *Evaluate probabilities.* Sophisticated traders view risk in terms of potential. In other words, just because risk has yet to present itself does not imply that it doesn't exist. I've heard a few astute traders talk about risk by way of physics, noting that quantum physicists view the world as a mathematical set of probabilities. Those probabilities, they point out, are real and shift over time. This is an important way for a trader to think about risk.

PERSISTENCE

Peter Lynch once commented that the stomach is the most important part of the body when it comes to investing. Others might make a similar case for the brain. However, I would offer that more paramount than either is the heart. As with so many other things in life, success is partially a function of who wants it most and who is willing to do what it takes to get to the top of the mountain.

- *Deal with loss.* You have to risk money to make money, and sometimes you *are* going to lose. Winners know how to pick themselves up off the mat quickly and study what they did wrong so they won't repeat it. Muhammad Ali managed to capture the heavyweight title three times, even after losses in between.
- *Become an expert.* Whatever path you choose, dedicate yourself to learning as much as you can about a particular area of interest you have. Whether it be technicals, fundamentals, psychology, a macro perspective, or an industry-specific analysis, immerse yourself and obtain an edge that no one can take away.
- *Be a student of the market.* The markets can turn on a dime; we must constantly evolve with them, if for no other reason than the financial

markets of tomorrow will be vastly different from what they are to-day. Learning is what keeps us mentally prepared, motivated, and skilled. Maintain an intellectual curiosity about the markets and question everything.

EXPERIENCE AND INSTINCT

Experience and instinct help in rapidly assessing the market environment. College basketball coach Bobby Knight uses the acronym C-A-R-R-E when discussing a mental framework with his players: concentrate, anticipate, recognize, react, execute. That framework applies to trading particularly well, and experienced traders instinctively comprehend this. The process of analyzing what works and what does not work enables a trader to listen to multiple viewpoints and comprehend all sides. Former Lehman Brothers technical analyst Steve Shobin has pointed out many times that "clues abound in the stock market." How a stock reacts to news, for example, is a telling piece of evidence. Instinct is the ability to see and hear those clues and to take appropriate action.

- *Watch the action.* There is no substitute for the perspective obtained from concentrating on the markets day in and day out for a number of years to see what works. Through the often painful and time-consuming process of trial and error, you begin to determine what works for you personally. Learning from mistakes provides chances to burn important lessons into your brain.
- *Find a comfort level.* Once you've had a chance to experiment with different approaches, you must be able to develop a comfort level with your chosen strategy. Comfort in the context of trading means you've developed a strategy that *you* believe in, that *you* inherently understand, that *you* can apply consistently, and that *you* can use to generate results. By comfort I'm *not* suggesting blind apathy. Traders must constantly adapt to the market, not vice versa, which also requires a trader to challenge his comfort zone at times for development (and perhaps survival).
- *Analyze potential scenarios.* Successful traders view the world in terms of scenarios. Analyzing scenarios and assigning probabilities to them ahead of time allows a trader to quickly adjust and react when/if they play out. Like a quarterback reading the defense and calling an audible at the line, successful traders anticipate the action before it unfolds.

- *Stay oriented.* Pilots deprived of visual references suffer spatial disorientation and become confused or mistaken about their position and motion relative to the earth. Too often, traders lose their bearings in a similar fashion and fail to rely on their indicators. This is a big problem in the current environment of information overload. Experienced traders have learned to tune out the noise and use their strategy as a compass that guides them in times of market confusion.
- *Pick your pitch.* View a portfolio in terms of opportunity costs (buying XYZ implies passing up a chance at ABC). Learning to wait until the rubber band is stretched sufficiently to react in either direction is a critical skill far more easily described than done. Executing at the right moment and selectively deploying capital are the key to realizing success. If your strategy and preparation have highlighted an attractive entry point where the odds are in your favor, be willing to swing the bat and capitalize on those opportunities.
- *Hear all sides but stick to your guns.* Experienced traders are able to listen to a number of views without losing conviction. There will always be another side to your trade. Successful traders seek out an argument against their positions and recognize potential issues they may have missed.

A FINAL NOTE

We live in a complex and ever-changing world filled with uncertainty. No place typifies that notion more than the daily fluctuations of the stock market. Every day, billions of shares are traded in a daring quest for wealth and fortune. Every day, traders win and lose.

Realize that in the investment world, the old adage holds true that experience remains the greatest of teachers. So read on. Spend a chapter inside the heads of people who have managed some level of success in this business, and think about how their common characteristics might apply to your own situation. My father, Jere D. Collins, ingrained in me the importance of observation and being a sponge. After spending a great deal of my career doing so, I remain convinced that playing such a role is key to evolving as a trader. Embrace the notion that each day provides new opportunities to learn, improve, and profit.

In the business of finance, or in life for that matter, there are unfortunately no precise how-to manuals to guide us on our daily journey. Success, regardless of how one defines it, is dependent on a unique mixture of genetic attributes, developed skills and abilities, intellectual curiosity, a tireless work ethic, and a little luck. Perhaps most importantly in the investment world, the old adage holds true that experience remains the greatest of teachers. Winston Churchill wisely offered, "Success is not final, failure is not fatal: it is the courage to continue that counts." Press onward, then, and focus on evolving. I wish you the best of luck in your lifelong quest to becoming a more successful trader—a *master* trader.

PART I

Technical Analysis

CHAPTER 1

Playing with Fear and Arrogance

Jeff deGraaf

> *You gotta play this game with fear and arrogance.*
> —Crash Davis, *Bull Durham*

In the market, arrogance without fear will eventually break you. Fear without arrogance will leave you paralyzed at the most inopportune time. The delicate balance of fear and arrogance fosters appropriate aggressiveness without the recklessness.

The combination may appear contradictory, but much like a seasoned sailor approaches the sea, a trader needs both to maximize returns while minimizing the risk of a debilitating blow. Arrogance fosters the killer instinct and the ability to dominate, to press while others show timidity. Fear is not only a sign of respect, but a deep understanding of the enormity and danger of the beast. To have fear is to understand that committed errors can be fatal, that markets are vast, and therefore unknowable, and that the unforeseen risk is usually the most dangerous and detrimental.

Contrary to what 99 percent of the investment population thinks, trading is not about being right. Being right is easy. Trading is about being wrong; and navigating this inevitable occurrence distinguishes the winners from the losers in the long run. History reveals a long list of financial disasters, a majority of which began and ended with the failure to proceed properly, fearfully, in the face of error. The road to riches is littered with the bodies of those who believed that being right required conviction and stamina. Conviction is viewed as a badge of honor among investors, traders, and portfolio managers—a sign of triumph and steadfast assuredness over others' pendulousness—but the line between conviction and stubbornness is at best vague. In most instances, conviction and stubbornness are indistinguishable characteristics differentiated only by their eventual outcome. To have conviction is to have the intestinal fortitude to see through the market's action and stay the course, understanding that the market will eventually reward the view. Stubborn investors carry the same intestinal fortitude, but the position eventually becomes a hopeless cause, or worse, part of a class action bankruptcy ruling.

The difference in attitude between conviction and stubbornness is only well defined after the fact. Though the probability of disaster may be small, the consistency of the 100-year flood striking financial markets every five or six years should serve as notice to play with enough fear to keep the arrogance in check. To fear the market is not to cower in its presence, but to be in continued awareness of its unforgiving attitude and its continual ability to wreak devastation.

Economist John Maynard Keynes once quipped, "The market can remain irrational longer than you can remain solvent." While these are about the only words from Keynes that I believe to be true, they are resoundingly so. What Keynes realized was that markets were powerful, and rational in the long run, but were influenced by a multitude of factors in the short run, some of which were inconsistent, illogical, and contradictory. By employing a combination of tactics, the short-term irrationality that often proves ruinous can be mitigated. Such tactics are not only unconventional, they are often the most controversial on Wall Street.

THE INVESTMENT PROCESS

Investors and traders both large and small share a similar objective: to earn a return on the capital employed. That return may be weighted against the risk taken (alpha), it may be in absolute terms (beta), or it may be measured against a benchmark for performance, such as the S&P 500, or the cost of borrowing the capital (leverage). In every instance, regardless of the methodology, investors are seeking a return on their capital.

Investors approach the market in several ways in an attempt to earn a return, but two primary schools of thought dominate: fundamental and technical analysis. By far the most popular of these disciplines is the use of fundamental analysis. The various elements of the discipline—finance, accounting, marketing, economics, and management—are rigorously taught throughout the country's business schools, and roughly 95 percent of Wall Street's analysts approach the market with a fundamental discipline. It stands to reason, as the approach is logical, methodical, and intuitive. The fundamental discipline uses company facts and specifics such as balance sheets and income statements as well as the study of industry and economic data to judge a company's merits as an investment. By comparing the current selling price with the theoretical price as computed by the analyst's assumptions, a buy or sell recommendation can be made. A market price above the analyst's estimated value would be considered a sell candidate, while a market price below the analyst's estimated value would be considered a buy candidate.

The technical analyst takes a different approach and uses data supplied from the market, such as price and volume, in an attempt to judge the dominant position of supply and demand (seller and buyer). In many ways the technical analyst is like a hunter tracking game, understanding that investors leave footprints, and those footprints are visible through the price patterns, volume flows, and other data presented in the charts. The technical analyst attempts to identify trends or turning points in the market or security using these inputs, and has little or no interest in the company specifics. Relying on the market to provide the message, the technician understands that if enough buyers or sellers are attracted to a security (for any reason) their actions will be noticeable through the price and volume displayed on the charts. The technical approach to investing is often skipped over at most business schools, and those classes where it is addressed tend to teach the discipline with snickers, snide comments, and the same incredulousness one may expect from a modern-day medical school teaching the merits of leeching their patients.

My initial exposure to technical analysis, as it was for most *technicians*, left me feeling skeptical. Being a quick learner, however, it became apparent to me that technical analysis provided a perspective much different from that of the fundamental process. It serves as a cold, hard reality check; the culmination of thousands of opinions backed by their capital. The devotees of technical analysis on Wall Street are rarely the young ivy-league MBAs with a hot hand; instead, they are the seasoned veterans, battle-hardened from years of experience. It is this rare breed who knows the true meaning of playing with fear and arrogance. They come to the work every day with admiration for the markets, and the technical discipline is an invaluable perspective into this world.

Proponents of both the fundamental and the technical disciplines have been engaged in a holy war of sorts for decades. It is a war that has wasted too much time and too much energy because it is a war that is unlikely to be won. As a Certified Financial Analyst (CFA) and Chartered Market Technician (CMT) charter holder, I will go so far as to say that both disciplines work and both disciplines fail at inopportune times. While each discipline has unique merits and attributes, neither deserves the religious fervor championed by its most ardent proponents, for both are fallible. In a business where the score is literally kept every day, it is surprising how often the means (forms of analysis) are held in higher regard than the ends (money being made). That is to say, the sequence and sophistication of arriving at the buy or sell decision is often looked upon with more prestige than the result of the recommendation. At the heart, there is an innate human desire to be able to account for and explain everything around us, from weather to bacteria. Fundamental analysis tends to fulfill this explanatory desire more adequately than technical analysis, which tends to be viewed as more of a faith-based discipline.

Importantly, neither discipline has been found to hold a clear or sustained advantage in generating excess returns from the market, most likely because both disciplines are as much an art as they are a science. The accuracy of linear mathematical tools will always be limited when nonlinear behaviors and emotions are present within the investment world. My allegiance has always been to the ends and not the means (within legal boundaries, of course), and if studying caribou migration patterns or lunar cycles improves the ends, the unorthodox means can be tolerated.

It is not a question as to whether fundamentals or technicals work. The question is, how and when do they work? The fundamentals are good at narrowing the pool of investable candidates and aligning ideas with a philosophical discipline or comfort level such as value or growth. Where the fundamentals tend to fail is in risk control, money management, and timing. In theory, buying a security based purely on the fundamental discipline will continually suggest buying or adding to a position as its price goes lower and lower and it becomes seemingly cheaper and cheaper. Using a purely fundamental approach, it is difficult if not impossible to know when the analysis is wrong, as at some point it will be. Continually buying at ever-lower prices represents what is known as the Martingale method in gaming situations. Essentially, it is a strategy that continually doubles down after each loss with the assurance that an eventual turn in the bad luck or string of losses will move the position to breakeven. Such a strategy requires unlimited resources and, less realistically, an extreme tolerance for pain since the position sizes and losses grow geometrically as the price moves against the position. It is a foolish strategy that reeks of arrogance and dances on a perilous edge of disaster. The flaw in the fundamentals is not in the rationale—it can provide an extremely useful guide—but in the timing and risk control.

The technical discipline acts instead as an unbiased arbiter providing risk control and checks and balances to the fundamental thinking. Technical systems are equal opportunity investors, with a willingness to buy or sell regardless of the securities' characteristics (i.e., growth or value, large or small, cheap or expensive). This is both an advantage and a disadvantage. It is advantageous in that technical analysis, when properly used, will identify areas of emerging strength or weakness and can reverse-engineer the attributes being most aggressively rewarded, or in vogue in the current environment. The disadvantage is that by not distinguishing on some other basis, an unrealistic number of names are presented as opportunities which are unlikely to be utilized. Using technical analysis in isolation requires throwing a lot of spaghetti against the wall to see what sticks, and that implies transaction costs and levels of frustration that become impractical. We find technical analysis to be best at identifying emerging opportunities before the fundamentals become apparent and well discounted, and then base our decisions on the pervasiveness of strength on an individual level and within the context of the group.

Historically, purely fundamental managers tend to suffer from a few systematic errors in the management of portfolios. Value managers tend to enter positions too early, falling into the value trap where the cheap security gets continually cheaper. Once the value begins to be recognized and the price bid up by the market, the value manager tends to exit the positions too early and not extract the maximum profit from the position.

Growth managers tend to enter positions after an established trend and when the fundamental data has been confirmed. The danger for the growth manager is the inherent price momentum in the strategy. As fundamental analysts, most growth managers will await fundamental confirmation before exiting a position. However, with growth, price momentum tends to deteriorate much more quickly than the fundamental confirmation, leaving the position severely impaired by the time it appears fundamental justification is confirmed. A simple trend-following discipline can reduce these costly errors and extract more profit and less risk from the various fundamental approaches used in isolation. By waiting for the trend to turn positive, value players avoid the opportunity costs associated with holding on to a position and awaiting their eventual turn. In many instances the same ideas that screened as cheap can be established at a lower cost basis by awaiting a change in trend, and avoiding the value trap. These same managers can then hold positions longer when the trend is supportive, even after the value has been fully recognized by the market. The growth manager, by monitoring a trend-following system, can screen for growth names that may be discounted by the market more quickly than with the fundamental process and increase returns by looking at ideas earlier.

Equally important, since growth tends to be momentum driven, the technical trends can assist the growth manager in assessing a potential turn in the growth prospects as prices begin to deteriorate before the fundamentals become apparent. By using an independent filter with no correlation to the underlying fundamental discipline, a consistent, lower-risk, higher-return methodology can be established.

KNOW THYSELF

In any business, it is imperative to know your advantages and disadvantages to maximize success. Playing to areas of strength and avoiding areas of weakness are even more critical in trading because margins tend to be thin. Serious introspection, however, is rarely undertaken; or advantages are assumed where none may actually exist. Know your advantages and stick with them; the more you drift toward your weakness, the less profitable you will be.

It is often assumed that large institutions have a distinct advantage over individuals. While that is true in terms of execution costs, access to management, and informational resources, the large amounts of capital that provide these advantages also saddle them with weaknesses such as impact costs, portfolio constraints such as tracking error, and quarterly performance measures. Since large institutions dominate the marketplace, their advantages are often the individuals' disadvantage and vice versa. By understanding slight nuances such as mutual fund tax loss selling in October, the disadvantage of one player can become another's advantage.

Like most drivers, most investors and traders believe that they have above-average ability. It is rare, even on a large scale, to have a clear informational advantage. An advantage in information or instinct is difficult at best, but even if one exists, maximizing the other advantages makes any information edge more profitable. There is no shortage of brains or complexity of investment ideas on Wall Street; but adherence to a discipline is one of the Street's rarest and most undervalued commodities. Discipline tends to minimize the largest mistakes made, which are those associated with trades done in the presence of emotion. Having a process or clearly defined discipline helps guide behavior when emotions are most likely to influence decisions, and creates boundaries within which one should operate. A person's IQ does not protect against emotion as sufficiently as discipline; and while that does not imply that serious traders and investors must adhere to a system in order to make money, a process that exploits personal advantage and avoids weakness will likely prove far more useful than assuming an information advantage.

If it were possible to correlate and show the returns between two investment classes—those operating with high IQs and those operating with discipline—I suspect those methodically following a discipline would have the highest correlations to returns. That may seem absurd, and certainly it need not apply on an individual level, but generally, discipline tends to be undervalued on Wall Street while intellect is overvalued.

One of the reasons for underappreciating discipline is the entertainment value offered by trading. Trading is exhilarating, particularly while winning, but even the lows provide an emotional charge that releases adrenaline, creating the modern-day equivalent of our ancestral anxiety produced during the hunt. The problem is that entertainment does little to maximize returns, and in most instances actually inhibits them. Having predefined rules, or following a process, is admittedly less entertaining and even borderline tedious, but if return maximization is the objective, it is almost assuredly more effective than following the emotional highs and lows of the capricious. Part of Wall Street's allure is the thrill of the kill, being in the game and matching wits with the brightest, richest, and most competitive people in the world. The gun-slinging subculture of the trader has obvious appeal (as evidenced by its representation in the media), but generally, playing consistently, playing methodically, and aligning positions with a process will also align returns with their maximized potential and away from the entertainment value glorified in pop culture. If an adrenaline rush is your objective, go play in traffic.

WHAT DO WE KNOW?

Few people enter into a position without some form of information, whether fundamental, quantitative, or technical. It is important, however, to make a distinction between information and knowledge. *Information* has specificity to it in terms of an event, situation, news, or data, whereas *knowledge* is a by-product, a culmination of experience and understanding. They are not synonymous, nor are they mutually exclusive, for information within the presence of knowledge is far more useful than information in isolation. Both information and knowledge are used as a security blanket, something to cling to when things go wrong, but both may be as detrimental as they are beneficial, because information and knowledge are often at the root of the conviction that becomes stubbornness. In part, information is dangerous, and highly unreliable, even when true, in that we have little way of knowing how pervasive the facts are among investors.

Even in this day and age, information is not disseminated instantaneously, and decisions rarely are made in a vacuum regardless of how seemingly independently one may approach the market. Stocks go up or down based on marginal supply or demand. Too much demand at the margin and stocks will tend to rise as investors bid up their value in the marketplace. Too much supply at the margin, and sellers will accept lower prices as buyers on the other side require compensation (lower prices) for the acceptance of the risk. It is what happens at the margin that determines the price, and if the catalyst for an investment decision is widely disseminated in the marketplace either through television, newspapers, or other highly trafficked areas, the usefulness of the information is likely to have diminishing returns and, at some point, no impact.

On August 29, 2005, Hurricane Katrina made landfall in southeast Louisiana. This Category 5 hurricane was the most costly in U.S. history. Much of the energy infrastructure was damaged or permanently impaired. While the horrific pictures and footage of the disaster's aftermath were lead stories and front-page news, there was no edge in the information. Oil made an interim high that day, and traded lower for the subsequent six months (see Figure 1.1).

With every piece of information there are ghosts, shadows, and the true light. Deciphering facts from fantasy and fiction can be a Herculean challenge, and in many instances not truly knowable on an *ex ante* basis. Strangely, what we know can hurt us, because the dissemination of information and the pervasiveness of the discounting of the information is never truly known. Whisper numbers, the inability of securities to rally/fail on good/bad news, and antiquated GDP figures are examples of information with marginal informational impact because of the market's discounting mechanism. Knowledge can provide a false

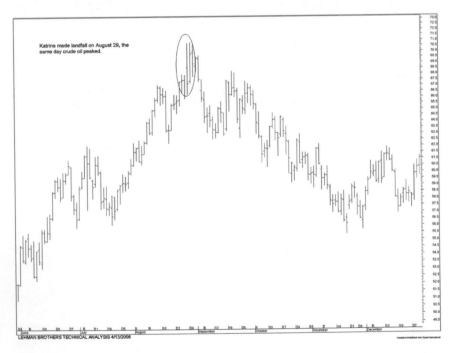

FIGURE 1.1 Crude Oil Prices at the Time of Hurricane Katrina

sense of security, and it can also lead us to believe something is important when in reality it is not, or worse, the facts as understood turn out to be false.

AN ABUNDANCE OF KNOWLEDGE IS DANGEROUS

Defense Secretary Donald Rumsfeld best said it when referring to the Iraq war: "There are known knowns. These are things we know that we know. There are known unknowns. That is to say, there are things that we know we don't know. But there are also unknown unknowns. These are things we don't know we don't know." This is applicable to the dynamic and fluid environment of trading. There will always be unknowable facts and unforeseeable events, but the danger lies in our knowns becoming unknowns. In reality the only thing in trading that is certain is the price, or, more precisely, the bid and ask. Everything else is an educated guess with varying degrees of confidence in accuracy. The point at which our knowns become unknowns is precisely the point at which conviction transforms itself into stubbornness, and hope begins to replace knowledge. If there is one lesson to pass on, it is that hoping in the markets is absolutely hopeless. If our only knowable fact is price, it is imperative that a process or strategy be implemented that maximizes the efficiency of decisions made with imperfect information. If knowledge is widely disseminated and accessible, it is far less likely to be useful.

That is not to encourage the use of nonpublic information, or any other illegal acts. It is, however, meant to encourage the assessment of information that is at the foundation of the decision-making process, and whether that information truly contains advantage. Being informed is important, but being informed and having advantage are completely different. If advantage is coming from reading the newspaper, watching television, or any other easily accessible source (God forbid a chat room!), your advantage is likely to prove illusory.

The most useful information tends to be in stark contrast to the consensus opinions available, but in harmony with the trend of the security. The best opportunities are likely to come from the most controversial ideas, but those ideas are best initiated only when the underlying trend or momentum confirms the thesis. Trading against the trend is arrogance without fear, regardless of your knowledge.

Knowledge is usually a mosaic of multiple inputs or information nodes that lead to a specific conclusion. The irony is that this complexity can often lead to worse predictability than a simplistic analysis. The greater the complexity of the model or decision tree, the greater the magnitude a small error has on the final output. As an example, it is well known that a fair coin when flipped enough will result in a relatively equal distribution of heads and tails or a 50 percent probability of a head. Guessing the outcome *ex ante*, before the knowledge of the outcome, there is a 50 percent chance of being correct. If the coin was flipped again the chance of guessing the second trial correctly would still be 50 percent, but the chances of guessing both flips (trails) correctly is reduced to only 25 percent (.50 × .50 = .25 or 25 percent).

The dangers of modeling are in the assumptions made and the high degree of forecast error that are usually inherent in such assumptions. The numbers and quantification of the process create a false sense of assuredness that leads to inherent errors that can be exploited, particularly if a consensus develops around highly unstable forecasts. If there is an 80 percent probability of being correct in any one assumption, yet the final output of the model is dependent on three such assumptions or variables, the probability of being right collectively begins to approach our coin flip scenario of 50 percent. With three variables that individually have an 80 percent probability of being correct, the combined probability of these inputs being correct is only 51.2 percent! (.80 × .80 × .80 = .512 or 51.2 percent.) While the confidence may be high on an individual input basis, unless the additional inputs added are a certainty, each will increase the error component of the forecast. As this number increases, the combined probability decreases exponentially.

In fairness, not all forecast errors are disastrous, but as the assumptions and forecasts increase, so too do the chances of errors and that the predicted outcomes will differ from the actual outcome. Modeling tends to create an illusion of control because of the certainty inherent in the mathematics involved. Modeling has its place, but there tends to be too much confidence in the output given the uncertainty of the input (garbage in, garbage out, or GIGO). The mathematics and rigors imbedded in a model do not cleanse the assumptions; there is no laundering of dirty or erroneous data through a magical model that then spits out clean and dependable answers. In fact, some of the best opportunities present themselves from too much reliance on output that is generated from input with very unstable tendencies.

Interest rate forecasts, as an example, are extremely unreliable, yet factors such as discount rates and growth forecasts are dependent on certain interest rate assumptions where small changes have a big impact on the final results. Historically, collective interest rate forecasts published in the *Wall Street Journal* at the beginning of the year accurately call the direction of short-term interest rates one year out less than 50 percent of the time! When the time, effort, and intellect spent on forecasting the future direction of these rates just one year out is worse than the flip of a coin, it becomes easier to see how errors in assumptions can create confidence where little should exist. These failures present opportunity for those not dependent on illusory knowledge, but are able to exploit the errors embedded in the certainty of forecasts.

When a consensus develops regarding an outcome that is highly dependent on such forecasts that prove historically difficult to predict, a low-risk, high-reward, contrary opportunity often develops. Contrary opinion, because it is behavior based, tends to be fairly robust in that it continually provides opportunities regardless of the asset class. It is one advantage in the market that presents itself time and time again. On an individual basis, it is easy to be confident with any single input, but when confidence is carried over to a combination of inputs, it becomes dangerous. What was thought to be a known can quickly become an unknown. Trading is a classic example of decision making with imperfect information, and creating a framework within which to operate is paramount to success.

There are several costs associated with trading, and while execution costs such as slippage and commissions are important, they are not necessarily the critical costs. Anyone who is interested in maximizing returns needs to have the intellectual honesty to assess the economic costs associated with errors of commission and errors of omission. The errors of commission are the costs associated with taking action. A losing position is an example of an error of commission. It is an explicit cost associated with the action of buying or selling, and tends to have the greatest impact on a trader's mind-set. The cost of omission is less explored, but is equally critical to maximizing return. Errors in omission are the cost of not having taken action. Failing to trade and profit from a name that doubles, triples, or quintuples is considered an error of omission. Such errors are much less painful because they are not explicitly felt; but recognizing these errors and engaging in a process that helps eliminate them can greatly change the structure of returns. In a single year, one or two trades that capture the big move can differentiate a great year from a bad year.

A distribution of annualized returns for constituents of the S&P 500 over the last five years exemplifies the power outliers (winners and losers) have on a portfolio (see Figure 1.2). By not owning the top 10 performers in the S&P, annual equal-weighted returns are reduced from 6.3 percent to 5.5 percent. These are classic errors of omission. Contrarily, by eliminating the bottom 10 performers from the S&P, returns improve from 6.3 percent to 7.2 percent. The power of the old Wall Street saw, "Cut your losses and let your winners run," is exemplified in such figures.

True return-maximizing traders need to understand and minimize both types of errors because the cost of omission can often be greater than the cost of commission. It is not practical to own every big winner in

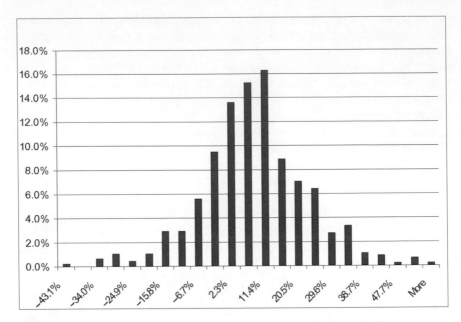

FIGURE 1.2 Frequency Annualized Five-Year Returns for S&P 500 Constituents

a portfolio, but it is practical to have had an opportunity to do so by having a look. The best way to consistently have a look at potential big winners is to employ a trend-following discipline. By definition, a big winner is a name that has embarked upon a sustained uptrend, and any trend-following system will identify such candidates well before their strength has faded. Relative-strength systems define this process; by investing in the top-performing relative-strength names, it is virtually impossible not to be involved in the biggest winners and leaders of the market. There are few ways technically or fundamentally to know how long a trend will endure and to what extent, but that does not minimize the need to reduce the errors of omission that are often overlooked and discounted as trivial.

Statisticians revel in normal distributions, which define virtually every data set and are ubiquitous throughout the physical world. A normal distribution has the average (mean) data point close to the middle (median) data point; the frequency of data is greatest near the average and tends to decline in a step function on either side of the average. Most data, when plotted, will take on normally distributed characteristics, whether it is annual rainfall in Kalamazoo, Michigan, or the height of residents in New York City (Figure 1.2 is a normal distribution). Data tends to fall around the average and thin out at the extremes.

In our world, trading is dependent on reducing the errors of omission and creating an asymmetrical distribution where a few large winning trades skew the results positively and force the average trade positively away from the median. By cutting losses early enough (fear), and letting winners ride (arrogance), a distribution of trades will take on the characteristics of positive skew, a distribution that tends to maximize returns and reduce entertainment value.

The majority of time and effort on Wall Street is dedicated to the buy decision, but buy decisions are only one-half of the equation, and probably the least important half. Sell signals, which tend to be approached with far less rigor and testing, are more critical because they tend to be emotionally based and—let me stress this again—decisions made or influenced by emotion are unlikely to maximize returns. Sell decisions based on fundamental disciplines have a tendency to fail in terms of risk control and in most instances produce far too much drawdown risk to be effectively implemented consistently. A technical discipline, if used in no other area, is critical in the sell process, because it is not subjective—it is price and performance dependent. The majority of the time spent on developing a process, a discipline, or a framework by which to trade should be spent on the various elements of selling, not buying. Attribution of returns will likely be affected more by the sell discipline implemented than the buy decision.

It is critical for traders to own their own system and ideas, to familiarize and understand the intricacies, tendencies, idiosyncrasies, inherent risks, and vulnerabilities on a *daily* basis. Point-to-point analysis (quarterly, monthly, or weekly) is useless because it fails to account for the intraday stresses imposed on an account. Using someone else's idea or system is unlikely to work because of the inconsistent match between personal tolerances for risk and reward. There is a great emotional need to be right, and the allure of consistent returns is high, natural, and dangerous. Remember that this is a risk business. To assume that a certain percentage can be extracted from the market every month like the compound interest on a certificate of deposit is a recipe for failure. If you are looking for consistent returns and low volatility, go buy a bond—you are not ready for the risks of trading.

Strategies that promote low volatility and consistently high returns tend to be dangerous in that the outliers or freak events will destroy the portfolio eventually. These types of strategies are popular because they tend to work a high percentage of the time, but beware of strategies that provide comfort and popularity. Those strategies with high win/loss ratios, consistent and steady returns, with minimal apparent risk, are likely to fail. That which is comfortable and easily implemented is prone to failure. Comfortable strategies attract capital and eventually diminish returns to the risk-free rate, if you're lucky!

Remember these four rules:

1. It is impossible for everyone to be rich.
2. It is impossible for everyone to get rich following a similar strategy.
3. Stable strategies tend to attract everybody.
4. See rule 1 to clarify the problem of rule 3.

Strategies with low winning percentages and lumpy and inconsistent returns are personally preferable because the risks tend to be obvious but manageable. The inconsistency of such strategies makes them unpalatable to even the most seasoned trader and institutions, a condition which virtually ensures durability.

THE LONG AND SHORT OF IT

Those looking for easy street through trading on Wall Street are likely to end up disappointed, discouraged, and potentially destitute. Trading is a difficult business with a high probability of failure. It requires an unnatural temperament, honest introspection, a reasonable intellect and, most importantly, discipline. There are several paths to success in trading, but few of them are well worn. Being successful requires a unique course that matches personal risk preferences, profit, patience, aptitude, and the exploitation of personal advantage. Know your weaknesses and avoid them at all costs. Be aware of the fallacies and the dangers inherent with knowledge and the conviction such knowledge can create. Be reluctant to fight the trend, and by all means play with fear and arrogance.

CHAPTER 2

Sector Analysis: Tools of the Trade

Frank Barbera

T he stock market has intrigued me since I began using technical analysis at the age of 17. While I was growing up in Los Angeles, technical analysis had a home on television long before the advent of FNN or CNBC in the early 1980s. Back in the mid-1960s, a local television station went on the air with the first full-time stock market channel in the country: KWHY, Channel 22. I was fascinated by the manner in which the market seemed to obey the rules set forth on the charts. Trend lines were drawn and then broken; markets would obey and seemingly reverse on command. Timing gauges suggested oversold conditions, and the market would promptly rally within days. I've been hooked on trading the market ever since.

Over the years I learned that the world of technical analysis is constantly changing, and that there is no single indicator that will always work—except the analysis of price itself. Anyone looking for a magic bullet to beat the market is very likely to be disappointed. Now, at age 43, I have spent the balance of the last 25 years studying every aspect of market behavior from Elliott Wave and the study of crowd psychology to Gann analysis and the squaring of price and time, to MACD and equivolume. In this field there have been many greats, from the early masters of Charles Dow, Robert Rhea, Edward Quinn, Paul Dysart, W. D. Gann, Sedge Coppock, A. Hamilton Bolton, and R. N. Elliott, to the more recent names of A. J. Frost, George Lindsay, Arthur Merrill, Edson Gould, Richard Arms, Justin Mamis, Alan Shaw, Robert Farrell, Robert Prechter, Paul Montgomery, Peter Eliades, John Bollinger, and Martin Zweig. In avidly studying the works and writing of many of these great minds, what emerges is a framework of thought, seeking in a detailed and copious manner to grasp the very subtle changes that take place below the surface within every stock market advance and decline. You can tell a lot about where the market is heading by understanding the nuances underlying each and every market trend.

Is the stock market rising with accelerating underlying force? Is momentum gathering or receding? Is the stock market rising in a manner where there is increased overall participation, or is it rising against a backdrop of narrow participation on the back of a select group of stocks or sectors? Has sentiment reached a truly historical extreme and is the crowd indulging in a one-sided love affair? One thing I have learned about financial markets is that they inhale and exhale just like a living breathing organism. They are prone to great excess and flights of fantasy, and thus, it is never a good idea to impose a limit on how far an extreme a given trend can move. Markets manifest crowd psychology in motion, pure and simple, and are the ultimate social mirror. The perpetual battle between fear and greed continues to dominate, and while timing indicators and analytical methodology will undoubtedly change, human nature with its ever-changing emotional states is the one great constant that will likely never change.

My early mentor John Bollinger once told me that it was not important to be able to forecast in advance a high or a low for a given market. Instead, he said, "You only need to be able to recognize the turn." John was never more on target, as understanding what underlies the change from up to down and from down to up is all any of us need in order to make money. The question of how far and to what extreme a given trend will go is a question best left for idle cocktail chatter with friends over dinner. More important is to keep your eye on the ball, and in any market, the proverbial bouncing ball is the technical condition of the underlying primary trend. The first rule of technical analysis is that *a trend in motion will remain in motion until it gives definite signs that it is about to reverse*. In my experience, the following five major tools within the world of technical analysis yield valuable output on the current status of the major trend: relative strength, breadth, momentum, volume, and sentiment.

THE FIVE TOOLS OF TECHNICAL ANALYSIS

Before going on, it is important to spend a moment defining some of these terms. *Breadth* refers to the degree of participation that is taking place within a given stock market trend. For example, if we are looking at a rally in oil stocks, just how many energy issues are participating in that particular advance? Are all segments within the energy sector participating in the move, including the large integrated oils, the oil service and drillers, the exploration and production companies (E&P), the natural gas stocks, and alternative energy? Just how widespread is the advance? For a more general bull market led by large moves in the S&P or the Dow, is the move unfolding with leadership in all major sectors, including financials, technology, energy, cyclicals, consumer, pharmaceutical, and retail issues, or is the move unfolding in one area to a greater degree than in others? A true bull market in the stock market will kick off with powerful rallies in a broad array of stocks. In essence the rising tide lifts all boats.

Strong stock market rallies are always accompanied by a large surge in volume and very high readings on momentum gauges. *Momentum* refers to the amount of force behind a given advance. The greater the impelling force at the outset, the longer and more enduring the advance is likely to be. *Volume*, representing the total number of shares traded, should expand in the direction of the primary trend, which, in a rising market, would entail expanding volume on rallies, and marked contractions in volume during corrections. Further, the duality of up volume versus down volume should score high ratios of up volume over down volume during strong advancing sessions (particularly at the outset of an advance) and more moderate ratios of down volume over up volume in ensuing corrections during a bull market advance.

While breadth, momentum, and volume are fairly straightforward, *sentiment* is an ever-changing bogey that needs to be used most carefully, as it can cause many problems. In its classic role, sentiment is used to identify when a given trend may be at an extreme, and when too much of the crowd is thinking in the same manner. As put forth by the "Theory of Contrary Opinion," if the majority of market participants are all bullish, and all believe the market is headed higher, then chances are fairly high that their money is *already in the market*. If the majority of capital available for investment is already in the market, then, by definition, there is very little money left on the sidelines available to come in and push prices still higher—and as a result, prices are near a high.

Conversely, if the majority of participants all believe that the market is headed lower and expect prices to continue to decline, then in all likelihood by the time most of these participants have their money in cash, all of the selling that can be done probably has been done. Put another way, if the consensus outlook is uniformly bearish, since no rational investor would intentionally hold on to shares he expects will continue to decline, most likely the majority of participants have left the market and the stage is set for a market bottom, as anyone who could sell has likely already sold. Thus, there becomes a lack, or void, in additional selling power, which is required in order for a bear market to drive prices even lower. It is under such circumstances, where cash levels are high, and investor expectations are very low, that even the slightest bit of improving news can spark a major advance as sidelined capital floods back into the market.

Sentiment gauges are probably the most susceptible to misleading readings over long periods of time, as the market is always changing its internal dynamics. Just as people age and change their philosophical views over time, so too does the stock market evolve. As an example, back in the 1970s, before the advent of futures and options trading, and before the rise of large institutional fund managers and hedge funds, the small investor was regarded as a good contrary indicator. At the time, the sentiment indicator of choice was the odd lot short sale index, which would spike up whenever small investors went into the market and sold short large quantities of stock. In the 1960s and 1970s the indicator worked pretty well, with high levels of odd lot shorting often indicating market bottoms, and low levels of odd lot shorting indicating market tops. At the time, many smaller investors also relied heavily on newsletter writers to make decisions on the trend of the market, and as a result, there was quite a variety of newsletters in circulation, each using varying approaches. Consequently, sentiment indicators based on prevailing newsletter polling became a useful contrary investment tool.

However, over time the market morphed, and some of these formerly useful tools became less effective. The advent of options trading moved the arena for speculative trading into the realm of puts and calls. By the mid-1980s, the put/call ratio had fully replaced the odd lot short index as the premier contrary opinion gauge, with high levels of put buying delineating market bottoms via high levels of fear, while a high level of call buying was often a key ingredient at market tops, reflecting excess levels of optimism.

Yet, by the late 1990s, the simple put/call ratio largely stopped working, as the rise of hedge funds and different trading strategies negated its meaning. Over the past few years, it has become common for hedge fund managers to short put options in order to establish a *bullish* bet on the market. The *shorting* of put options still shows up as a large *increase* in the quantity of puts versus calls. As a result, in the market of the 1990s and 2000s, a high ratio on this gauge hasn't meant what it did in the 1980s when a high ratio was a sure indicator of a market bottom and the presence of high levels of fear (as the puts were being purchased, not shorted).

Back then, the options market was dominated by small retail investors, not institutions. Today, in the era of the hedge fund, high levels of put volume do not necessarily imply anything about a market high or low, as it is impossible to tell how many puts are being purchased and how many are being sold short. Both cases—the purchase of a put and the short sale of a put—are recorded as transactions and show up as put volume. This is a good example of how the very fabric of the market has changed, with the relative size of the former options retail market (seen in the 1980s) now dwarfed by the rise of large institutions practicing far more sophisticated strategies.

Another example relating to the trading of options is the rise of the exchange-traded fund (ETF) market, also seen in recent years. Back in the 1980s there were no exchange-traded funds. Today, there are ETFs on different countries, currencies, commodities, and specific stock market sectors, many of which trade options with the results getting mixed into the aggregate options data. For the technician, this is massive-scale data pollution, and it is so widespread that generically reported aggregate options volumes no longer mean very much. On a given day, the options data on one stock—the NASDAQ QQQ back in 2000–2003, Google in 2005, Apple in 2006, the oil service HOLDERS (OIH) in 2005, or the S&P Spiders (SPY)—might be so high that, in dollar volume terms, it would equal or surpass all of the other equity options totals combined. Further, an ETF like the SPY or the QQQQ (as the NASDAQ ETF is known now) provides enormous cross-trading hedge strategies to institutions that may be long the underlying basket of stocks and short both the calls and the puts in combinations on the ETF as protection.

This institutionalization of the market has profound implications for many other areas of thought implemented in the realm of technical analysis. As a long-time student of Elliott Wave, I can go back to the Dow charts of the 1920s, 1930s, 1940s, 1950s, and right up to the mid-1980s and see very clear Elliott patterns. These were markets centered on a U.S. centric retail market where people would walk the streets and look at the ticker tape in the broker's office. Real market aficionados, back in the day, would spend their time in the broker's office staring at a quote machine. That was a retail (individual) driven stock market, where retail order flow governed the ebb and flow of the market.

Not any more! Over the past 20 years capitalism has gone global and the rise of institutions (of all kinds from mutual funds to banks, to nonbank financials, to hedge funds) has placed greater decision-making power in the hands of fewer decision makers. As a result, Elliott Wave counts are less crisp than were seen in decades past. Some of Elliott's rules must be bent more today because the widespread nature of crowd psychology seen in the 1950s retail stock market has been funneled down into the hands of Wall Street powerhouses like Fidelity, Janus, and Franklin in what is now an institutionally based, order-flow, new-millennium stock market.

Mind you, this is not to say that tools like Elliott analysis are no longer useful; rather, it is to point out that market dynamics have changed and, in so doing, tend to produce an altered set of final results using the same set of tools. I have found that formerly strict interpretations for tools like Elliott, and even basic bar charting, now need greater latitude, making some of these tools even more of an art than a science. While this may seem discouraging at first, it has actually opened a whole new playing field for more serious investors. In my work, I have found that it is possible to carve out a niche in segments of the market where individual investors can still gain a definitive upper hand against their larger institutional brethren using the power of the PC and, in particular, the power of the spreadsheet.

SECTOR TRADING

To gain an edge on large institutions, the area of sector analysis offers a whole new horizon for making outstanding stock market returns. Down through the years there have always been sector booms, including the great energy boom of the early 1980s, the gambling craze of the early 1980s, the technology boom of 1984, the pharmaceutical stock boom of the late 1980s, and, of course, the Internet and technology stock boom of the late 1990s. Each boom always had its super stocks: Global Marine and Parker Drilling in the late 1970s in the oil service sector; Dome Mines and Campbell Redlake in the gold boom of 1980; Resorts International, Caesar's World, and Bally's in the 1980s gaming craze; Wang Labs, Boroughs Corp, Sperry Rand, Control Data, Commodore International, Compaq Computer, and Digital Equipment in the early 1980s tech boom; and of course, names like Inktomi, Broadvision, Yahoo!, Lycos, AOL, and VerticalNET in the tech/Internet boom of the late 1990s.

I have observed that in recent years, the dramatic increase in hedge funds has amplified to a great degree the flows of capital directed at sector trading. When one sector is hot due to amplified earnings leverage, fund managers are quick to discern the prevailing condition and pile vast quantities of highly leveraged capital into the sector. This has tended to lead to outsized movements in areas like energy, technology, gold, biotechnology, steel, and health care in recent years.

Within the world of sector trading, there is always another casino. One bubble ends, and within short order, another bubble begins to inflate. One can argue very persuasively that now more than ever, given the all-encompassing global linkages that have been created between capital markets, and the precariously high levels of debt and instability now embedded in the global economy, asset market inflation and the ongoing mass-scale creation of both credit and liquidity will continue, and *must* continue in coming years. In this newly globalized economy, were liquidity levels allowed to contract sharply, the resulting deflation would likely be felt globally and would likely pose too large a political problem for governments to accept. As a result, the global economy and global financial markets have become addicted to an exponentially increasing global liquidity mechanism. With the rise of hedge fund managers, which now control more than $1 trillion of potentially highly leveraged capital, volatility levels within sectors are also dramatically on the rise.

Today, a 25 percent decline within a sector can strike, ostensibly with little warning and be followed by a rapid 50 percent advance. Formerly stodgy stocks in sectors like steel and copper have become highly volatile market leaders, the result of a burgeoning global competition (between nations) for long-neglected natural resources, a trend that will likely persist for many years. In the stock market, making money in a particular stock is today more often dependent not only on the health of the company, but also on the status of the particular sector that company is in. The rotation of money within capital markets seems to be speeding up in recent years, and can sometimes paint with either a very narrow or a very broad brush.

For example, in late 2005, fund money worried about higher interest rates began pulling out of natural resource stocks, which had been leaders the entire year. The scope of the receding tide was quite widespread, triggering sharp declines in all of the following sectors at the same time: *energy*, including large-cap integrated, oil service and drilling, mid- and small-cap E&P, refining, natural gas, coal, and alternative energy; *base metals*, including copper, steel, and titanium; and *precious metals*—gold and silver. Years earlier, a decline in gold stocks would often have nothing to do with a decline in copper or oil stocks. In today's market, at times the linkages between these groups have been so pronounced that one would be hard-pressed to discern the difference between the chart pattern of a copper stock and that of a coal stock.

This phenomenon reflects the age of tactical asset management, where large institutional flows of money can flow in and out of very broad sectors, affecting a wide swath of groups which, for a period of time, can trade very much in tandem, even when affected by very different fundamentals. I would argue that in the new globalized, highly interdependent economy of the late 1990s and new millennium, global macroeconomic conditions play more of a role than ever before in determining how the current environment impacts various markets segments. In many ways, we are back to a brave new world, with money managers in the information age ironically, in some cases, really flying blind with very little real information to go on. Years ago, for example, the stock market was trained to live and die on the basis of trends in the domestic U.S. economy. U.S. economic data was the primary engine of market and sector moves. The largest economy in the world pretty much called the tune for trends within the stock market. Now, with the passage of time and thanks to the evolution of capitalism, whole new economies like China and India, and Asia in general, are rewriting the perceptions of whole industries.

Today, stodgy railroad companies achieve higher price/earnings (P/E) multiples than ever before, as the rails are seen as an extension of the ports, and the ports are the gateway to trade with Asia. An increasing U.S. trade deficit today is not bad for the dollar (at least so far), but instead means more backlogs at the ports and higher freight rates for railways shipping goods cross-country. Written off for dead in the early 1980s, overlooked and ignored in the early 1990s, who would have thought that the Dow Transportation Average based on rails and overnight shipping would gain sex appeal as the pick-and-shovel guys of the new-age global economy?

With the Rail Index up nearly 150 percent in the last two years, does a report on Chinese gross domestic product (GDP) growth or U.S. GDP growth have a bigger impact on the outlook for rails? Today, a major portion of the earnings at U.S. corporations and the S&P 500 comes from sales *outside the U.S. economy.* We are in a period that features the rise of the transnational corporation, true multinationals whose fortunes are tied more directly to the global trend for business than the fortunes of any country. Not surprisingly, in today's world, what is good for the corporation is often not so good for the host country—and in the end, the inevitable clashes between the boardroom and the national as well as the public interest seem destined to progressively intensify.

Among many examples of global economics at work and its profound impact in markets has been the megaboom recently in uranium stocks, a form of alternative energy. Their rise in recent years has been largely predicated on developing Asian economies and their choice to use nuclear power in coming years. The price of yellowcake uranium 308 has skyrocketed against the backdrop of a seemingly endless rising tide of new demand in Asia. Cameco (CCJ) and other uranium miners have exploded in price as more countries have announced plans to build more nuclear energy plants. Iron ore, another commodity, which at one point not long ago was entirely out of favor, has also risen dramatically in price, driving up the shares of Rio Dulce of Brazil, with Brazil now a major exporter of iron ore to Asia. The point to grasp is that much of what is playing out in markets these days is driven by truly global macroeconomic changes where, for an individual, real on-the-ground data does not exist or is not within easy reach.

In this area, large institutions like hedge funds most definitely have an edge, as they often have local experts who understand the real trends and can relay firsthand understanding. In my view, this places an extra premium on solid technical analysis for individual investors as unreported, global macroeconomic changes are still most likely to show up early on with bullish or bearish charts. To be clear, I believe that in the world of investing, there is no substitute for being well read and knowledgeable about how the world around us is changing, and about how those changes are likely to impact various industries.

Two more examples of industries that have been dramatically affected by the new and emerging globalized economy would be the U.S. auto industry and the U.S. airline industry, both of which have suffered at the hands of structural macroeconomic problems. Companies in the auto industry and much of the U.S. manufacturing sector in general have been hurt by cheap foreign labor and a globalized market that have put downward pressure on final goods prices. How can Detroit manufacturers, with their dramatically higher cost structure, compete against low-cost companies that use cheap overseas labor and have far fewer pension obligations? In a world headed toward peak oil and increased global competition for scarce resources, how can airline companies manage sequentially higher prices for fuel when constrained with high salaries and cost structures that only worked on the back of low fuel prices? Today, industries such as aluminum, base metals, heavy equipment, lumber, energy, chemicals, cement, building materials, railroads, gold and silver, and steel and iron all trade more and more based on the larger global economic trend.

While many basic industries have been profoundly affected by the opening of new sources of low-cost foreign labor, other industries remain relatively immune. Health care stocks, for example, are still primarily driven by domestic trends with sectors like HMOs, hospitals, generic drugs, big pharmaceuticals, medical appliances and equipment, health care distribution, dental, and even biotechnology and life sciences all still function independent of the global framework to a high degree. Other domestically driven sectors remain insurance, retail apparel, banking and brokerage, aerospace/defense, waste management, gaming and casinos, pollution control, utilities, security and protection, home entertainment, media and advertising, lodging, food and beverages, and restaurants. A good breakdown of industry groups can be found on Yahoo.com, showing the service sector to be the least affected by global trends (http://biz.yahoo.com/ic/ind_index.html).

Thus, for every economic environment, there is a time to be in certain sectors and a time to avoid those sectors. In the past, for example, rising short-term interest rates and the Fed tightening monetary policy would be tough on the profits for financials, or perhaps the real estate investment trusts (REITs). Increased supplies of oil flowing from the pumps at OPEC, or the onset of a serious slowdown in the global economy, could spell trouble for the energy sector, or maybe even the commodity sector in general. Today, stock market sector investing should begin with an awareness of the global fundamentals and the use of technical analysis to help spot some of these trends in their early stages.

UNDERSTANDING RELATIVE STRENGTH IN SECTOR ANALYSIS

At its best, technical analysis can often help identify new trends early in the advance, enabling an investor to hone in on what could be an exciting story and the early stages of a super bull move. In my work, I utilize several approaches to deciphering a good sector trade. One of my favorites is to buy into sectors that are out of favor for a period of at least six months, if not more—preferably one year to 18 months. One positive element involved in this approach is that normally, when a sector is depressed, properly used technical analysis can help you better control your risk. Thus, in this approach, I am ideally looking for sectors that have declined in a meaningful manner over a period of months, and are usually near the bottom of list in sector rankings like *Investor's Business Daily* (IBD) or *Barron's* with its Dow Jones Industry Group rankings.

These rankings are normally very comparable with Dow Jones Sectors, providing something of a broader overview, and IBD rankings something of a more subsector-specific overview. For example, while the Dow Jones tables have five categories for health care (health care providers, medical equipment, medical supplies, biotechnology, and pharmaceuticals), the IBD tables (which have approximately twice as many groups, 200 versus 100) have over a dozen categories for health care including microgroups like medical—dental supplies, medical—dental services, medical—nursing homes, medical—genetics, medical—biomed/biotech, medical—HMO, and medical—generic drugs. Often I start with the Dow Jones Sectors and then move on to the more specific IBD tables, which highlight closely linked baskets of stocks that at times can become downtrodden, unloved, and unwanted. With today's lower brokerage commissions, it is more possible than ever before to structure baskets of these stocks in portfolios without running up a large commission tab. For the *Investor's Business Daily*, index components are featured in regular Monday columns and at Investors.com, while for the Dow Jones Sector Indexes, the complete list of components is included in each issue of *Barron's*.

In my efforts at bottom fishing, one reason I tend to look for groups near the bottom of the list is that within the institutional stock market of the last 20 years, money is always rotating and looking for lower-risk investment ideas. Very often, in a sector that has been depressed for a lengthy period, value will be created as leading companies in that sector often manage to continue making forward progress despite unfavorable industry conditions. Over time, mergers and acquisitions—the ones with synergies—can also take place and often end up consolidating market share and restoring pricing power to sectors that perhaps had been engaged in a competitive price-cutting binge. Very often, some of the best turnaround trades take place within sectors that have just completed an extended period of corporate consolidation wherein stronger product pricing is the end result.

A widely followed corollary to this approach is the "Dogs of the Dow" approach, which posits a contrary opinion approach to buying each year's worst-performing, highest-yielding stocks in the Dow Jones Industrial Average. Over long periods of time, the results of the Dogs of the Dow have been fairly significant, and in my view it has a great deal to do with buying into the value that gets created during a period of extended underperformance. Of course, the key in this approach is knowing when the sector underperformance is coming to an end, and not wasting an investment lifetime looking for a turn in a sector that may not be at hand for some time to come. In this vein, the basic relative strength ratio used in technical analysis is an invaluable tool.

In order to calculate relative strength, we simply divide the sector index by the S&P 500 value and come up with a relative strength ratio line. When the line is declining, it indicates that sector is underperforming the S&P, while a rising ratio line indicates outperformance. Typically, I look for instances where a sector has remained below a long downtrend line in its relative strength versus the S&P 500. A good example of this would be back in 1987, when, following the stock market crash of 1987, the large drug companies fell into an extended period of underperformance vis-à-vis the S&P (see Figure 2.1). For all of 1987 and 1988, pharmaceutical stocks lay fairly dormant, tracing out a large ascending triangle base. The breakout from this base took place in early 1989 and was confirmed with the relative strength line breaking above its long-standing downtrend.

While the breakout in relative strength above a long downtrend line can be an excellent indication of more strength yet to come, it is possible on occasion to gain even more insight as to when a sector is beginning to outperform. To do this, I like to use a momentum indicator known as the moving average convergence-divergence (MACD). The beauty of MACD is that it is a *nonbounded* momentum indicator, meaning there is no set scale that prices are confined to both above and below zero. Indeed, higher beta sectors like biotechnology, precious metals, and gaming will likely generate greater extremes above and below 1.00 on MACD. Being

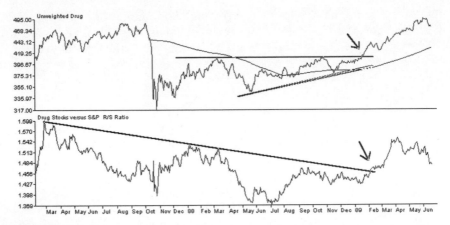

FIGURE 2.1 Drug Stocks versus the S&P 500 (top) with the Relative Strength Ratio (bottom)

nonbounded gives MACD the advantage of being able to highlight truly pronounced momentum divergences, on both price and relative strength, and it is those positive divergences that will often signal major trend changes in markets.

The classic MACD gauge is based entirely on closing prices. It is calculated by computing a 12-day exponential moving average of price, and a 26-day moving average of price, and then subtracting the 26-day moving average from the 12-day moving average. However, with prices experiencing much higher volatility in recent years, I have found that a ratio-based calculation actually works even better, and hence I *divide* the short-term moving average by the longer-term moving average. This division yields what I dub a ratio-adjusted MACD (henceforth referred to simply as MACD), upon which we then calculate a signal line, which is most often a 9-day moving average of the MACD ratio. To be clear, MACD uses *exponential* moving averages, as opposed to *simple* moving averages, because exponential moving averages place a greater weight on the most recent data, giving MACD maximum responsiveness to near-term changes. For the ratio-based MACD I use in my work, neutral readings are a value of 1.00, which acts as a kind of zero line for this gauge.

In my sector work, I like to compute MACD based not on price, but on the relative strength ratio curve. By basing MACD on the sector relative strength (R/S) ratio, we are looking for an early sign of when the relative strength itself is beginning to shift. Put another way, whenever a group is declining, the momentum behind downside underperformance has a maximum, and is then eventually followed by dissipating relative underperformance. In the case of the drug stocks in 1987–1988, the low in relative strength was seen in May–June 1988 and formed a double bottom, or "W" bottom. Note that as the R/S ratio slumped to new lows in July 1988, the MACD based on the R/S ratio was *not* making new lows, and in fact was only one-third as negative as had been seen during the decline in May 1988. This positive momentum divergence accompanying the decline to token new lows in the R/S ratio in July 1988 told us that drug stocks were still underperforming the market, but that the amount of negative momentum underpinning their underperformance was easing substantially.

In the two years following the relative strength breakout in early 1989, the drug index advanced by nearly 200 percent, with many leading stocks doubling and tripling in price. In Figure 2.2, note that the breakout in the drug sector is confirmed at the same time, with a breakout in the R/S ratio. Notice also the strong positive divergence on the MACD, indicating the imminent upside reversal in drug stocks.

A huge bull market in drug stocks followed the breakout in the R/S ratio. This was the key signal heralding a new period of much better relative performance in the sector and eventually a full upside breakout in sector relative strength versus the overall market. In Figure 2.3, we see what happened to drug stocks in the following few years, with the group drastically outperforming the rest of the broad stock market, and all stock market averages gaining nearly 200 percent in two years following the breakout. The next charts show similar declines in the aerospace stocks (Figures 2.4 through 2.6) and in the semiconductor stocks (Figures 2.7 and 2.8), which also produced huge results after undergoing poor periods of relative strength lasting between a year and 18 months.

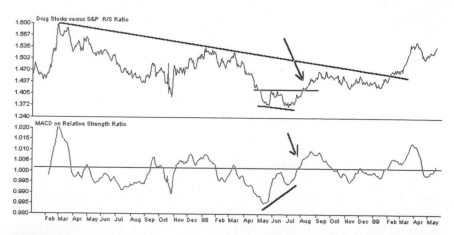

FIGURE 2.2 The R/S Ratio of Drug Stocks versus the S&P (top) with Ratio-Based MACD (bottom)

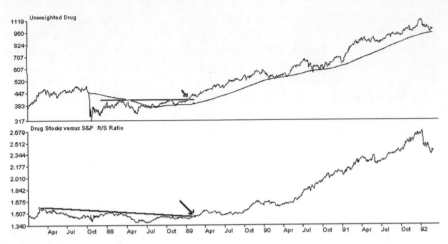

FIGURE 2.3 Drug Stocks Explode to the Upside Following Their 1988 Buy Signal

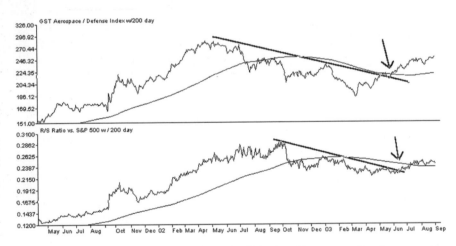

FIGURE 2.4 Aerospace Index (top) and R/S Ratio of Aerospace Stocks versus the S&P 500

In Figure 2.4, we again see an elongated bear market ending with an upside breakout. In Figure 2.5, note the positive divergence on MACD leading into the March–April 2003 lows. This was followed by a rise in the aerospace defense index over the next two years (Figure 2.6). Switching to semiconductors, Figure 2.7 shows a long downtrend in semiconductor stocks, which lasted nearly 12 months. Following the upside breakout in

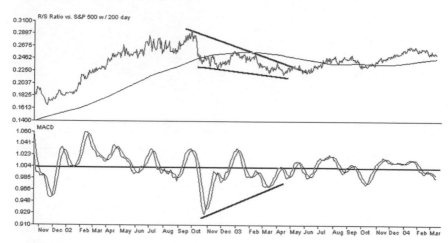

FIGURE 2.5 The R/S Ratio for Aerospace Stocks versus the S&P 500

FIGURE 2.6 Following the Breakout in May 2003 the Aerospace Defense Index Rose Nearly 200 Percent in 25 Months

relative strength, the semiconductor index advanced almost 400 percent in the next 15 months (Figure 2.8).

What about those instances where the period of R/S underperformance is stretched out beyond 12 to 18 months? In these situations, I would advise making a few changes. Begin by lengthening the periodicity for MACD to create something of a more medium- to long-term gauge performing the same type of analysis. Over the last few years, I have found

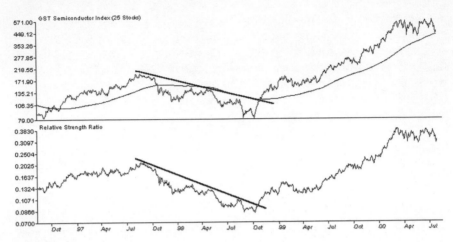

FIGURE 2.7 A Breakout in Relative Strength Accompanies the Turn in Semiconductor Stocks

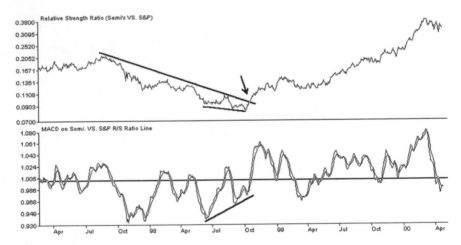

FIGURE 2.8 The MACD Provides an Early Hint at the Developing Trend Change with a Positive Divergence with Relative Strength

that a more medium- to long-term MACD can be constructed with good success using a 24, 48, 12 sequence, wherein the first exponential moving average is 24 days, the second 48 days, with medium-term MACD computed by subtracting the first MA from the second. In this instance, the signal line should also be lengthened to 12 periods, again using the classic exponential moving average.

In addition to the modified medium- to long-term MACD, it is also a good idea to run a 200-day simple moving average on both the index (i.e., sector) and the sector R/S line. Only consider a long position once the R/S ratio has crossed back above its 200-day moving average. In my work, I would use the medium-term MACD as the setup for the buy and then buy once the relative strength ratio crosses back above the 200-day average, using this crossover as a bullish confirmation.

Let's look at a recent example using my index of 40 health care stocks in the period 1999–2000. As can be seen in Figure 2.9, the relative strength ratio for health care stocks peaked in late April 1996, the sector lagging the market badly in 1997, 1998, and 1999. Of course, 1999 was the year of the great technology Internet boom and no one cared about boring old health care stocks. From the Asia crisis of 1998 right into the NASDAQ peak in March 2000, health care stocks were passé, with the relative strength ratio in a straight-line decline, remaining consistently below its 200-day moving average. Perhaps people would no longer be getting sick and require medical attention?

As Figure 2.9 shows, the bottoming process in late 1999 in health care stocks had several defining features. First off, the long-standing downtrend line was overcome early in 2000 after having remained intact for nearly two years. Two-year downtrends are a big deal, because they do not occur all that often, and their reversal often signals the beginning of a truly major advance. Next, we see that as the relative strength ratio actually crossed above its 200-day moving average, this really marked the

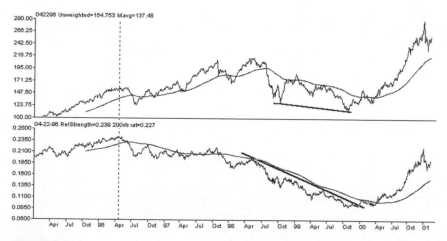

FIGURE 2.9 Health Care Stocks Underperformed the Market in 1998 and 1999 but Broke Out on the R/S Ratio in Early 2000 (bottom)

beginning of the major uptrend in the health care index, which confirmed it by quickly moving back above its own 200-day moving average.

Bringing MACD into the equation, it is important to remember that we are looking for a *pronounced* loss of downside momentum in the declining pattern of relative strength. In this instance, using the medium-term MACD, the signal came in late March 2000 when the relative strength ratio closely approached its former lows with a reading of .096 on March 28, 2000 (versus prior lows of .092 on December 31, 1999, and .0899 on October 28, 1999) while at the same time, MACD barely dipped below zero. Note that during the course of the major downtrend, while the April 1999 and late October 1999 bottoms on MACD did manage to hold slightly above the initial momentum low of August 27, 1998, the amount of the divergence was not that substantial in either case. These were only marginally higher lows. In my work with sectors, I have noted that very often, longer-range (two years or more) periods where a sector underperforms the market (i.e., a period of poor relative strength) will often trace out this type of triple negative excursion (three moves below 1.00) on the medium-term MACD. An example is shown in Figure 2.10. Note the elongated (triple) base with MACD moving up to zero several times. The tip-off on these patterns is the last decline, which invariably is very shallow on MACD.

Invariably, the third cluster of readings below 1.00 should be a major hint that the end of the downtrend is at hand or, at a minimum, very near. Following the third negative cluster of MACD readings (with each cluster

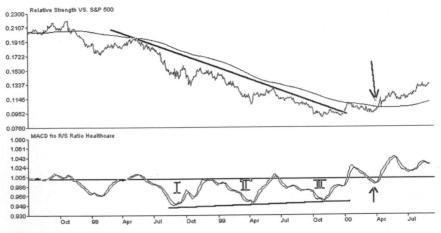

FIGURE 2.10 The R/S Ratio of Health Care Stocks versus the S&P (top) and the MACD Based on the R/S Ratio (bottom)

separated by a brief move back up toward 1.00), we would normally look for the more positive action on MACD moving back above 1.00. In this case, the setup for a major turn was perfect, as MACD surged above 1.00 and then reversed back below 1.00 to only a very shallow reading as the ratio virtually retested its former lows. The pronounced divergence on MACD, which then recrossed to the upside, was followed by the R/S ratio breakout back above the 200-day average, which was solid evidence that a major turn was at hand.

How important can something like this be for an investor to recognize? Well, over the following two years, the mighty NASDAQ collapsed, losing nearly 75 percent of its value and with many technology stocks losing 80 percent or more of their value (see Figure 2.11). During the great bear market of 2000 to 2002, which sector succeeded in moving *up* instead of down? You guessed it—the health care stocks, acting as a safe haven for money in a terrible market environment. Figure 2.11 shows the NASDAQ Composite (top clip) and the health care index on the bottom. Note that as NASDAQ collapsed, money rotated into health care.

For those interested in sectors that may from time to time be involved in a secular bear market relative to the S&P, I would suggest using weekly charts in lieu of daily charts and running the standard 12-26-9 MACD on your weekly charts. This type of analysis would apply to stock sectors in multiyear bear markets, which are known to happen with more frequency than might be imagined. Gold, for example, went through a 20-year bear market from 1980 to 2000, during which time the gold stocks suffered

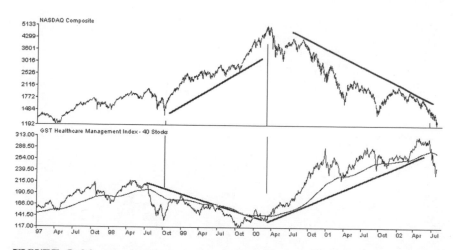

FIGURE 2.11 The NASDAQ Composite (top) and the Health Care Index (bottom), 1997–2002

several huge bear market declines (see Figure 2.12). How do you find a turn in a situation like this? Use weekly charts, and draw the same type of trend lines on the R/S ratio. Here again, watch the weekly MACD based on the R/S ratio line to give corroboration of a potential bullish reversal. In the case of the gold stocks, between 1996 and 2000 we saw a triple negative excursion (see Figure 2.13), which was followed by a strong surge above 1.00 on MACD and a series of higher, less negative readings on MACD in 1999 and 2000. Figure 2.13 shows the end of the long downtrend with the timely trend line breakout on the R/S ratio.

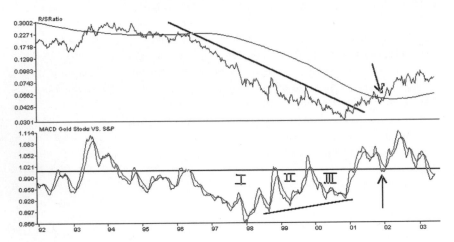

FIGURE 2.12 Gold's Secular Bear Market, 1993–2000, with R/S Ratio (top) and Weekly Version of MACD (bottom)

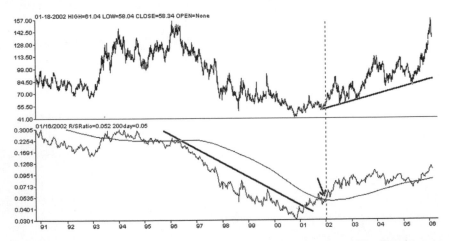

FIGURE 2.13 The End of Gold's Long Downtrend with a Trend Line Breakout on the R/S Ratio

USING BREADTH IN SECTOR ANALYSIS

Another gauge I like to use in looking for important trend changes in stock market sectors is the medium-term advance/decline (A/D) ratio, which I plot for every sector that I follow. In order to use this type of gauge, you need to be following a fairly substantive group. For smaller microgroups like *Investor's Business Daily's* medical—dental or medical—nursing homes, breadth work is really not possible in the truest sense. Later I provide a kind of short cut that can yield similar results for narrower microgroups, but for now, I want to focus on the role of breadth gauges on larger sectors.

What could constitute a large enough sector? In my view, any group with 20 or more stocks, and ideally any sector with 25 to 30 or more stocks that tend to move in the same trends. Twenty stocks is really the minimum requirement to get real value from sector-related breadth indicators. How many groups are there with 20 or more stocks? Strangely enough, there are quite a few, including health care, technology, energy, oil service, gold and precious metals, biotechnology, semiconductors, consumer staples (including food, beverage, tobacco), cyclicals (including base metals, paper, chemicals, coal), home building, aerospace defense, alternative energy, steel, chemicals, Internet, large-cap banking, regional banking, insurance, pharmaceuticals, utilities, apparel retailing, transportation, consumer electronics, paper and forestry, leisure (including hotels, recreational services, restaurants, and travel and tourism), financials (including brokers, asset managers, and investment services), software, and telecom. The beauty of investing in today's market is the fact that the ever-increasing number of ETFs allow you to trade one stock that directly follows the trend of a number of these groups. A number of the most popular ETFs, such as the oil service (OIH), energy (XLE), semiconductor (SMH), retailers (RTH), and biotech (BBH), trade huge volumes and provide excellent liquidity. Some newer additions include aerospace and defense (PPA), leisure and entertainment (PEJ), consumer staples (XLP), and home builders (XHB). A complete list of all ETFs including iShares, HOLDRs, PowerShares, and others can be found at www.amex.com.

In order to compute the medium-term A/D ratio for a particular sector, the group's components must be parsed each day into advancing and declining issues. In my work with the gold stocks, for example, I keep a universe of 30 gold stocks and tally the breakdown of advancers and decliners each day. I determine the net tally of advancing or declining issues by using closing prices or a daily median calculation. The daily median is computed by averaging the high and low for each stock each day, and then comparing the daily change in median prices. Both approaches will yield similar results, although at certain turns, where a group may experience key reversal days, the median approach may yield even more information. That said, the medium-term A/D ratio is calculated by tabulating a 50-day exponential moving average of advances over declines.

Here again, we end up with a ratio-based indicator that will normally move back and forth between low values in the area of .70 to .80 and high values in the area between 1.30 and 1.40. Depending on the overall beta of the sector, the amplitude of the gauge will vary. In the case of very high beta groups like gold and biotech, which are three to four times as volatile as the S&P, high-end figures can get as high as 1.80 to 2.00 and low-end figures as far down as .40 to .50. For the gold stocks, I have found that the parameters of 1.30 for overbought and .70 for oversold act as good guidelines. (See Figure 2.14—while this may look like someone's EKG, the chart gives a good idea of the kind of range this indicator can cover.) The same is true for biotechnology stocks and other volatile groups like home builders and oil service stocks. On the more conservative side, lower-beta groups like consumer staples and drugs will have a narrower range on the A/D ratio with parameters more akin to 1.20 to 1.25 overbought, and .80 to .85 oversold. For the majority of sectors with a market-oriented beta, 1.30 works well as overbought and .80 as oversold. My advice would be, when tracking a particular group, to download at least four years of prior history to establish parameters before making any investment decisions. A good vendor for historical stock data is Track Data's "DialData" product, which contains a huge historical database for equity prices.

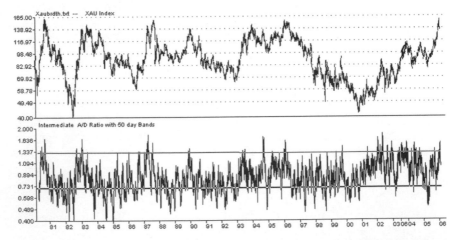

FIGURE 2.14 Volatile Gold Stocks with the Medium-Term A/D Ratio, 1980–2006

When employing the medium-term A/D ratio, in addition to the presence of overbought and oversold values, which often highlight potential buy/sell zones, positive and negative divergences with price also become extremely important and speak volumes about potential trend changes when they are present. Figure 2.15 shows a classic example of a bottom, where we see the XAU (gold and silver mining index) tumbling in late 1997 and forming the extreme oversold low on the A/D ratio in early December. After a trading rally of 10 days' duration, prices then come back down and fall to new lows in early 1998. However, as prices drop to lower lows, the A/D ratio is successful in holding at a higher, less negative low, and in the process sets up a positive divergence with price. Invariably, this type of positive divergence will signal a substantial rally, as it did on this occasion with XAU gaining better than 30 percent in just three months.

An example of the opposite condition, a market top, was seen in the telecom stocks where I maintain a group of 30 large- and mid-cap telecom names. Note the classic head and shoulders pattern in Figure 2.16 on the major price high seen in early 2000, just before the major crash. Note also that the medium-term A/D ratio peaked on the left side of the top, on the left shoulder, and made lower highs even as prices pressed to new highs to form the head of the pattern. Here again, the successive minor rallies to higher highs took place against a backdrop of weakening group participation, a telltale signal that the long uptrend was ending.

Once you accumulate enough data on a group, you will notice that these signals happen with a high degree of regularity and attend many of

FIGURE 2.15 The XAU Gold Index with the Medium-Term A/D Ratio, September 1997 to June 1998

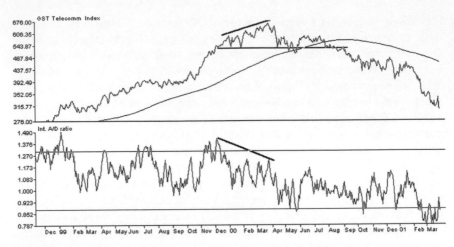

FIGURE 2.16 Telecom Stocks in 2000 with a Bearish Divergence on the A/D Ratio

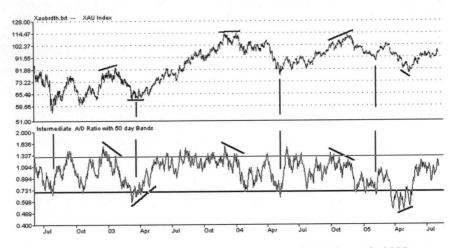

FIGURE 2.17 The XAU Gold Index and A/D Ratio, July 2002 to July 2005

the most important turns. In Figure 2.17 we see the XAU gold index and its A/D ratio between 2002 and 2005. Note the oversold divergent readings attending the March–April 2003 bottom and the April–May 2005 bottom. In addition, fully oversold spikes also highlighted the washout declines of July 2002 and April 2004. Conversely, on the high end of the range, we note the bearish divergences that attended the peaks of early 2003, late 2003, and late 2004.

USING VOLUME IN SECTOR ANALYSIS

Another useful area that will add value to any sector trade is the incorporation of volume-related indicators. Here again, it is important to parse each day's sector trading into columns of advancing and declining volume. There are at least two approaches one can use in determining each day's total up and down volume. Perhaps the simplest approach is to look at the daily closing change for each stock on the list, and if the stock is closing higher, all of the day's volume is assigned as up volume; all of the day's volume is assigned as down volume in cases where the share price declined. Yet, as Larry Williams pointed out years ago, with his Accumulation-Distribution Gauge, and Marc Chaikin with his Money Flow Gauge, assigning all of the day's trading volume to one direction based solely on the direction of the day's close can be quite misleading. Perhaps, where volume indicators are concerned, a better approach would be to compute a daily median, averaging the high and low for each security and then assigning volume based on the day-to-day changes in median.

An even more discrete determination of up and down volume would be to use Williams' approach, and calculate a volume percentage for each stock on the list. To do this, the following formula can be used:

$$(\text{Close} - \text{Open}) / (\text{High} - \text{Low}) \times \text{Total Daily Volume}$$

This formula can even be applied to individual stocks. By summing the last 12 days worth of up and the last 12 days worth of down volume, we arrive at a fairly helpful 12-day oscillator of up-to-down volume. An example of this gauge applied to an individual stock is the chart of Citigroup shown in Figure 2.18, where net 12-day down volume totals approaching −5 million have picked up at any number of important bottoms over the last few years. Notice how extreme readings in net down volume correlate with important lows.

Because individual stocks will sometimes create division-by-zero errors using a short-term ratio of up-to-down volume, for individual stocks I tend to look at a net oscillator, netting the up less down volume. That said, readers need to be aware that where individual stocks are concerned, this indicator will be reset often when stocks split. The point of mentioning the application to individual stocks is really to highlight the effectiveness of parsing up and down volume as tools.

By parsing the day's volume into buying pressure and selling pressure, we can highlight low-risk entry points, not only for a stock, but to an even more effective degree with a large sector, such as banking or energy.

When applied at the sector level, in other words, creating an aggregate up volume series and aggregate down volume series for, say, a list of

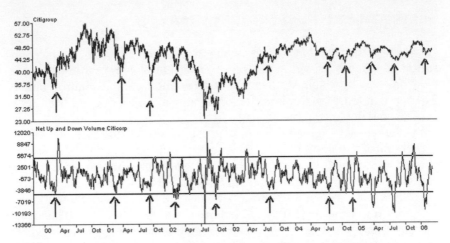

FIGURE 2.18   Citigroup Stock with a Net Up-to-Down Volume Oscillator

25 to 30 stocks all in one sector, we arrive at yet another powerful technical timing tool. When it is developed into a sector tool, I definitely favor
using an up-to-down volume ratio, as the ratio automatically takes into account the higher levels of trading volume that tend to unfold in the market
as time marches on. Traders and investors are encouraged to get creative
with these gauges, as changing the periodicity in the span of the indicator
will allow the user to identify different kinds of trading opportunities. In
my work, I tend to use a 12-day period for identifying short-term high and
low extremes, and a 25-day period for more important medium-term high
and low extremes. In Figure 2.19, we see a good example of the power of
the up-to-down volume ratio. In this instance I have applied the ratio to a
basket of 50 technology stocks. Note the rhythmic movements back and
forth between overbought and oversold territory, and in particular the
positive divergences that accompany a number of important bottoms. The
up-to-down volume ratio tends to lead the market at turns, and oversold
readings tend to generate worthwhile trading rallies.

Depending on how many constituent stocks make up a particular sector, the overbought and oversold parameters for an indicator like up and
down volume will vary to a modest degree. Smaller sectors composed of
20 to 30 stocks may tend to fluctuate over a slightly wider range of .50
oversold to 2.00 overbought with 1.00 neutral, while larger sectors of 30 or
more stocks may see those parameters shrink by a certain margin, with
readings above 1.50 to 1.75 indicating overbought and readings between
.70 and .80 oversold. As in the prior instance with advances and declines, I
recommend downloading at least four years of history for whatever group
is to be followed and then setting up best-fit parameters on that pilot data.

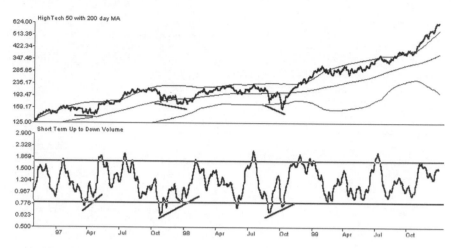

FIGURE 2.19 Barbera's High Tech 50 Index with Up and Down Volume

Usually, with four years of history the extremes of overbought and oversold territory become fairly evident. While on the subject of establishing indicator extremes, I might add that it is very important to keep an eye on the direction of the primary trend.

SCALE SHIFTS

During bull markets, all indicators tend to trade with a bias to the high end of the range, while in bear markets indicators tend to shift to new, lower extremes. This is what I call indicator *scale shift*, and where truly major market moves are involved, it will happen.

Sticking with the example of technology stocks, we see that during the secular bull market of the 1980s and 1990s, the up-to-down volume ratio on my High Tech 50 was overbought at 1.75 and oversold at .80. See Figure 2.20, noting how the scale of parameters of overbought and oversold tend to shift downward in a bear market and upward in a bull market.

Now, fast-forward to the secular bear market in technology stocks in 2000 to 2002, and we see the scale drifting lower, with readings of 1.50 overbought and readings of .65 oversold. This is life in the big city, as virtually all indicators will tend to move to deeper oversold values in a bear market, and to shallower oversold values in a bull market. Keep an eye on the 200-day average: When it is turning down after an elongated advance, the technician should be especially on guard for the possibilities of a downward scale shift in the indicators. Under these circumstances a good

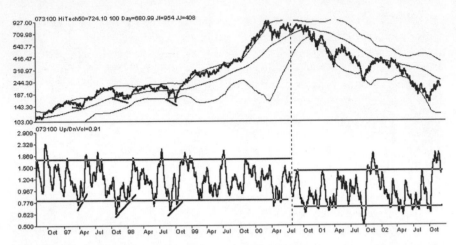

FIGURE 2.20 Overbought and Oversold Indicators Drop Lower in Bear Market (Barbera's High Tech 50 Index with Up-to-Down Volume)

approach, which can provide temporary relative overbought and oversold extremes, would be to run a 200-day medium- to long-term trading band around a gauge like up-to-down volume using 1.50 standard deviations, which I have found through trial and error works pretty well. Figure 2.21 depicts this with the Bollinger Bands overlaid on the High Tech 50 up-to-down volume gauge. In a transition environment, where long-term moving averages are changing direction, the outer trading bands can be good relative overbought and oversold values.

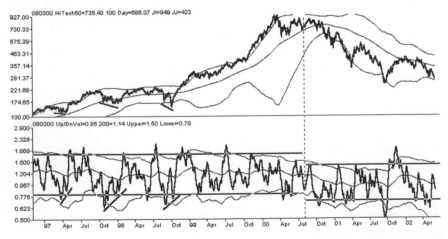

FIGURE 2.21 Barbera's High Tech 50 Volume Gauge with Bollinger Bands Overlaid

In addition to gauges of breadth and volume, we also see the scale shift phenomenon at work in more classic gauges like the nine-day Wilder Relative Strength Index (RSI), which is a common momentum gauge. The RSI is what is known as a *bounded* momentum gauge in that the scale is fixed to readings between zero and +100. This contrasts to MACD and Rate of Change readings, both of which are nonbounded momentum gauges. The classic RSI scale suggests that values above +70 are over-bought and readings below +30 are oversold. In reality, in strong uptrending bull market moves, the nine-day RSI will often move up to record readings in the +80 area and end up a subsequent correction in the low +40 zone. This upward scale shift away from the traditional +70 and +30, to +80 and +40 parameters, is the bull market "80/40" rule for the nine-day RSI. Alternatively, in bear markets, we often experience a downward scale shift to parameters of +60 overbought and +20 oversold. This is the bear market "60/20" rule for the nine-day RSI.

In Figure 2.22, a serious bear market in commodities in 1998 and 1999 saw the CRB Index, a widely watched gauge of commodity prices, trace out a classic bear market pattern with overbought readings peaking at +60 on the nine-day RSI, and oversold values troughing just below or near +20—again, the "60/20" bear market rule.

Figure 2.23 shows an alternate view, once again of the CRB Index, this time circa 2003 through 2005. Here we see a great bull market under way and another great example of scale shift behavior. Note the manner in which small declines are arrested and reversed to the upside as the RSI troughs above +30 in the +40 zone. These are examples of the "80/40" rule

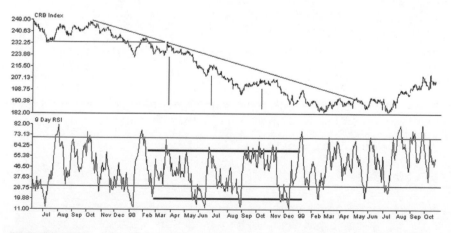

FIGURE 2.22 CRB Index in Bear Trend, with the RSI Shifting down the Scale

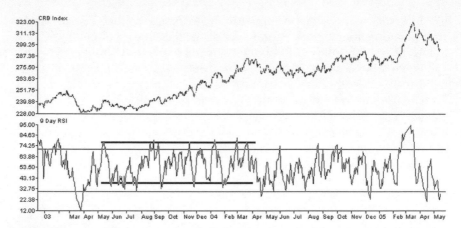

FIGURE 2.23   CRB Index in Bull Trend, with the RSI Shifting up the Scale, 2003 to Mid-2005

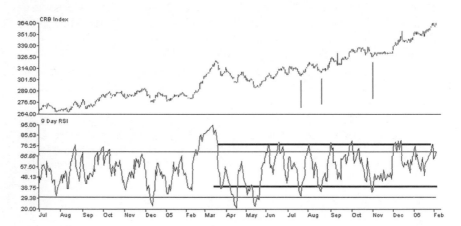

FIGURE 2.24   CRB Bull Trend Continuing into 2006, with the RSI Shifting up the Scale

for bull markets. Figure 2.24 once again shows the CRB Index in a bull trend, with the RSI shifting up the scale in the bull market.

SENTIMENT

Finally, I want to touch on the use of sentiment gauges in sector analysis as yet another tool that can be helpful in identifying important extremes. In the area of sentiment, I continue to prefer gauges that come from real flow-of-funds data rather than surveys of investor sentiment. The reason for this is that survey data does not necessarily indicate what people are actually doing with their capital. On many occasions, people may feel one way about a market (i.e., "Oh, the next 10 percent is down") but may not necessarily act accordingly (i.e., sell).

Gauges that depend on trading on options and order flow tend to be fairly helpful, although as I alluded to earlier in this chapter, one needs to be extremely careful in constructing and maintaining these gauges. I believe that on a sector level, if one carefully goes through the daily options trades for closely related stocks in the same sector, it is still quite possible to build out valuable timing tools. Always concentrate on including only near term at-the-money options data, as these days, deep in-the-money options trades are generally the playground of large hedge funds.

The CBOE Volatility Index (VIX) is also an especially useful tool, as implied volatility goes to the very heart of sentiment. This is a great place to start if one is keenly interested in tracking sentiment. In my work, I use individual VIX and implied volatility calculations to build out sentiment indicators for groups like gold and oil services, where high volatility can lead to very profitable trades. Figures 2.25 and 2.26 show an example of the Hamzei Analytics UniVol Index for the oil service sector, which signals bottoms with an upward price spike, and an example of my own work using gold stocks, where I compute a daily dollar-weighted put/call ratio. As in the past, high readings on this gauge suggest the presence of great fear and are an excellent indication of a major trading rally, often highlighting an important bottom. Low readings on the VIX and put/call (P/C) ratio indicate optimism and need to be handled with great care. They are important

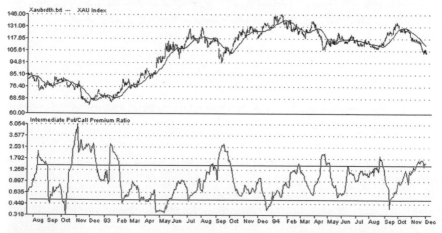

FIGURE 2.25 The XAU Gold Index with a Dollar-Weighted Put/Call Ratio

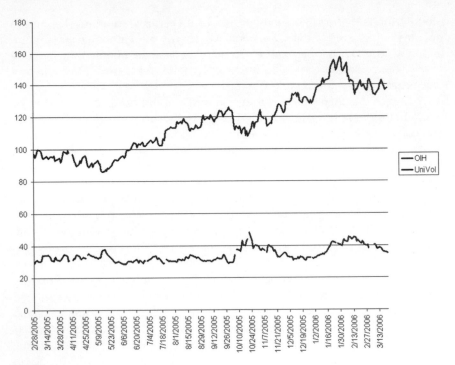

FIGURE 2.26   A Spike in UniVol Highlights a Bottom in OIH ETF

only at the end of an elongated trend, once other gauges begin to diverge. At that point, low readings could well signal a major top.

Rule number one—a cardinal rule—when looking at low overbought readings on the VIX and put/call ratio is to *ignore low readings at the beginning and middle of an advance*. If breadth, momentum, and volume indicators are all acting well and there are no bearish divergences on these other gauges, then low sentiment readings should be seen as confirmation of the primary trend. Put another way, in the early and middle phases of a bull move, the bulls are correct. Contrary opinion gauges like sentiment come into play *only* during the latter phases of an advance, months into it, when participation has been noticeably dwindling for some time, momentum gauges are diverging, and volume is weakening. As can be seen in Figure 2.27, in 1994 gold stocks ended a long bull move, and only at the very end—once breadth, momentum, and volume gauges had been deteriorating for months—did the low put/call readings signal a genuine downside reversal. Note the extended pattern of bearish divergence on both the MACD and the A/D ratio and how the very low P/C reading in early 1994 established the sentiment backdrop for a major top. Usually, after the initial powerful surge

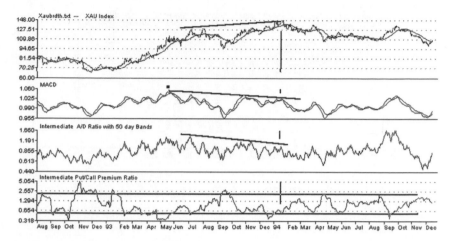

FIGURE 2.27 Gold Ends Long Bull Move After Breadth, Momentum, and Volume Gauges Deteriorate, 1993–1994

is complete in a sector, the first decline will be a large correction (20 percent or more), which is then followed by a series of higher highs. New highs following a sizeable correction need to be scrutinized more carefully, as normally it is in that window that risk of a primary trend reversal is highest.

CONCLUSION

In summary, I believe that for investors willing to put in a certain amount of time every week, the ability to market-time individual stock sectors can boost overall investment returns quite dramatically while at the same time minimizing portfolio risks. In my experience it is usually best to pick no more than two or three sectors where you can come to a better understanding of industry fundamentals, and where volatility levels are fairly high so that within any given year there are likely to be several large-scale moneymaking opportunities. High-volatility (high-beta) sectors like gaming, oil service, biotechnology, gold, and technology sector trading offers the potential of 20 percent returns virtually year in and year out, something that is not true of the broad market (ala the S&P 500), which quite frequently will see entire years pass with moves of 5 or 6 percent or less. Invariably, sector trading equals opportunity, and those opportunities are enhanced each passing week with the introduction of more ETFs, many of which specialize in individual sectors. For the small investor, the ETFs now provide the vehicle while technical analysis can provide the equally important intellectual capital.

CHAPTER 3

Evaluating Probabilities to Improve Profitability

Kevin Tuttle

Within the industry there are countless shoot-from-the-hip managers searching for the holy grail of profitable trading. Sadly, this journey has no clear destination. However, for those on a quest to increase the probability of profitable trading, you have purchased the right book. The sole premise of this chapter is to help devise a long-term and time-tested road map for successful investing, tailored to your style of management.

Before we embark, I believe it necessary to clarify my inherent belief regarding technical analysis and its application to all tradable markets. In my humble opinion,

real condition
reliable data

> *Technical analysis is nothing more than interpreting a graphical illustration depicting, as a whole, investors' psychology in relation to the existing condition of the markets. As such, technical analysis should be employed for the sole purpose of commandeering a greater comprehension of the market's supply and demand elements that underlie its position at any given time.*

Simply, technical analysis should serve as a mechanism that assists in both the evaluation of the current risk/reward condition of the market and the determination of the next likely progression of price action. This deduction is essential to increasing the probability of investing profitably.

If you take away only one aspect from this chapter, it is my hope you recognize the need to cultivate an exclusive system based on the changes in today's market dynamics and reject yesterday's straight-line-thinking

non-linear

philosophy. Hence, be able to establish the framework for a dramatic change in your long-term investment decision-making processes.

To understand straight-line thinking all we have to do is listen to the abundantly pronounced wisdom regarding the question of how to invest: "You can't time the market." "You'll be better off if you buy and hold and not trade the market." "Invest for the long haul." All of these constitute straight-line thinking and occur when a trend has been in place for such a long time that people don't recall when it wasn't, or they just weren't around to witness it. In general, such thinkers unconditionally believe everything will remain status quo.

Given the fact that U.S. equity markets from 1982 to 2000 were in the *also* most magnificent uptrend ever produced, these comments made sense at *1935–1968* the time. But what if you were a money manager in 1966 and held these same philosophies? Would you have still been in business in 1982? During that 16-year interim, the market (referring to the Dow Jones Industrial Av- *or SPX* erage) roughly began and ended at 1,000, yielding a negative real return after taxes and inflation. Clearly no one could have predicted with 100 percent accuracy what was going to transpire during that period. The same goes for today's markets and the next 5, 10, and 15 years.

I believe that the industry has entered another major transition period which will amplify the complexity of market dynamics for the foreseeable future. This has set all investment professionals climbing toward a mountaintop where only a few can stand. Today's success requires the design and adaptation of an investment philosophy that maximizes the efficiency of research expenditure, lowers risk, and increases the probability of success.

A DYNAMICALLY CHANGING SYSTEM

Over the years of managing assets I've designed a dynamically adaptive system that encompasses a three-tier investment pyramid (see Figure 3.1). When employed properly, this framework can accommodate any type of manager/investor and his individual philosophy of the market. Throughout this chapter I articulate my theory of "evaluating probabilities to improve profitability" and how to design your own unique system.

The investment pyramid consists of:

- A solid foundation ("Long-Term Market Theory")
- A strategy set atop ("Simplify the Complexity")
- A proven trading methodology ("Quantitative Screening and Technical Analysis")

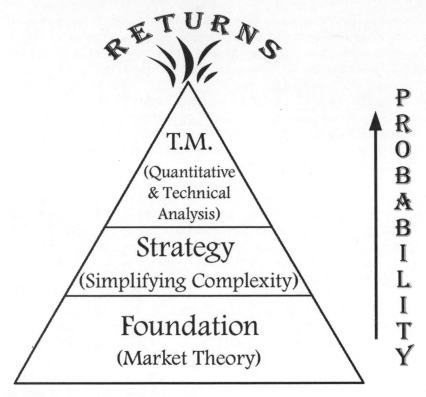

FIGURE 3.1   TAM Investing Pyramid

The nucleus of this system pivots around increasing the probability of success through identifying the market's <u>inflection points</u> within the context of a long-term technical view that underlies a quantitative and technical screening process of elimination. This results in a fundamental shift of mind-set and provides a rigorous daily technique that is set in stone. It also prevents loss of focus on the daily road map and aimless driving down a winding highway.

THE FOUNDATION: 100-YEAR DOW CHART AND LONG-TERM MARKET THEORY

When I want to understand what is happening today, I try to decide what will happen tomorrow; I <u>look back because a page of history is worth a volume of logic.</u> (Oliver Wendell Holmes, nineteenth-century author and poet)

That men do not learn very much from the lessons of history is the most important of all the lessons history has to teach. (Aldous Huxley, early twentieth-century English novelist)

To create a road map, a traveler must first examine the trip he wishes to embark on and plot an appropriate course—the foundation. This is similar to the creation of a long-term technical outlook. Once established, it will allow further progression upward within the pyramid. Thus, I felt it apropos to present two quotes that underscore its importance to the core of any investment decision-making process.

We are all aware of professionals who are straight-line thinkers and rattle off the all-too-common phrase, "The market will maintain a bullish stance and should be bought on all dips." As previously noted, I do not subscribe to this statement or its thought process. The market is a continuously varying organism and the model must adapt correspondingly. Not unlike all levels within the investment pyramid, the foundation is dynamic and must provide the ability to adjust as the market's long-term technical condition changes. Failing to adapt will inevitably confirm failure itself.

Before reviewing the long-term market philosophy, it's important to make a few disclosures:

- The material presented is not solely technical in nature. The chart incorporates the 10-year smoothed average price/earnings (P/E) ratio of the S&P 500 as a broad measure of the market's fundamentals. Although not without imperfections, in my judgment it's the only true time-tested fundamental metric with long-term reliability.
- The pyramid is representative of U.S. equity market investing but can be applied to any and all tradable markets. The reason: Investor psychology may change given the analyzed market, but the supply and demand metrics always remain resolute.
- The Dow Jones Industrial Average prices are in logarithmic form, while the P/E ratios are arithmetic.
- The data is considered to be factual in nature and sources believed to be reliable.
- The presented information is a matter of opinion from Tuttle Asset Management, LLC and should be considered as such.

Foundation and U.S. Equity Market Theory

Extreme excesses in market valuation, due to immense price appreciation over extended periods, can take years to correct and

*allow earnings to once again draw closer to prices (www
.tuttlemgmt.com/TAM/Investment-Philosophy-and-Strat.html)*

The following interpretation of the Dow Jones Industrial Average
chart depicts a mega macro technical view over the last 100 years. As
shown with simple trend lines, it's plain to see that throughout the last
century there have been four periods of significant growth—one extreme
downtrend and three (now possibly four) major consolidation periods. On
a more micro scale there have been numerous periods of deterioration,
consolidation, and growth within these larger periods. For the purpose of
this illustration on the underlying foundation we only need to take into
consideration the larger macro point of view for now.

In Figure 3.2 I include a 10-year smoothed average P/E multiple, provided by Robert J. Shiller's web site (www.irrationalexuberance.com), for
long-term fundamental valuation analysis. Mr. Shiller is a professor of economics at Yale University and was the co-author of a paper posted in the
Journal of Portfolio Management called, "Valuation Ratios and the Long-
Run Stock Market Outlook," in July 1997. Therein he concluded that using
a 10-year smoothed P/E multiple accurately represented valuations over
longer periods of time and is directly applicable to my theory.

There are some who do not subscribe to the correlation between
technical trends of market valuation and historical prices. Despite these
opposing views, I believe the long-established and time-honored P/E valuation ratio is exceptionally relevant because of the direct relation to fundamental measurement. The straight-line thinkers who disagree with our
over/under valuation analysis believe long-term valuations will, under no
circumstances, retrace back to historic lows. They propose shifts in corporate policy, changes in investor behavior, or even the development of a

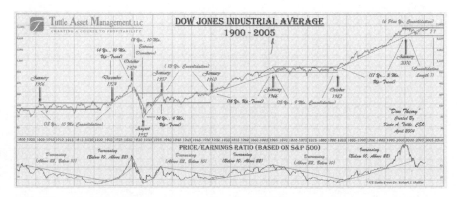

FIGURE 3.2 TAM Dow Jones Industrial Average 100-Year Chart

greater global economy as reasons why this will never happen. Unquestionably there have been times past where valuations fluctuated to extremes. Yet this is precisely why we must not ignore the implication of such movements and the possible repercussions thereof.

Table 3.1 and Figure 3.2 can assist readers in following along with the long-term market interpretation. They depict the different time periods discussed, the corresponding price action, and the P/E ratio trend direction. If you wish to obtain a full reproduction, you can log onto our web site at www.tuttlemgmt.com.

As illustrated in the table and chart, the first (and thus far the longest) macro consolidation began in January 1906 at the 105 resistance level and didn't break out until December 1924, almost 19 years later. All the while, and conceivably more important, the P/E ratio remained in a downward trend, from the overvalued above-22 level to the undervalued below-10 level, virtually the entire period. In 1922 the P/E ratio finally broke above its downward trend and began its ascent back above 10 in 1925. Notably, the market's last retest of the bottom side of the channel was in 1921, and in December 1924 it finally broke the 105 technical resistance level.

Once the market broke free of this consolidation, it gained over 300 percent in just under five years and ended its reign just below 400 in October 1929. Noticeably during this time the P/E multiple blasted off like a rocket and reached an above-32 multiple, which was then followed by the Great Depression, initiated by the great market crash of 1929 (Black Tuesday).

The Great Depression's extreme downtrend and corresponding uptrend does not fit the typical consolidation/uptrend technical price pattern. The downtrend lasted approximately three years, compared to the other consolidation periods, which lasted from 13 to 19 years. However, the corresponding P/E multiple does fit the cycle of valuation change and had the same overall effect as the longer-term consolidation/uptrend patterns. In other words, the vast drop-off during the Great Depression achieved the same result as a longer-term consolidation—it wrung out the excessive overvaluation within the market.

In 1932 the P/E multiple, after being trounced and declining below the undervalued 10 level, broke above its downtrend and the market began its next rise. The ensuing uptrend beginning in August 1932 only endured for just over four years before it entered a second and much longer consolidation period. This is where in January 1937 the market hit the bottom side of the "floors and ceilings" resistance from the 1929 crash—Black Tuesday—at approximately 195. This began another 13-year consolidation. Also in January 1937 the P/E valuation reached the overvalued 22 level, broke its uptrend, and commenced another downward cycle.

TABLE 3.1 Analysis of Major Dow Jones Inflection Points

Date Range		Price Action	Duration	Price/Earnings Ratio
Jan. 1906	Dec. 1924	Consolidation	18 years, 10 months	Declining from above 22 to below 10
Dec. 1924	Oct. 1929	Uptrend	4 years, 10 months	Increasing from below 10 to above 22
Oct. 1929	Aug. 1932	Extreme Downtrend	2 years, 10 months	Declining from above 22 to below 10
Aug. 1932	Jan. 1937	Uptrend	4 years, 4 months	Increasing from below 10 to above 22
Jan. 1937	Jan. 1950	Consolidation	13 years	Declining from above 22 to below 10
Jan. 1950	Jan. 1966	Uptrend	16 years	Increasing from below 10 to above 22
Jan. 1966	Oct. 1982	Consolidation	15 years, 9 months	Declining from above 22 to below 10
Oct. 1982	Jan. 2000	Uptrend	17 years, 3 months	Increasing from below 10 to above 22
Jan. 2000	Present	Consolidation ?	5 years +	Declining from above 22 to ?

By January 1950 the market broke free of another major macro consolidation period and began a 400 percent move higher that lasted over 16 years. In 1966, following the latest uptrend, the P/E multiple crossed back below the 22 level as the market stalled out in the region of 1,000. The ensuing consolidation lasted nearly as long as its previous advance—16 years.

In 1982 the majority of the P/E valuations had been washed out and the market began its largest uptrend as of yet. This uptrend lasted almost 18 years and provided over a 1,000 percent return during its tenure. Even the "Black Monday" crash in 1987 held the market's mega long-term uptrend and merely looks like a blip on the radar. Coincidently, prior to this time of immense upward momentum, most of today's straight-line-thinking money managers and analysts weren't even in attendance.

As we all remember, in January 2000, following the massive bull market, the P/E multiple hit an astonishing level of 43 while the market began one of the top five downturns in American history. This downturn came to rest in March 2003 at approximately 7,200 for the Dow Jones Industrial Average. Simultaneously the P/E multiple descended and broke its upward trend once again. However, it continued to remain above the historic overvalued level of 22. Since the March 2003 bottom the market has again approached the previous highs without ever once having the 10-year smoothed average P/E multiple drop below the overvalued 22 level. Consequently, one obvious question remains: What comes next?

The ability to look back is one of the most important tools we have in the assistance of understanding today. For this reason, following this review of historical technical price trends and their correlation to the P/E multiple, we are obliged to make some observations.

- Subsequent to every macro technical uptrend, a macro consolidation *either one* period or excessive sell-off has immediately followed and correlated in length of time.
- Consolidation periods have ranged from 13 to almost 20 years in length, not including the excessive market sell-off of the Great Depression.
- P/E valuation trends have corresponded to every technical market uptrend, consolidation period, and massive downturn.
- Breakouts from consolidation periods or new uptrends have not resumed without first having the P/E ratio multiple drop below the undervalued level of 10.
- Market breakdowns have all occurred after the P/E multiple breached the 22 overvalued level and were preceded by it breaking its upward trend.

- The first market sell-off and corresponding bottom of a macro consolidation period normally constitutes the floor of the large technical channel that has begun.
- All historic technical market channels have contained a plethora of 30 to 40 percent price fluctuations.

Distilling data to increase probabilities—that's the name of the game! Resulting from this work, it is my contention that in all likelihood the market has entered yet a fourth consolidation period whose channel logically ranges from a 7,200 low to a 12,000 high. Also inherent within this contention is that the channel will not end until the P/E multiple again crosses back below the undervalued 10 level. Most likely this will not transpire for many years to come and will be aptly related to the length of time of the latest bull run—nearly 18 years. Based on our belief the channel began in 2000—well, you do the math.

Just recently we realized we are not alone with this thought process and have seen other prominent market technicians who have come to similar technical conclusions by using unrelated secondary indicators that support this thesis. For example, in late 2005 John Bollinger (the creator of the Bollinger Bands) and Dick Arms (the creator of the Arms Index, TRIN), appeared on CNBC's *Street Signs* with anchor Ron Insana. Both, using their own indicators, presented similar technical conclusions regarding a long-term technical channel within the U.S. equity markets over the next 10 to 15 years, which neighbored the same range as ours.

Having established a logical long-term technical view of the market (the foundation), it's time to begin forming the next level of the pyramid (the strategy). This is where determining the market's position on the discovered course comes into play.

THE STRATEGY: SIMPLIFYING THE COMPLEXITY

Years ago, an astute businessman and treasured friend sent me the following quote, which has sat atop my desk for nearly 10 years. It exemplifies the logical reasoning contained within the investment pyramid:

> *There is a master key to success which no man can fail. Its name is simplicity. Simplicity, I mean, in the sense of reducing to the simplest possible terms every problem that besets us. Whenever I have met a business situation which, after taking careful thought, I could not reduce to simplicity, I have left it alone. (Sir Henri Deterding, former president of Royal Dutch-Shell)*

There is no question the markets are complex and require us to break down the investment process into more manageable parts. Simplicity is now a necessity in today's market environment. Let's face it, every day there is more and more investment information available to assimilate. There are only 24 hours in a day, only seven days in a week, and a person must sleep, not to mention balance time with family. The information overload dilemma facing money mangers today is nothing short of a double-edged sword. This deluge can overwhelm even the best team of money managers. The main challenge is how to extract the trusted information without overthinking or second-guessing the investment choices.

Thus far I have stated two, seemingly contradictory thoughts about my interpretation, which need to be clarified before continuing. The first is that we must look back at past mega long-term trends within the markets to gain understanding and consequently a better insight into tomorrow. The second is that the markets are dynamically changing and becoming increasingly difficult to navigate. "If everything is changing, then why look back to gain an understanding?" you may ask. My belief is this: No one can build an all-inclusive model—fundamental, economic, political, or otherwise—that incorporates all data relevant to market action. However, the market's price action already incorporates all the relevant factors within itself. In other words, by analyzing the price and volume movements of the market, one is already gaining comprehension of all the intrinsic thoughts and opinions on all the data disseminated to investors/institutions in a graphical illustration.

The Strategy

The overall purpose of our strategy can be summed up as follows:

> *To determine, with reasonable probability, where and when the tops and bottoms may occur within the mega long-term consolidation channel by using technical analysis and corresponding secondary road signs.*

Previously we deduced a clear-cut fact from the historical precedents set in the pyramid's foundation: All historic technical market channels have experienced massive price fluctuations ranging from 30 to 40 percent.

When market technicians speak about channels in relative terms, there is an inherent implication that it is nothing more than a pause, with small price fluctuations, which gives the investment time to create a new base before continuing on with additional advances/declines. Let there be no mistake: The fluctuations contained within these macro long-term channels bestowed absolute devastation to many market participants. The fact of the matter is that, barring the 1929–1932 Great Depression's extreme downturn of 89.5 percent, all the other bear markets have occurred in the context of these massive channels and carried very heavy price tags. Not to downplay the most recent debacle, the 2000–2003 bear market, we should look at all the most destructive bear markets within the last 100 years (see Table 3.2).

Determining where the market is in relation to the foundation's theory allows money managers to reallocate and shift investment strategy by changing their net long and net short exposure. Half the battle of choosing a successful investment is properly determining the overall direction of the market; otherwise it's like rowing a canoe upstream with a spoon.

I personally decided to become proficient in traditional trend line analysis and momentum divergence theory because of its reliability in the type of analysis and management we do at our firm. Therefore, at this point I will digress for a moment and discuss how to increase the probability of ascertaining the next likely progression by giving a few examples of traditional trend line analysis and a combination of road signs. The following is not intended to teach technical analysis, but rather to show the importance of properly using it.

Road signs refer to various secondary technical indicators that help increase the probabilities of a successful outcome. In my interpretation there is only one primary indicator on a technical basis—price. All other indicators used in technical analysis are secondary. That being said, there are countless secondary indicators that technicians can pull from their toolbox. However, many money managers, whom I call "armchair

TABLE 3.2   Top Five Stock Market Declines other than the Great Depression

Years Involved	Percent Decline	Channel Number
1906–1907	48.5%	First Channel
1937–1938	49.7%	Second Channel
1969–1970	36.8%	Third Channel
1973–1974	46.5%	Third Channel
2000–2003	38.7%	Fourth Channel?

technicians," use many of these indicators improperly for three common reasons:

1. Not implementing the proper trend line and/or time frame in the technician's analysis.
2. Lack of understanding of the philosophy underlying the indicators, and improperly utilizing the interpretation.
3. Employing only one indicator to make an investment decision.

The first and most common improper use of technical analysis is rudimentary yet inexplicably true. The abundance of miscalculations and bad investment decisions because of improperly drawn trend lines is surprising. One would think, since the root of technical analysis is interpreting trend lines, that the basics would be second nature. To illustrate this point, let's do a brief self-realizing quiz. Of the two charts shown in Figures 3.3 and 3.4, without giving either the stock's name or the year this occurred (I have to keep you honest), which figure has the proper trend line drawn for a change of trend?

Tough call, can't decide? Don't feel bad, you're not alone. In Figure 3.3

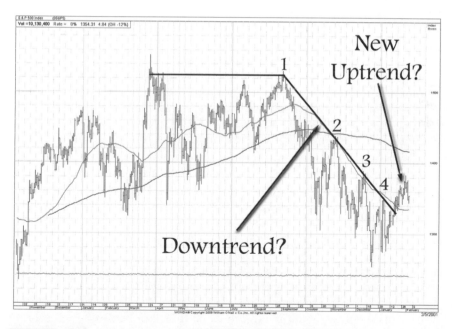

FIGURE 3.3 Self-Realizing Quiz, Part 1 (*Source:* WONDA Copyright 2006 William O'Neil + Co., Inc. All rights reserved. Reprinted with permission from William O'Neil + Co., Inc. Further reproduction prohibited.)

FIGURE 3.4 Self-Realizing Quiz, Part 2 (*Source:* WONDA Copyright 2006 William O'Neil + Co., Inc. All rights reserved. Reprinted with permission from William O'Neil + Co., Inc. Further reproduction prohibited.)

you can see a downward trend line that has four points and corresponds to the 50-day moving average (50-DMA). Illustrated at the bottom right, the price breaks above this line and again above the 50-DMA. Seems reasonable; the downtrend must be over, right? Then again, is the new downtrend line drawn correctly?

If you said, "Yes, the downtrend line is correct," then I have to be the bearer of bad news: You're wrong. When drawing a new trend line you should never come off an absolute peak or trough. There may be times when they do coincide with the overall trend, but for the most part they have the tendency to give many false positives (case in point). A proper change-of-trend line should be built off the first retest of the prior break of trend (floors and ceilings), as seen in Figure 3.4. Why is that more accurate? Because most peaks and troughs are just that, emotionally driven spikes and/or abnormalities in price that don't truly correspond to the overall trend.

If you got it correct, give yourself a hand. If you chose Figure 3.3, don't worry; many people make the same mistake. Nevertheless, look at what would have happened to a long side investment made with the first chart (see Figure 3.5).

I cheated; it's not a stock at all but rather the S&P 500. In spite of that, the same concept applies to any situation, which brings us to a related issue—time frame. While making determinations for the strategy and look-

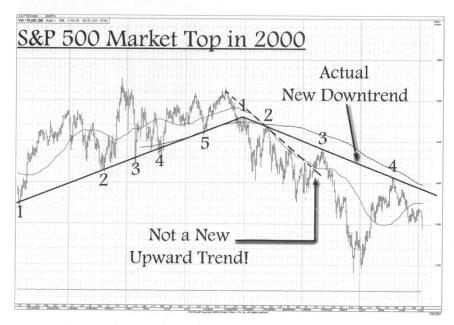

FIGURE 3.5 Answer to Self-Realizing Quiz (*Source:* WONDA Copyright 2006 William O'Neil + Co., Inc. All rights reserved. Reprinted with permission from William O'Neil + Co., Inc. Further reproduction prohibited.)

ing for an approximate top or bottom within a long-term (5- to 10-year) market channel, you can't use a short-term daily chart to establish your conclusion. This may seem simple on the surface, but it happens all the time. As you are assuredly aware, trend lines differ according to time frame. For this reason both long- and short-term charts should be employed at all times. Never make an investment decision based solely on short-term trend lines without first confirming them against the longer-term trend. This is especially true in today's market where the majority of stocks have a profusion of overhead resistance from years prior.

The second example of using technical analysis improperly is comprehensible, but even so remains incorrect. It is not only important to use secondary indicators to help confirm trend line analysis, but it is critical for success that they be *understood* completely and utilized properly. By means of my favorite secondary momentum indicator, I'll give you an example. The stochastic oscillator is one of the most misused and misinterpreted momentum indicators in the technical universe. When applied incorrectly it creates a huge number of false positives and becomes a very poor tool for confirming changes in trend.

Without going into the inner workings of how the stochastic is calculated, let's just say it is a momentum oscillator with two moving averages, a slow (%D) and a fast (%K). The stochastic calculates where on a percentage basis the current price of the stock is in relation to a prior period of time—traditionally 9, 14, or 20 periods. Not unlike the moving average convergence divergence (MACD) indicator, the second slow stochastic is nothing more than a moving average of the fast—traditionally 3, 5, or 6 periods. These two bands fluctuate within a 0 to 100 percent range with an undervalued and an overvalued line at 20 percent and 80 percent, respectively. One primary misuse of this indicator is to sell an investment as the stochastic crosses above the 80 percent line and buy below the 20 percent line. This creates many false positives because the stochastic can sustain itself above or below these lines for extremely long periods of time (see Figure 3.6, Point 1).

Another common misperception, which on the surface sounds reliable, is to sell the investment as the fast stochastic moves through the slow stochastic and returns back below the 80 percent overvalued line, and vice versa. This also presents many false positives. As demonstrated in Figure 3.6 (Point 2), the market never broke trend on either of these occasions.

With that being said, you must be wondering, "Then why is it your favorite secondary indicator?" When used properly—for divergence—it is one of the most accurate and reliable of all the momentum indicators to

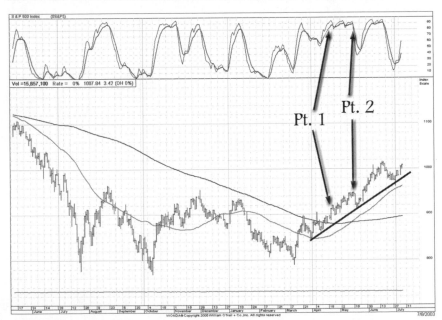

FIGURE 3.6 Misuse of Stochastic Oscillator Creates False Positives (*Source:* WONDA Copyright 2006 William O'Neil + Co., Inc. All rights reserved. Reprinted with permission from William O'Neil + Co., Inc. Further reproduction prohibited.)

Use 2 sets of KD with different (%, %) say 9, 3, 3, then 14.

help identify a change of trend. As they say, a picture is worth a thousand words. The S&P 500 chart in Figure 3.7 gives two short-term picture-perfect stochastic divergences, one negative and one positive.

The true essence of a stochastic divergence can be viewed by noticing two things. The first is a lower low in price—from the beginning of the arrow to the end of the arrow. The second is a higher low for the stochastic—again, from the beginning to the tip of the arrow.

Nevertheless, what makes it absolutely picture-perfect is the point where the second stochastic turn occurred on both, the negative and the positive. By looking closely at the second bottom of the positive stochastic turn and the second top of the negative stochastic turn, you'll see that the slow stochastic (%D) on both occasions barely touched the overvalued and undervalued lines of 80 percent and 20 percent. This gives a true indication of momentum shift. Simply put, the amount of directional price momentum declined/advanced on the second top/bottom. Hence the adage, "Before you learn the tricks of the trade, learn the trade."

The third and most widespread fault in technical analysis is the use of only one indicator to make a decision. This typically occurs when money managers already have an opinion of what they hope to see before they

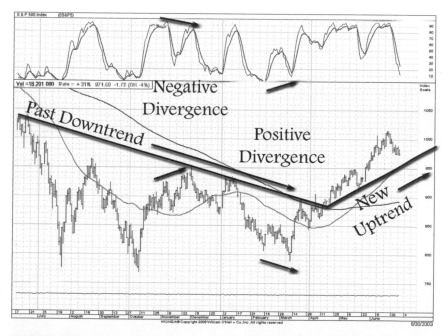

FIGURE 3.7 Proper Interpretation of Stochastic Divergences (*Source:* WONDA Copyright 2006 William O'Neil + Co., Inc. All rights reserved. Reprinted with permission from William O'Neil + Co., Inc. Further reproduction prohibited.)

begin their analysis. Let's get one thing very clear: Technical analysis should be utilized to assist in forming an opinion. Too often managers seek evidence to support their existing view while dismissing the indicators that do not. These armchair technicians tend to manufacture what is not present, rather than read the story being told by the chart.

Over the years, understudies have asked me, "Why use more than one secondary indicator for momentum?" In view of that recurring question I feel apropos to share my answer in an overly simplistic example. The premise of the investment pyramid is to increase the probability of predicting an event by stacking different, yet related, types of analysis. Statistically one can ascertain that when one of a pair of correlated events occurs, there is an associated probability of the other occurring. Following that logic, as more independent events take place simultaneously that individually correlate to a second event happening, then reason has it the second event has a higher probability of occurring. Let's take a closer look at probabilities using a non-market-related example, which is offered solely to demonstrate how a confluence of separate factors can change probabilities.

- If a dog lives in Florida it has a 20 percent probability of having fleas.
- If a dog has long hair it has a 20 percent probability of having fleas.
- If a dog has no flea collar it has a 20 percent probability of having fleas.
- If a dog sleeps outside it has a 20 percent probability of having fleas.
- If a dog always digs in the dirt it has a 20 percent probability of having fleas.
- If a dog only gets bathed once a month it has a 20 percent probability of having fleas.

If I told you that a dog lives in Florida, would you put money on the likelihood the dog has fleas? Of course not; no one in his right mind would make a decision based on a 20 percent probability. On the other hand, what if I told you that the dog lives in Florida, sleeps outside, has long hair, has no flea collar, always digs in the dirt, and only gets bathed once a month? Would you put money on that flea-ridden mutt? Sure you would. By using a very simple probability calculation you would have ascertained there is a 73.79 percent probability the dog has fleas. Realizing this, would you want to make an investment decision based on just one indicator?

The past examples of some common missteps by technicians are not intended to sound condescending or all-knowing, and certainly not to distract from the investment pyramid theory. They are mentioned to stress the importance of knowing more than just the basic usages of the tools in your box. You wouldn't use a power saw if you only knew how to plug it in, would you?

Thus far the foundation has increased the probabilities of success through a macro technical interpretation of the market. The strategy was then set forth to increase probabilities even further by technically determining where and when tops and bottoms may occur by using trend lines and secondary momentum indicator tools. We now move on to trading methodology and examine how the confluence of secondary momentum indicators increases probabilities.

TRADING METHODOLOGY: INCREASING PROBABILITIES THROUGH QUANTITATIVE SCREENING, TECHNICAL ANALYSIS, AND MOMENTUM DIVERGENCE THEORY

Once a manager has decided on where the market is in relation to the theory and, with reasonable probability, determined the next ensuing trend of the market, it is time to put brains behind brawn and step up to the next level of the pyramid. For purposes of simplicity, this chapter assumes the money manager's market direction of choice is bullish. In other words, the market is at the bottom of a long-term market channel. Okay, great! But now what do you do? Buy anything that moves? Of course not; there are over 10,000 equities and multiple other types of investments, including the onslaught of new exchange-traded funds (ETFs) coming to market every year.

The objective here is to stack the pyramid even higher by narrowing down the investment choices and once again, increase the probability of success and potential profits. This involves two steps—quantitative screening and technical analysis.

Quantitative Screening

There are countless ways to go about quantitative screening which have to be determined by the money manager's investment style. I am what you would consider a trend and momentum manager. As such, my proprietary screens are designed to generate the highest quality stocks (fundamentally and technically) with the greatest probability of advancing quickly. There are a whole host of different quantitative software packages available and it is only through trial and error that you will find the one suitable for you. Many companies will give you a one-month free trial if you ask, which I highly suggest.

When beginning to write a quantitative screen you must first determine what is important to screen for—fundamentals and/or technicals. As stated previously, the pyramid is designed to be dynamic, or should I say dynamically changing? The quantitative portion, out of all the others levels in the pyramid, varies the most. The screens should be constantly tweaked and analyzed to see if the program misses something important, delivers too many choices, or just plainly needs to be shifted from searching for long to short investments.

I have put together a simple quantitative screen example. Let's first assume the market is entering a new bull trend cycle. Consequently, you may want to screen for stocks that have been doing well in the downturn but have been under pressure from the general market. As such, your fundamental screen may have these requirements:

- Must have 20 percent year over year quarterly earnings growth.
- Must have 15 percent year over year quarterly sales growth.
- Must have positive cash flow.
- Must have projected annual earnings growth above the following annual projected.
- P/E multiple must demonstrate growth at a reasonable price (GARP).

This may seem somewhat familiar to those who follow the CANSLIM formula created by William O'Neil. However, you can also write an opposing screen for times when you believe the market is at the top of the market channel and search for short investments. The fundamental screen, whatever criteria decided upon, will substantially reduce the number of equities from the vast number available to trade. Nonetheless, it may still leave you with too many to review on a daily or even weekly basis. At this point the technical quantitative screening criteria come into play. They may look something like this:

- The 50-DMA must be trading above the 200-DMA.
- The 150-DMA must be upward sloping.
- Price must be within 20 percent of a 52-week high.

A collective fundamental and technical quantitative screen with the eight criteria mentioned so far should provide a reasonable number of equities to scroll through for final scrutiny and potential addition to one's watch list. Most money managers will add an additional piece of criteria depending on the amount of assets they are managing and the time frame in which they wish to be able to get in and out of a position. Therefore, the final element of most screens will almost certainly be for average dollar volume minimums. This will ensure that the equity list being generated will fit the management and investment style.

Assume a money manager is managing $100 million and won't exceed a 5 percent position in one stock at any time. Also assume they want to have the ability to trade in and out of the position within a one-day period. Given a position size of no greater than $5 million, logically they wouldn't be interested in an investment that only trades $10 million in average daily dollar volume (ADV). To be liquid enough to buy and/or sell the entire position within a one-day period, a money manager may not want to exceed 10 percent of ADV. In other words, the equity has to trade a minimum of $50 million a day on average. This additional factor again reduces the number of investment choices produced, which in turn assists with a manager's time management.

At this point the long-term technical overview of the market has been established—foundation. The position and direction of the market has been determined—strategy. By stacking the quantitative screen atop and capturing a concise list of eligible candidates, the probability of profitable trading has been increased substantially. The majority of the battle is accomplished. But before betting on that "flea-ridden mutt," there is still more work to do. Now comes the tough part. The apex of the pyramid is where you examine the screen results for technical patterns with confirming indicators, create a watch list, set price alerts, and invest appropriately when the time arises.

Technical Analysis and Momentum Divergence Theory

Scrolling through 300 to 400 stocks to add just a select few to a watch list may seem tedious at first, but trust me, it is well worth it in the end. The main objective now is to once again increase the probability of investment success by combining simple trend line and volume analysis with corresponding divergence of secondary momentum indicators. This area is subject to a multitude of different factors, interpretations, and personal preferences.

As touched on earlier, the first step is to properly identify the trend lines. I can't stress enough the absolute necessity of drawing the support, resistance, and trend lines accurately. The next goal is to identify peaks, troughs, chart patterns, and breakouts/breakdowns from subsequent trends. Not to beat a dead horse, but this is again where the aforementioned adage, "Learn the trade, not just the tricks of the trade," comes into play. There are countless books, magazines, and newsletters available on chart patterns and trend line analysis. Education from experienced technicians is definitely a key, but the greatest education one can receive comes from continuous practice, scrutiny, and trial and error.

Having identified a proper chart pattern while scrolling through your quantitative screens' results, the next step is to check for volume confirmation. Remember, technical analysis is based on the law of supply and demand. This is why volume analysis is crucial for gaining an increased comprehension of patterns revealed and buying/selling pressure within the overall base. A simple way to properly interpret volume is through confirmation of the pattern versus a divergence from the pattern. This is somewhat different from how the secondary momentum divergences occur.

Thinking about this logically, before a stock has the ability to go higher, there must be a reduction in the number of sellers wishing to get out of the position. Once the sellers dissipate, demand can take over and the stock can move higher, or vice versa. As a result, when a stock breaks out of its base the volume should confirm by being a minimum of 15 percent greater than ADV. When this occurs you have yet another component to add to the weight of evidence.

Following this methodology many technicians, including myself, have confidence in another small yet important analysis of volume. The belief is that if the volume does not exceed the previous price peak's volume, the position is more than likely going to retest the breakout level. If this does occur it is not necessarily unfavorable. An equity that retests the breakout level with declining volume adds another level of confirmation and confidence in the position purchased. What's more, if the investment was missed at the breakout, it provides another opportunity for entry. Also, during turbulent market times, many technicians will actually wait for the low-volume retest confirmation to gain further assurance of a first-rate breakout before investing. (See Figure 3.8.)

Another noteworthy use of volume analysis is with the divergent peaks and troughs. For example, when price displays a lower low within a basing pattern or downtrend and presents a reversal having less ADV, there is now a new road sign that indicates a possible turn. This indicates the stock or index is declining further on less conviction and the majority of the sellers have gone to play golf. Using the same investment example as before, this is very evident, as seen in Figure 3.9.

The volume examples lead us directly into the next discussion: confirming divergence of multiple secondary momentum indicators. My favorite secondary indicator, the stochastic, has already been discussed in the strategy section. For that reason I only cover two others here that are most commonly used by market technicians—the relative strength indicator (RSI) and the moving average convergence-divergence (MACD).

The RSI is not to be confused with a stock's relative strength in comparison to a particular index. Rather, the RSI is a momentum oscillator that only needs the information from its own previous price action to be calculated and is not compared with any other stock or index. Without diving into the actual calculation, the RSI looks at the previous magnitude

FIGURE 3.8 Textbook Long Position Technical Setup with a Low Volume Retest (*Source:* WONDA Copyright 2006 William O'Neil + Co., Inc. All rights reserved. Reprinted with permission from William O'Neil + Co., Inc. Further reproduction prohibited.)

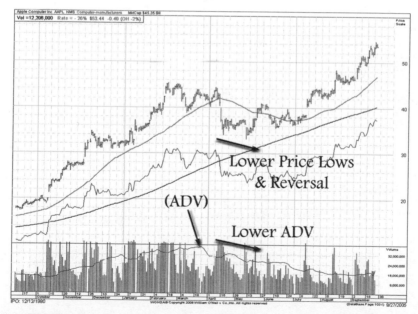

FIGURE 3.9 Divergent Trough (*Source:* WONDA Copyright 2006 William O'Neil + Co., Inc. All rights reserved. Reprinted with permission from William O'Neil + Co., Inc. Further reproduction prohibited.)

of average gains and losses over a certain period (usually 14). It then smoothes the data by using the previous period's RSI and plots the oscillating results between 0 and 100. Not unlike the stochastic, the RSI is used with 80/20 over- and undervalued lines and becomes much more reliable—producing fewer false positives—when used for divergence analysis. In Figure 3.10, the RSI is attaining higher lows as the price is hitting lower lows. This divergence indicates greater underlying strength of the position as the price declines.

The final momentum oscillator to be discussed is again extremely popular—the MACD. This secondary momentum indicator is one of the simplest to use and provides a vast amount of information, but is plotted somewhat differently. The MACD is nothing more than calculations formed from two moving averages (usually 12 and 26 periods). These calculations provide two oscillators which fluctuate around a zero line with no limits above or below. The difference between the two oscillators produces a histogram that also fluctuates around this zero line.

A common mistake by some armchair technicians is to believe that the two plotted lines are the two averages. In reality, the faster line plotted

FIGURE 3.10 RSI Momentum and Price Divergence (*Source:* WONDA Copyright 2006 William O'Neil + Co., Inc. All rights reserved. Reprinted with permission from William O'Neil + Co., Inc. Further reproduction prohibited.)

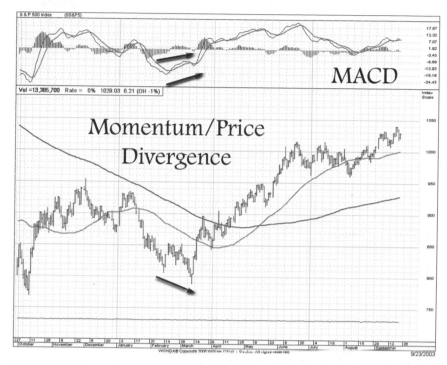

FIGURE 3.11 MACD and Price Divergence (*Source:* WONDA Copyright 2006 William O'Neil + Co., Inc. All rights reserved. Reprinted with permission from William O'Neil + Co., Inc. Further reproduction prohibited.)

is the difference between the 12- and the 26-DMA, which produces a rate of change (ROC). The slower line is a smoothed average of this difference (usually nine periods) or a slower ROC. If the MACD is rising, then the difference between the two moving average periods is widening, indicating the ROC of the faster moving average is higher than that of the slower moving average and there is positive momentum. The histogram is then used to determine if the slow is above the fast or vice versa, and by how much. Both the histogram and the ROC lines should be used when determining price/momentum divergence (see Figure 3.11).

PUTTING IT ALL TOGETHER

Throughout this chapter I have touched on multiple tools that managers have at their disposal. All that's left is to plot the course and read the road signs by combining and implementing all that we have covered. The following scenario delivers just that and is from my personal trading experience.

Looking back at Figure 3.7 in the strategy section (the S&P 500 Index), this is where and when I determined a possible change of trend in the overall market. This was not only confirmed with trend lines and the stochastic as shown, it also incorporated volume analysis, the RSI and the MACD. Once this was accomplished, the quantitative screen generated one equity—UTStarcom Inc. (UTSI: NASD). At the time the equity showed the following characteristics:

- Above a 100 percent year-over-year quarterly earnings growth.
- Above an 80 percent year-over-year quarterly sales growth.
- Above $1.00 per share in cash flow.
- About an 18 P/E multiple with above 40 percent projected fourth quarter earnings growth.
- Within 20 percent of a 52-week high.
- Increasing institutional ownership (being accumulated).
- An upward-sloping 150-DMA with the 50-DMA above the 200-DMA.
- Meeting the volume requirements.

In other words, it was hitting on all cylinders. Next I noticed a potential cup-and-handle chart pattern, with the volume confirming action and the possible change in trend indication given with the three divergences confirming secondary momentum indicators. Therefore it was placed on my watch list with a $24 alert. At that moment it met all the requirements. The pyramid's foundation was in place, the strategy was set, the quantitative screen was kicking off a select group of potential candidates, scanning yielded a small group to add to the watch list, and the alerts were set. The probability of success increased to a considerable level and now it was time to put money on that flea-ridden mutt. (See Figure 3.12.)

On May 13, 2003, UTStratacom Inc. broke out of the pattern at $24 a share and never looked back until it formed a double top pattern at $45 a share, which happened to coincide with its long-term resistance from the initial market breakdown in 2000.

Now let's switch to a short-side example using the same theory in reverse. By looking back at Figure 3.8 in the example of properly drawn trend lines, you can see the change in trend being discussed. Once the inflection point was determined and a new downtrend was in place, it was time to transpose the quantitative screen to provide short-side analysis. One short candidate brought forth was Network Appliance Inc. (NTAP: NASD).

In Figure 3.13, you will notice the following:

- All three momentum indicators showed a divergence.
- Volume was also divergent at the second top.

- The chart pattern revealed a "two-headed monster"—a <u>head-and-shoulders top with two heads</u>—having a $100 neckline that corresponded to the recent upward trend.

At that point the stock was added to the watch list. Once the neckline was <u>broken on massive volume,</u> over 100 percent of ADV, the position was entered. Within a month the stock hit $50/share and within three months it dropped below $18/share. Not bad for another flea-ridden mutt.

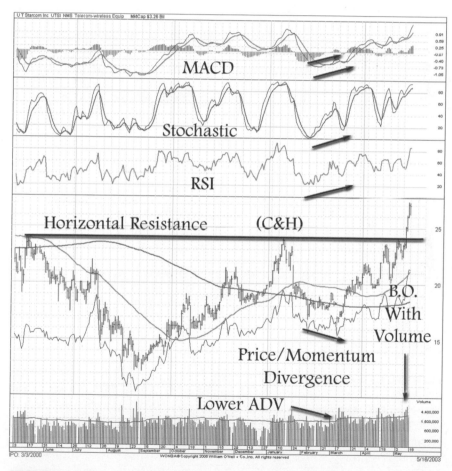

FIGURE 3.12 UTSI Long Investment Example (*Source:* WONDA Copyright 2006 William O'Neil + Co., Inc. All rights reserved. Reprinted with permission from William O'Neil + Co., Inc. Further reproduction prohibited.)

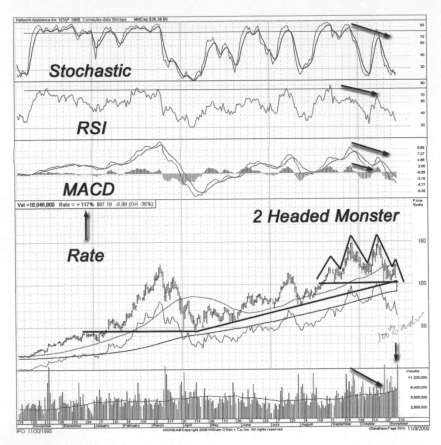

FIGURE 3.13 NTAP Short Example (*Source:* WONDA Copyright 2006 William O'Neil + Co., Inc. All rights reserved. Reprinted with permission from William O'Neil + Co., Inc. Further reproduction prohibited.)

SUMMING UP

In this chapter I have given you much to contemplate. However, it remains only a taste of what can be used to completely understand the investment pyramid, technical analysis, quantitative screening, and divergence theory. Through the edification and implementation of your own investment pyramid you have already begun to take the first step toward the mountaintop. It is now your responsibility to further expand the comprehension of technical analysis through personal research and practice. I sincerely hope this chapter assisted you in the quest for developing a unique and dynamic system that will last for years to come. I wish you good luck and continued success in this everlasting pursuit to better yourself and the others who surround you!

CHAPTER 4

The Secret Science of Price and Volume

Tim Ord

There are two components that drive a stock or index: price and volume. In order to recognize buy and sell signals, a trader needs to understand how these two components work together to form chart patterns. Much has been written and discussed regarding price patterns and what particular patterns are considered bullish or bearish. Very little is said, however, about how volume affects these bullish or bearish patterns. While price is an important part of a chart pattern, equally important is volume. By introducing volume to a price chart, the analysis of a bullish or bearish picture will be reinforced.

Before exploring this further, we need to define the terms *swing* and *leg*, as they will be utilized through this study of price and volume. A swing is a high or low in a stock or index at which direction changes. A leg is the distance between two consecutive swings.

Volume on rally legs and decline legs can reveal a great deal about which way a market is heading. Volume is the force in price movement. For example, if more volume is present on the rally leg than on the decline leg, then there is more force to the upside than the downside. That should lead to an advance.

MEASURING VOLUME FORCE

The correct way to measure the volume force in a leg is by taking the average volume per time frame. This technique works on all time frames, from a five-minute chart to a monthly chart. To keep it simple in the following examples, only a daily time frame is used. By measuring the average daily volume (ADV) on the up leg rallies and then the ADV on the down leg declines, one can determine which way a market is pushing. (Note: Use the *average* daily volume and not the *total* volume for the leg. Total volume will yield misleading information.) For a stock to have an uptrend, for example, the force needs to be higher on the rally phase than the declining phase.

Figure 4.1 shows an example of a daily bar chart of a market, with the volume for each day noted at the bottom of the bar. As Figure 4.1 shows, the market rallied for four days on volume of 3,000 per day, for total volume over the span of the four-day rally of 12,000. The market then declined for three days, with daily volume of 3,000, 5,000, and 4,000, for a total of 12,000. It would appear at first glance, based on the volume over each time frame, that the up force is equal to the down force. However, it is not. The ADV on the rally phase was 3,000. The average daily volume on the declining phase came in at 4,000. The force to the downside was one-third stronger compared to the upside. As this example illustrates, the leg with the highest average volume has the most force and indicates the direction of the market break.

In Figure 4.2, the ADV is higher on the rallies within the trading range than on the declines in the trading range. This implies the break will be to the upside. By contrast, Figure 4.3 shows ADV heavier on declines and implies the breakout will be to the downside.

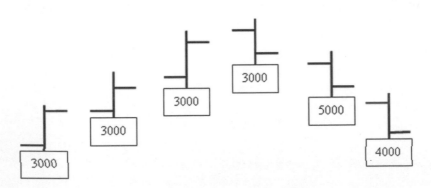

FIGURE 4.1   Daily Bar Chart with Volume Noted at the Base of Each Bar

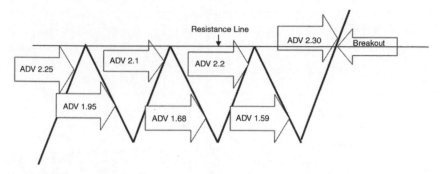

FIGURE 4.2 Average Daily Volume of Sequential Moves, Showing Greater Volume during Rallies than Breaks (Volume of 2.25 could be thousands, millions, and so on.)

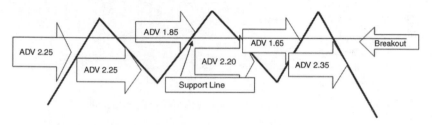

FIGURE 4.3 Average Daily Volume of Sequential Moves, Showing Greater Volume on Declines than Rallies

BEMA GOLD STUDY

With a fundamental understanding of the insights that can be gleaned from volume comparisons, let's take a look at a particular stock to show how this method applies in the real world of trading. Bema Gold (BGO) provides a good visual display of supply and demand, which is the reason I have selected this issue as an example. Figure 4.4 shows how the price increases as volume expands and price declines with decreasing volume. We know, based on price/volume analysis, that if volume is increasing as the price is advancing, while volume is decreasing when the price declines, then the trend is still bullish.

The conclusion that one can draw from this example is that *stocks trend in the direction of the highest volume, and stocks correct or consolidate on lighter volume.* By measuring the volume between the high swing and low swing, and comparing it to previous swings, one can see

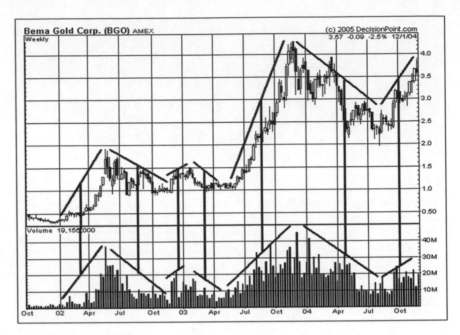

FIGURE 4.4 Bema Gold (BGO) Chart (*Source:* Chart courtesy of DecisionPoint.com.)

the force of a particular move developing in a stock. In an uptrend, the stock should have higher volume during the rally than during the downward correction. In a downtrend, the stock should have higher volume during the decline than during the upward correction phase. (Keep in mind that a swing is a high or low in a stock or index at which direction changes.)

Figure 4.5 shows the ADV of each swing in Bema Gold. Looking at the chart, one can see that ADV evaporated going into the August 2004 low. From that low, the ADV increased by more than 65 percent on the next swing up, confirming the reversal. This is the way the market works. To trade more successfully, one needs to study the volume and trade in the direction of the flow of the heaviest volume.

In addition to studying the daily volume, a trader can add up the volume between swings and then find the average daily volume in order to determine the force in that swing. One would have to repeat that process with other swings and compare them with each other to see which way the force is pushing. This can get tedious. I have developed a software program to do this for me, measuring the average volume of swings, which I call Ord-Volume. With the click of a mouse button, I can see these forces behind a stock and which way those forces are pushing. Figure 4.6

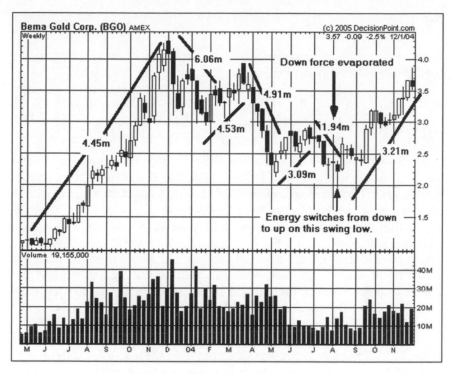

FIGURE 4.5 Bema Gold Chart Showing Average Volume of Up and Down Moves (*Source:* Chart courtesy of DecisionPoint.com.)

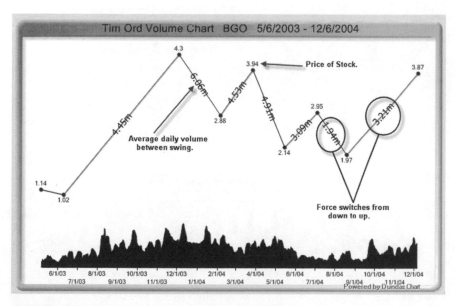

FIGURE 4.6 Bema Gold Chart Showing Ord-Volume

shows Bema Gold for the same time frame as the other charts, but this time displayed in Ord-Volume format.

SWING HIGH TO SWING LOW

In Figure 4.6, find the area where the force changed from down to up. The leg going down to the low of $1.97 had average daily volume of 1.94 million shares. The leg going up from $1.97 had average daily volume of 3.21 million shares, which is more than a 50 percent increase in volume compared with the down move. The swing low of $1.97 is where the market switched from down to up.

In hindsight, of course, it's fairly easy to see where the force changes from one direction to another. While that is all well and good, it is not particularly useful when trading in real time. Fortunately, we have also discovered that when a market *approaches* a low or a high—particularly on a retest—the volume shrinks dramatically.

As Figure 4.7 illustrates, the force during the previous down leg (prior to the $1.97 low) was an average of 4.91 million shares. Going into the low of $1.97, however, the down force decreased by 60 percent to an average of 1.94 million shares. For the down leg to continue, the volume should

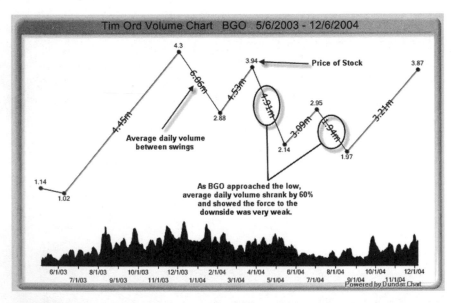

FIGURE 4.7 Bema Gold Chart Showing Daily Volume Shrinking on a Retest of a Low

have had an increasing force. Therefore, going into the $1.97 low, the average daily volume (or force) showed that this market did not have the energy to continue downward and a low was close at hand.

BUY AND SELL SIGNALS

There are several rules for buy and sell signals using Ord-Volume. The two main ones are:

1. A buy signal is triggered when a stock closes above a previous important low at which the current Ord-Volume low shrinks by about 50 percent or greater against the previous up leg or previous down leg. Both conditions indicate the stock is in strong position. Once a buy signal has been generated, the upside target will be the previous swing high. If volume is equal to or greater than the previous high, then the target will become the next higher swing high, and so on.

2. A sell signal is triggered when a stock closes below a previous important high at which the Ord-Volume of the leg shrinks by about 50 percent or greater against the previous down-leg or previous up-leg. Both conditions indicate the stock is in a weak position. After a sell signal, the downside target will be the previous swing low. If volume is equal to or greater than the previous swing low, then the next lower swing low will be the target, and so on.

These two buy and sell signals work on all stocks. To illustrate, I've chosen Bema Gold because it gives a clear illustration of how volume and price work together. As Figure 4.8 displays, the Ord-Volume going into the low of $2.14 is 4.91 million shares. The Bema stock price then starts a bounce from $2.14 and rallies to $2.95 before turning back down. On the decline from $2.95, Ord-Volume shrinks to 1.94 million shares, which is 60 percent less than the average volume of the previous down leg—generating the setup for a buy signal.

A buy signal is triggered on a close above the previous low, which in this case is $2.14. Notice that on the rally from the $1.97 low, Ord-Volume increased more than 50 percent, showing that the energy in this stock had switched from the downside to the upside, confirming the bottom.

Figure 4.9 illustrates a sell signal using Ord-Volume on Sysco Corp. (SYY) stock. The sell signal set-up for Sysco is as follows: On the up leg to $38.04, Ord-Volume was approximately 50 percent less compared to the previous up leg. This shows that the force (as exhibited by the Ord-Volume) was nearly half of what it was on the previous up leg. This is a sign of a

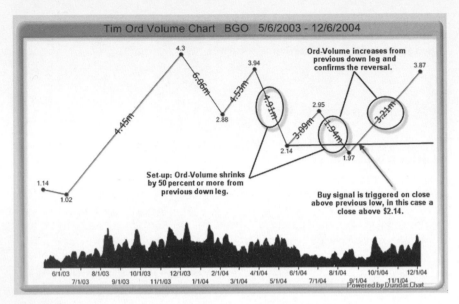

FIGURE 4.8   Bema Gold Ord-Volume Chart Showing Buy Signal

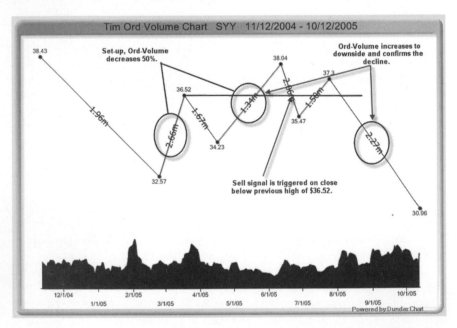

FIGURE 4.9   Sysco Corp. (SYY) Chart of Ord-Volume Showing Sell Signal

weakening market. The sell signal was triggered on a close below the previous high of $36.52. Notice the increased force (Ord-Volume) on the down leg from the $37.30 high, confirming the reversal to the downside.

USING THE WYCKOFF METHOD

As these examples have illustrated, volume plays a very important role in identifying strength, weakness, and reversal in markets. For the next section, I have expanded and simplified the works of Richard Wyckoff, who was famous for developing successful strategies to analyze and forecast the market. Wyckoff incorporated volume and price in the creation of buy and sell signals for stocks. He created these techniques in the 1930s. They worked very well then, and they still do today. This methodology has stood the test of time.

Because the Ord-Volume method and the Wyckoff method both have price and volume as their centerpiece to determine price direction, a stronger sense of market direction can be achieved by combining the two. In studying the Wyckoff methods, I have come to the conclusion that what is most important about price and volume is *how they interact* on retests of a previous high or low, as well as the *percentage relationships* between the volume on the retests of the previous high or low. These volume relationships define whether the market will pass through these previous highs/lows or reverse at these points.

The rule, in simplest terms, is as follows:

If the market cannot take out the previous high on near-equal or greater volume, *it will try to take out the previous low of the same degree* on near-equal or greater volume. *By the same token, if the market cannot take out the previous low on near-equal or greater volume, it will try to take out the previous high of the same degree on near-equal or greater volume.*

I have taken this rule further and broken it down into buy and sell triggers. By following these smaller buy and sell triggers, I believe traders will have the potential to become more successful. These techniques work on all time frames.

To generate a buy or sell signal, a test is needed of a previous high or low. The volume must shrink by 8 percent or more, and the stock must close back inside the trading range. These conditions will trigger a buy or sell signal. (Remember, the volume percentage relationships work on all time frames, whether 5-minute, 60-minute, daily, weekly, or monthly.)

The volume percentage relationship, which shows the force behind the move, is what generates the signal. A test of the high or low should be accompanied by lighter volume (force) for that test to hold and reverse the market.

Rules for Buy/Sell Signals Using Price and Volume

I have developed several rules for the buy and sell signals using price and volume. To illustrate each rule, I use line charts, which provide a visual picture. I also refer to these rules according to their particular signals later in this chapter.

Rule 1   A test of a previous high or low occurs with a decrease in volume of 8 percent or more. The market then closes back within the trading range, implying a reversal. As confirmation, the market needs to touch and break the high or low, and then close back into the trading range. (See Figure 4.10.)

Rule 2   A test of a previous high or low occurs with volume variations of 3 percent or less, implying that the high or low will be exceeded. (See Figure 4.11.)

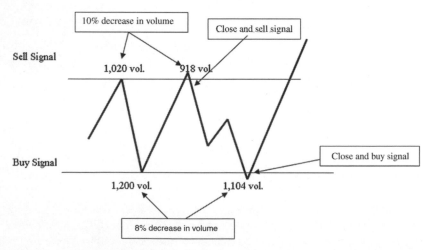

FIGURE 4.10   Line Chart Depicting Rule 1 with 8 Percent or Greater Decrease in Volume

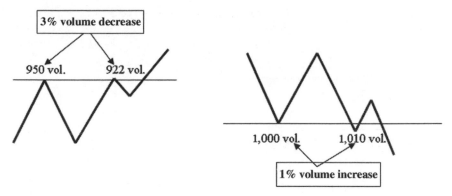

FIGURE 4.11 Line Chart Depicting Rule 2 with Volume Changes of 3 Percent or Less

Rule 3 Always compare volume relationships to the first high or low, even on a third or fourth retest. The volume relationships for buy and sell signals remain the same. (See Figure 4.12.)

Rule 4 The higher the percentage decrease in volume beyond the 8 percent threshold on the test, the more likely the test will be successful.

In Example A depicted in Figure 4.13, the decrease in volume was 5.5 percent, which is not sufficient on the retest to assure a reliable reversal signal. In Example B in Figure 4.13, volume declined by 27 percent compared with the previous high, providing more assurance of a reversal. (These same percentage relationships also work on tests to the downside, providing assurances of a bottom being established and a reversal to the upside.)

Understand that the specific volume figures themselves are not important on the retests of previous highs and lows; rather, it is the percentage relationships between the volume compared with the previous high or low. These volume percent relationships will determine if the market will likely pass through or reverse at these previous highs and lows.

Rule 5 Markets that have very light volume (with a shrinkage in volume of 20 percent or more) on the attempted retest of a previous high or low may not get back to these levels. These markets that fail to achieve previous swing highs or lows on very light markets are capable of producing strong reversals. (See Figure 4.14.)

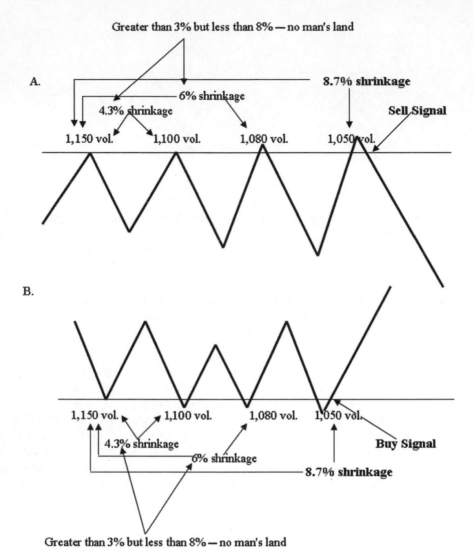

FIGURE 4.12 Line Drawing Depicting Rule 3 with Volume Percentage Relationships

Example A

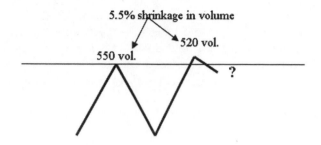

Volume did not shrink enough on the retest to assure a reliable reversal signal.

Example B

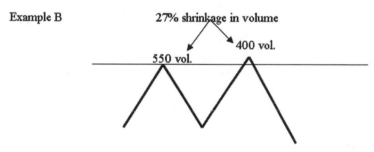

FIGURE 4.13 Line Charts Depicting Rule 4, with Two Examples of Volume Percentage Relationships on Tests of Previous Highs/Lows

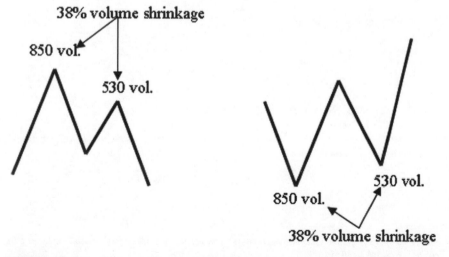

FIGURE 4.14 Line Drawings Depicting Rule 5 of Strong Reversals on Volume Declines Greater than 20 Percent

Rule 6   Markets that break to new highs or lows on near-equal or increased volume may then reverse back into the trading range. The last high or low will be tested if not exceeded. The way to determine if the market will reverse or exceed a previous high or low on a test is the volume. (See Figure 4.15.) Here are two important considerations:

1. If volume is at least 8 percent less on a test of a high or low, expect a reversal.
2. If volume is within 3 percent or less on a test, expect continuation.

Rule 7   Markets that break to a new high or low on a decrease in volume of 8 percent or greater and close outside the trading range imply a false break, and will eventually return to the trading range. (See Figure 4.16.)

Rule 8   Tops and bottoms of gaps work the same way as previous highs and lows, as well as previous support and resistance zones. The same volume percentage relationships work with the gaps as with retests of previous highs and lows. (See Figure 4.17.)

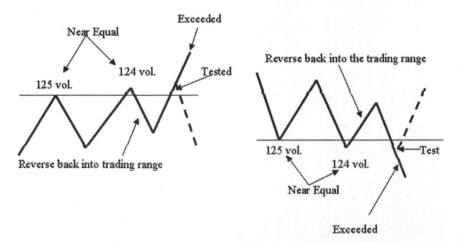

FIGURE 4.15   Line Drawings Depicting Rule 6, Showing New Highs/Lows Put In on Near-Equal Volume

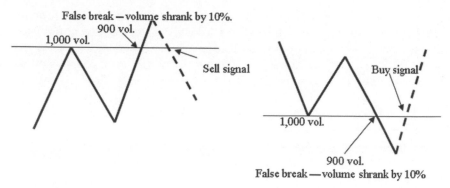

FIGURE 4.16 Line Drawings Depicting Rule 7 of False Breaks on Volume Declines of More than 8 Percent

Example A

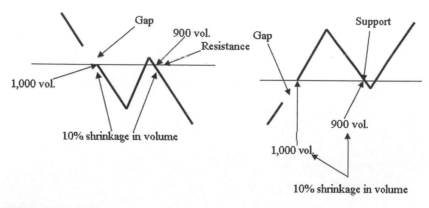

FIGURE 4.17 Line Drawings Depicting Rule 8, Showing Volume Percentage Relationships and Gaps

PUTTING THE CONCEPTS TOGETHER

Now we are going to show these concepts in practice, using charts of the Standard & Poor's 500 Index (SPX). Keep in mind that the specific volume is not important; rather, what matters is the percentage increase or decrease in volume compared with the previous high, low, or gap level. The amount of the percentage increase or decrease will determine whether the market will pass through or reverse at previous highs or lows.

In the first example, the SPX made a low near 1,080 in late January 2002 on volume of 2.7 billion shares. (*Note:* In Figure 4.18 and subsequent charts, volume figures in billions are abbreviated as "b".) That low was retested a few days later on volume of 2 billion, for a 26 percent decrease in volume, and closed above the previous low. This triggered a Rule 1 buy signal.

The SPX then rallied to the next upside target, which was the gap level at 1,120. It tested the gap level with a 15 percent decrease in volume and closed below the gap level, triggering a Rule 8 sell signal. The index subsequently declined to its next downside target of the previous low near the 1,080 area.

On tests of a multibottom market, always compare the current test with the highest-volume day in that bottom pattern. In this example, the comparison is of the current test to the first day the low was made in late January. The SPX tested the first low, which was put in on volume of 2.7 billion shares, and retested that level a few days later on volume of 2 billion

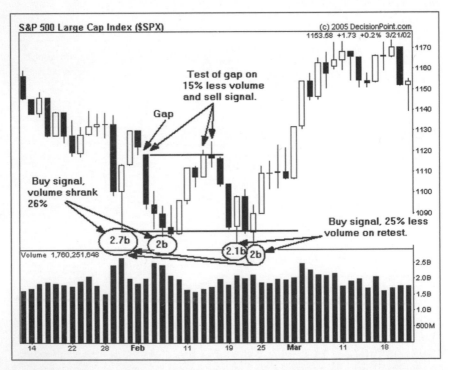

FIGURE 4.18   Chart of S&P Index (SPX) Showing Percentage Volume Comparisons on Retests of Lows and Gap Areas in January–February 2002 (*Source:* 004 Lows in July and August on Declining Volume, Triggering Buy Signals (*Source:* Chart courtesy of DecisionPoint.com.)

shares, which was approximately 25 percent less volume. This condition triggered a Rule 3 buy signal for both days.

As Figure 4.19 depicts, after the bullish signal was triggered again at the 1,080 area, the next upside target was the previous high, set near 1,120 in mid-February. Notice that as the SPX came close to testing that mid-February high, volume increased to 2 billion shares—an increase compared with volume at that high level of 1.7 billion shares. Testing previous highs on higher volume is a bullish signal (Rule 2). A couple of days later, the S&P Index broke above the mid-February higher on higher volume, confirming a valid breakout.

Earlier in this chapter we examined how to utilize Ord-Volume (the average volume between swings) in two issues: Bema Gold and Sysco Corp. Now let's look at those two issues for how buy and sell signals are triggered using the price-and-volume method in the same time frames.

Figure 4.20 is a daily chart of Bema Gold, focusing on the low made in May 2004 in the low $2.00 range. Bema Gold shares bounced off that low and traded higher for a few months, then declined in late July and also in

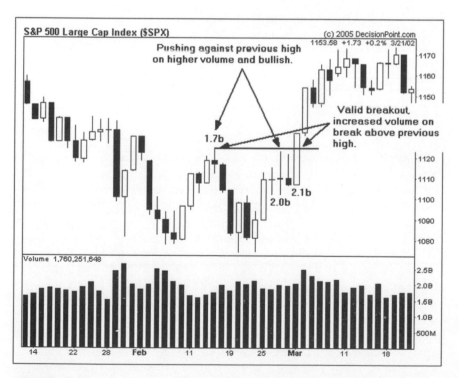

FIGURE 4.19 Chart of SPX Showing Retest of High on Higher Volume, Confirming Valid Breakout (*Source:* Chart courtesy of DecisionPoint.com.)

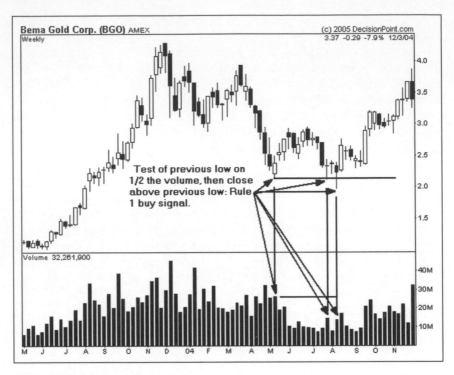

FIGURE 4.20 Bema Gold Chart, Focusing on the Retest of the May 2004 Lows in July and August on Declining Volume, Triggering Buy Signals (*Source:* Chart courtesy of DecisionPoint.com.)

early August 2004, testing the previous low made in May. Note that on the tests in late July and early August, volume was approximately half of what it was at the May low. This shows that the force to the downside was only half as great, meaning the energy to the downside was waning.

Two signals were actually triggered, one in July and one in August. Since both the July and August lows exceeded the May low on reduced volume and subsequently closed above the May low, both events triggered buy signals (Rule 1).

Figure 4.21 is a weekly chart of Sysco Corp., focusing on early to mid-2005. The first focal point is the high near the $36/share area in late March. In mid-May, Sysco broke above that level. However, volume on the break was about half of what it was when the high around the $36 level was establish in late March. This implies a false break to the upside, indicating that, at some point, this stock would reverse back into the previous trading range. In mid-June, Sysco did drop below the previous high near 36, triggering a sell signal (Rule 7).

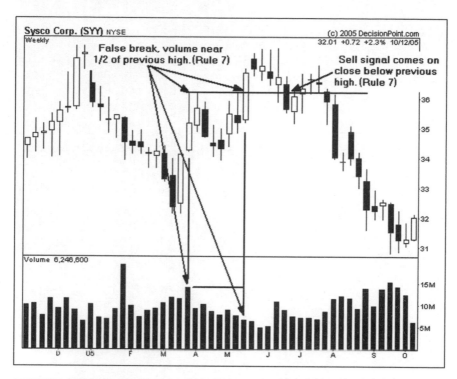

FIGURE 4.21 Weekly Sysco Chart Showing Retest of March High on Decreased Volume, Indicating a False Break and a Return to the Trading Range (*Source:* 004 Lows in July and August on Declining Volume, Triggering Buy Signals (*Source:* Chart courtesy of DecisionPoint.com.)

CONCLUSION

Volume plays a very important function in stock and index trading. Early on in my own career trading stocks and indexes, I did not follow volume studies as there was little information available to explain what the volume figures meant. Through years of studying the old masters on volume patterns, and adding some of my own ideas to this discipline, I have become confident that volume is a determining factor in predicting price direction for both stocks and indexes. In fact, I usually refer to the volume chart *before* I consult a price chart.

Understanding how volume compares to price, it is much easier to interpret and determine the price direction of an issue. By following these methods and rules, I believe one can gain a better understanding of how volume interacts with price, and thereby increase one's accuracy in predicting future price patterns.

PART II

Fundamental Analysis

CHAPTER 5

The Keys to Biotech Investing

David Miller

Fundamental analysis has often been thought of as the bedrock of investing. Even technical analysis was once explained as piggybacking the fundamental research of others by detecting the movement of large sums in and out of stocks. With the explosion in derivative instruments, the shortening of investment horizons, and program trading regularly accounting for over half of daily trading volume, I think the argument can be made that the impact of fundamental analysis is eroding.

One place where fundamentals still matter more often than not is in the biotechnology space. I define biotech as companies, regardless of market cap, whose valuation is primarily derived from a drug not yet on the market. Genentech (DNA) and Amgen (AMGN) are not biotech companies under this definition. They are pharmaceutical companies mislabeled as biotechnology companies. If you are looking for biotech companies, your index of choice is the NASDAQ Biotech Index (NBI) and not the AMEX Biotech Index (BTK). Although not all the stocks in the NBI meet my definition, the majority do.

Biotech stocks are valued largely by sentiment because they have few revenues, and the day when those revenues are responsible for their market cap is often many years away. Fundamental analysis here is less about accounts receivable outstanding or P/E ratios than the speed of disease recurrence and clinical trial stage. If you only take one thing away from this chapter, you must understand that investing in this sector is nothing like you are used to. Rules that work elsewhere either do not apply or can get you into serious trouble.

FIVE RULES

The best place to start, therefore, is to share our firm's "Five Rules of Biotech Investing." These rules are an integral part of our daily research activities.

Rule 1: Never Fall in Love

Biotech stocks are unusually likely to be objects of affection. Many people find their first biotech investment when doing research on a medical condition of a friend or family member. That's a situation ripe for emotional attachment. In any case, it is hard not to fall in love with an investment with such huge potential returns and whose products can cure terrible diseases.

All biotech investors have had their portfolio decimated by a biotech love affair gone bad. The most important thing you can remember is that the purchase of a biotech stock is an investment. It is not an act of charitable giving to sufferers of the target disease. As an investor, you are allowed to be dispassionate in your evaluation of new developments. When verifiably bad news comes knocking, sell first and ask questions later.

Rule 2: Diversify, Diversify, Diversify

Diversification is the difference between living to invest another day and financial ruin in biotech investing. You must spread your risk capital over a wide number of biotech stocks to protect yourself when (not "if") bad news arrives. The odds you must live with are that only 1 in 10 development-stage biotechnology stocks succeed.

Biotech stocks are so news driven, instant declines of 50 percent are common when bad news hits a company's lead product. You go to bed feeling happy and wake up the next morning with no chance to sell before the stock opens down in a very big hole. If you're short, you can expect overnight gains of 20 to 40 percent, so diversification is necessary no matter what side of the trade you take.

Here's a rule of thumb: If you invest in 10 biotech stocks, you would be doing well if 4 to 6 of them succeed. Significant losses are the name of the game here, so you must plan for them.

Rule 3: Early Clinical Success Is No Guarantee

Drug development goes through three phases of human clinical trials, each more rigorous and informative than the last. The worst thing an investor can do is become too excited about preclinical data—data from animals or test tubes. While such data is interesting, it should not be the basis for any sizeable investment in a company. Government statistics tell us that for every 1,500 drugs reaching the preclinical stage, only one is approved for sale.

In Phase I trials, humans are given the drug for the first time in an effort to examine safety and the proper dose. Demonstrations of efficacy here are enticing, but there are three to seven years of additional hurdles ahead, so keep your wits about you.

Excellent Phase II trial data is worthy of serious consideration, but not all Phase II trials are created equal. Let your attention and money gravitate toward randomized, controlled Phase II trials. They generate the best-quality data. Be far less enthusiastic about nonrandomized Phase II trials, especially where the study drug is used in combination with other drugs.

Good Phase III data is wonderful, but investing after this stage usually reduces the potential gain. Care is still warranted. I see far too many post–Phase III investors believing they have effectively eliminated all but sales risk. What they are actually doing is trading clinical risk for regulatory risk. FDA rules seem straightforward, but they are not. Applying logic to the regulatory process is a common mistake of investors who like waiting to the later stages of the process—particularly those investing in cancer drugs.

Rule 4: Reward Good Data, Punish Bad Data

This is where most biotech investors get into trouble. They fall in love, and then they apply the broadly misunderstood concept of dollar cost averaging. Bad news hits and investors start rationalizing about it being a temporary setback. Pretty soon the "If I liked it at $15 I should really like it at $4" thought process kicks in and a portfolio disaster is in the making.

As I stated previously, when bad news hits, sell first and ask questions later. Pare back or eliminate your positions when bad clinical data come out. Add to your position (even at higher prices, yes) when good clinical data arrive.

If you spend much time investing in biotech, you'll see what appears to be good clinical data announced but the stock goes down. Short sellers, who may or may not be smarter than you about the data, are particularly aggressive in the biotech sector. You have to respect the direction of the stock price, but you cannot defer to it. If the stock moves opposite the way you expect from looking at the data, you must be willing to devote the time and resources necessary to understand why. If you have neither time nor resources, you must rethink your position.

The higher the quality of the data and the better the results, the more comfortable you can be with deploying additional investment capital—provided you don't break Rule 2 in the process.

Rule 5: Commit to Hard Work

Biotech investing is 100 percent data and news driven. It is impossible to be a consistently successful biotech investor without working hard to keep up on the developments affecting your chosen investments. This means hours of research each month for each biotech company in your portfolio. It also means being a slave to news tickers, with the related ability to be able to drop what you're doing and pay close attention to your investment if crucial news hits the wires. While hard work is a cornerstone of any good investment strategy, biotech investing is likely to take more time than most other sector investments.

The trade-off is that your hard work is rewarded handsomely when it affords you a competitive advantage over other investors. While good research always puts you ahead as an investor, I've not found any market sector where you can secure such a significant head start via old-fashioned basic research.

DEVELOP YOUR THEMES

Fundamental research in the biotech sector is difficult. The human body is inordinately complex. You could spend a 70-hour week at a cancer conference and probably only come away with an understanding of a single type of cancer—assuming you had a good grasp of the medical terminology going in.

So do you have to be a trained medical professional to invest in the sector? It would be stupid to deny that it helps, but the answer is no. You have to have time, you have to be bright, and you have to be dogged. Having help from trustworthy fundamental research shops is also a good thing.

Because the sector is so complex, it tends to move thematically. Themes are part and parcel of most any sector, but they are particularly strong in the biotech sector. This might be a defense mechanism triggered by complexity. It might be an outgrowth of the clubby nature of professional biotech investors. Whatever the reason, theme investing works—boosted, no doubt, by the fact that biotechs trade heavily on perception.

The following themes, combined with the five rules previously listed, should give you a head start.

Theme 1: Look for Smart Regulatory Strategies

Every biotech investor's nightmare is to receive news of a successful trial only to have the FDA decide the trial did not meet its standards. Such disconnects usually revolve around the arcane science of biostatistics (which does not resemble the statistics classes you took in business, political science, or engineering programs).

Industry convinced Congress and the FDA to create something called a Special Protocol Assessment (SPA). This is a negotiated agreement between a biotech company and the FDA over exactly how a clinical trial is to be run and analyzed. If the company follows the SPA contract, the FDA essentially agrees in advance to approve the drug if the trial is successful. The FDA gives itself a few outs, most notably reserving the right to change its mind if the state of the art in treating the target disease changes radically while the trial is under way.

SPAs apply only to Phase III pivotal trials designed to lead to drug approval. If you are looking at a company with a drug in a pivotal Phase III trial, ask them whether they have an SPA for the trial. A negative response should have you looking elsewhere in most instances.

Theme 2: Therapeutic Index

There is no such thing as a safe drug. I'm constantly surprised at how many otherwise intelligent people believe safe drugs exist. With very few exceptions, every human being on the planet is different. The differences are not just external, they are internal as well. Give a drug to a billion people and it will kill or severely maim at least one. Does that seem odd? Consider the fact that the innocuous peanut kills several people each year. Consider that many clinical trials pair a drug against a sugar pill and the people who take the sugar pill experience side effects not explainable by their underlying disease.

Take a drug's benefit and (conceptually) divide it by the potential side effects. You've just calculated the drug's therapeutic index. That's biotech-speak for good risk/reward, but it reaches beyond that concept. Not a day goes by where the idea of therapeutic index doesn't affect our research process.

If a drug removes wrinkles, that is certainly a benefit. What if a common side effect is 5 percent of patients suffer a severe rash requiring medical attention? That risk is likely enough to have patients, doctors, and most importantly the FDA willing to think twice.

If a drug causes lung cancer to go into remission for several months, that is certainly a benefit. What if a common side effect is 5 percent of patients suffer a severe rash requiring medical attention?

Patients, doctors, and the FDA are likely to pay little attention to that particular side effect.

That's therapeutic index in action. The most valuable drugs are those with great benefits and the least possible side effects. Therapeutic index, therefore, is a handy way to compare competing drugs. The drug with the higher therapeutic index will likely be the winner in the marketplace. The concept of therapeutic index has become increasingly important as a defensive mechanism after a string of drugs were withdrawn by manufacturers due to safety issues.

Therapeutic index can also be employed more generally as a theme. When the FDA is particularly concerned about side effects as a general policy (as we saw in the middle of the 2000s), then you will need to skew your investments into drugs with a particularly high benefit to the patients. You would skew away from lifestyle drugs (treatments for wrinkles, erectile dysfunction, moderate pain, mild obesity, sleeplessness, etc.) and toward drugs treating hardcore diseases like cancer where the risk of the treatment is more easily outweighed by the risk of no treatment.

Theme 3: Death of the Blockbuster Drug

This theme has been an underpinning of our research for some time, but it first appeared explicitly in our research in June 2004. It has proven to be a reliable, though slow-developing, theme. We use it to determine which companies deserve greater due diligence efforts. Recently this theme has gained considerable popularity.

A blockbuster drug is one selling over a billion dollars each year. These drugs are currently the backbone of the pharmaceutical industry. Drugs not destined to reach this goal are abandoned or outlicensed by pharmaceutical companies. If a biotechnology company creates a blockbuster drug, it immediately becomes a target for a larger company.

Blockbuster drugs will become less common. All of medical science is moving toward the idea of personalized medicine. While the advent of personalized medicine has been heralded as "just around the corner" for a couple of decades now, we are on the threshold of a new approach to the personalized concept. Blockbuster drugs will decline in number as these new approaches make their way into clinical practice.

Biotech and pharmaceutical companies will create blockbuster platforms instead, featuring several drugs sharing the same general mechanisms and construction. Each blockbuster platform will resemble a toolbox. Physicians will perform detailed analysis of a patient's condition—down to the protein level—and select drugs specific to the patient's disease from the toolbox. No single drug in the toolbox will match enough patients to sell a billion dollars on its own. If you combine all the drugs in the toolbox, however, the platform itself on will achieve blockbuster status.

Movement toward the idea of personalized medicine gained ground in the first part of the twenty-first century, but the real opportunity lies ahead. To apply it as an investment theme you must be able to recognize the following signposts.

Signpost: Low-Cost, Rapid Test Kits   In the not-too-distant past, diseases were rather monolithic. You had breast cancer. You had heart disease. You had schizophrenia. Everyone else with breast cancer, heart disease, or schizophrenia was considered to have the same disease you did.

Science has disabused us of this notion, even if community clinics haven't caught up to that reality. Line up a dozen breast cancer patients and you are likely to find at least six different types of breast cancer. The same applies to nearly any other disease you can think of. Each disease has its own specific markers at the protein and/or genetic level, differentiating one patient from another. A marker is like a UPC code for the specific kind of disease seen in a patient.

We are not far from the day when you will be given highly specialized tests to determine the exact specifics of your disease. Only when those specifics are known will the doctor be able to select the right drug from his toolbox. One of the first signposts, therefore, will be the widespread availability of fast and inexpensive tests for specific diseases.

These tests will be commodities, so companies producing them are likely to be suitable only for a first-to-market trade. At first, these testing kits will be approved alongside personalized drugs. An example of this is Genentech's Herceptin for breast cancer. It only works in about 20 percent of patients with a particular protein marker, so the drug and a test to detect the protein were approved simultaneously. As this signpost matures, tests will receive FDA marketing approval on their own. Eventually, a single test kit will screen for a multitude of proteins and/or genetic markers of disease.

Signpost: Developers Embrace Patient Targeting   Clinical practice, unfortunately, has not caught up with the science. We have a laundry list of excellent targets for personalized medicine, but few approved medicines to use.

The companies developing these drugs deserve part of the blame for pursuing their use on the entire patient population. Why attempt to use a targeted drug on an entire patient population? Bigger markets and faster clinical trial enrollment. By definition, these therapies will not work in the entire patient population, so the patient pool for sales and for clinical trials is smaller. Drug developers are currently willing to take the risk that the drug will fail in the broader population in exchange for the reward of faster trials and more sales.

The lung cancer drug Iressa is a perfect example of this. The drug works on a marker found in 10 to 15 percent of lung cancer patients. Astra-Zeneca (AZN) ran trials in the broader lung cancer population, hoping the drug would have enough activity to secure approval on a broad label. Initially, this strategy worked. In the long run, the FDA reached an agreement with Astra-Zeneca to modify the drug's label. This effectively removed the drug from the market. The drug has essentially no sales now as researchers develop tests to determine in advance which patients will be helped by the drug. If Astra-Zeneca had developed the test upfront and used it to screen patients into their clinical trials, the drug would have been approved earlier at much less expense.

Biotech and drug companies who hope to develop blockbuster platforms must test personalized (targeted) therapies in only those patients who have the target. That may seem like a no-brainer, but it rarely happens. To see if a biotech is thinking correctly about targeted therapies, examine the eligibility criteria for the company's clinical trials. Then compare it to the advertised mechanism of action of the drug. If patients enrolling in the trial are limited to those who have the target for the drug, then the company is properly targeting the drug. The more companies you see doing this, the more certain you can be this signpost has been reached.

Signpost: Active Immunotherapy Success   Companies who have the best shot at being first with a blockbuster platform are those who specialize in training the patient's own immune system to fight the disease. "Active immunotherapy" is the technical term for this, and it is a technology pursued for a couple of decades with only isolated success. Three or four types of active immunotherapy are nearing maturity. Each has varying chances for success. Unfortunately, comparing and contrasting the approaches is beyond the scope of this chapter.

Active immunotherapies all have one thing in common: They work by training the immune system to recognize a specific disease marker. Because the immune system is highly specific, this makes active immunotherapy an ideal platform technology. Once the base system for training the immune system is validated, many disease markers can then be used as targets. It is realistic to expect active immunotherapy companies to be among the leaders in creating blockbuster platforms.

The signpost to watch for here is successful results from active immunotherapy companies. Watch late stage clinical trials for success and pay attention to how the FDA adjudicates drug applications seeking approval for active immunotherapeutics.

Signpost: FDA Ceases to Be a Barrier Speaking of the FDA, it is a significant barrier to the rise of the blockbuster platform. Current rules regarding trial size, endpoints, and threshold levels of statistical significance are not amenable to an era of personalized medicine. Trials will take too long to enroll the large numbers the FDA likes to see when personalization narrows the pool of potential patients significantly.

The FDA will need to see the platform as the key approvable. Once the platform is validated as safe and effective, adding tools to the toolbox should be made much easier from a regulatory standpoint. The current FDA has a hard time conceiving of such a system, and therefore will treat every tool as a new drug.

When the FDA adopts new rules specifically to ease approval of targeted medicines, this signpost has been met.

DANGERS OF CHARTING BIOTECH

Most of this book represents ways of investing based on something other than fundamental analysis. I have no problem with that. Successful investing is tough and only people who do it as a hobby have time for pedantic diatribes about whether charting, trend following, fundamentals, or behavioralism is the "proper" way to make money in the markets. Whatever works, do it.

Applying typical technical analysis to biotech is a risky proposition, especially since many chartists eschew fundamental analysis. Charting is about playing the odds. Outperformance comes by limiting losses and letting winners run. To be effective, chartists are expert at employing stop-losses and trailing stops.

In biotech, you often see beautiful chart patterns. The patterns tend to become very clear just before monster bursts in the stock. To a die-hard chartist, these charts patterns are like the Greek sirens of the deep—pretty, but deadly.

The biotech sector is incredibly news driven. Long gaps of sentiment-based trading are interrupted occasionally by news forcing investors to recalculate the fundamental value of their investment. Those beautiful chart patterns often coincide with known news events. If you're the type of chartist who only looks at charts and doesn't give even a cursory check to the fundamentals, this spells trouble for you.

Currently in the biotech sector, bad news is punished by a 40 to 60 percent decline in the stock. Good news is rewarded by 20 to 40 percent gains. If a company releases news after the close of trading one evening, a biotech stock doesn't open weak and then slide to a 50 percent loss. It opens 50 percent down. We use the shorthand term "overnight risk" in our day-to-day operations to describe the abruptness of this move. These big moves in the stock happen without any ability to cover a short position or dispose of a long position between the last trade of the day and the first trade after the news release.

The overnight risk is so violent it cancels out chart-based stops. That's fine if you read the chart in the right direction. If you are on the wrong side when news hits, the resulting move can wipe out months of the typically incremental successes a day-trading or swing-trading chartist depends on to generate his/her returns.

Many chartists look only for breakout/breakdown patterns. Breakouts play out differently in biotech than other sectors. Take, for example, a breakout in a technology company caused by a good earnings-per-share (EPS) number. Three months hence, the cycle will be repeated. An analogous event for a biotech company would be good clinical trial news. The difference between the two is that the next significant news for the biotech company might come a year later, when the drug is finally approved for sale.

Short-term traders of biotech breakouts need to realize biotech specialists broadly anticipate these news events. Specialists often fade breakouts mercilessly to cash in on their good fortune. Selling the news certainly happens in other sectors, but other sectors rarely have news gestation periods measured in years.

If you are paying close attention, you probably just thought of Rule 4. Look at any biotech chart over a period of years and it looks like stairs. When good information is released, the stock will step up to new levels. During the step-up period, the best value is often not immediately after the news is released (at the breakout). There is usually a pullback. Those pullbacks are the place to add on the rally—or at least do the majority of any additions. Gauging the depth and duration of the pullback is, in fact, one of the few safe uses of charting for biotech investing.

THE CASE FOR BIOTECH

So far we have five rules, a set of themes, and more than a few warnings about how biotech is a tough place to spend your investing capital. Many professionals have learned of biotech's uniqueness the hard way and they avoid the sector altogether.

I want to close this chapter by making the case for investing in biotechnology stocks.

Tech, But Not Tech

Biotech stocks have traditionally been linked to the performance of what I call "hard" technology stocks like software, chips, telecom equipment, and so on. The various biotech indexes generally orbit the path of the NASDAQ. A notable exception to this, though it is not completely obvious on the charts, was the performance of biotech stocks in 2000.

When MicroStrategy's (MSTR) accounting fraud broke the back of the bull market in 2000, tech fund managers were desperate to place their money somewhere. Hard tech was obviously getting killed, so they ran to the only other place arguably meeting the investment thesis of their fund: biotech. Unfortunately, biotech was experiencing a bubble of its own as rookie biotech investors mistakenly believed genomics companies (biotech's version of the internet "picks and shovels" trade) had similar timelines as telecom equipment companies. Biotech stocks were killed over the next two years, with many of them trading for less than cash at the bottom in 2002.

So many people were burned in that trade that biotech has been verboten for them ever since. The biotech space became the province of a relatively small group of funds.

Rationally, biotech has little in common with technology companies. There are few good reasons beyond convention for biotech and technology to trade in tandem. This divergence between hard tech and soft tech can be useful to an overall portfolio strategy designed to outperform the market.

No Overnight Obsolescence

Most companies have serious innovation risk. A leading software package or chipset can be made obsolete nearly overnight with little or no warning to investors. Patents are available, but the pace of technology advancement is so fast that patents are made obsolete nearly as fast as they are granted. Sales incentives, unique ways of targeting an audience, and innovative consumer products are also copied almost overnight.

Overnight obsolescence is nearly impossible in biotechnology. The 10-year development path from first human trial to FDA approval gives investors plenty of warning about competing products. This development path is populated with dozens of looks at competitive data in a manner only corporate espionage could duplicate in the hard-tech sectors.

Countercyclical

Technology company valuations have become hostage to the economic cycle. Lack of consumer spending eventually results in decreased business spending. Both events decrease the need for chips and software.

Biotech companies are largely immune from cyclicality in the economy. In fact, these companies are countercyclical because the technology they consume is generally cheaper to acquire in tough economic times— ditto for employees. This is significant since R&D and human resources are among the largest expenses at these companies. For those biotech companies with revenue, health care has long been considered countercyclical. In good economic times or bad, people still become sick. The business of treating these individuals steadily increases independently of economic considerations.

Benefit from Rising Rates

Rising interest rates are tragic for most companies. Not only do rising rates make it more expensive to carry their own debt, but rising rates increase the all-in prices of their products. Companies taking advantage of the carry trade are particularly squeezed by rising rates.

Biotech companies love it when rates increase. None of these companies has appreciable debt. What debt they do have is usually in the form of convertible notes with generally low fixed interest rates, often payable in shares. Furthermore, these companies depend on investment income to extend their cash. Higher rates mean increased income from these investments.

Overnight Risk Not Unique

I am going to turn my warning about overnight risk on its head for a moment. Conventional wisdom holds that overnight risk is biotech's soft spot. I would point out that the same risk exists for hard-tech investors. MicroStrategy lost 65 percent of its value overnight. Enron, WorldCom, and other fiascos are all examples of significant overnight risk.

To be clear, there is a key difference. Overnight risk exists for every development-stage biotech company as a regular part of investing in this sector. In hard tech, it is a potential risk likely to affect only a few companies.

CONCLUSION

There are several unique advantages to investing in the biotech sector. There is no denying profits are more difficult to come by here than elsewhere. I am convinced, however, that is because most investors approach biotech like they would approach any other technology company. I hope I've made it clear: That's a recipe for disaster.

The five rules given in this chapter will help you avoid disaster. The themes I've shared should give you a head start on developing a rational investment thesis for this section of your portfolio. All that's left is the hard work necessary to understand the fundamentals of these companies. The risks are considerable, but the long-term rewards for making the right choices are fantastic.

CHAPTER 6

Investigative Investing: Themes and Methods for Uncovering Value

Kai-Teh Tao

Today we live in a world where traders can easily buy and sell three- or four-letter stock tickers with a click of the mouse. What is often forgotten is that these symbols represent real businesses that employ workers and produce revenues and products that fulfill a particular need. By discovering these companies and each of their stories before the public becomes aware of them, an astute investor can capitalize on market inefficiencies and generate strong risk-adjusted returns.

However, fundamental investing requires a lot of hard work. The quest to find the next winner is a constant treasure hunt. One has to turn over many stones before discovering the nuggets hidden beneath the dirt. The good news is that the tools and skills necessary to be successful are readily available to the investor who is willing to go that extra mile and investigate a lead. Wall Street analysts have traditionally shown a linear bias when projecting future earnings growth, utilizing the same growth rate based on historical numbers and assuming lackluster growth during times of difficulty. With dynamic markets and changing business conditions, these linear projections may be insufficient to adequately value a company's future prospects.

At my firm, we begin with the premise that all businesses are cyclical. We center our investment strategy around capturing inflection points in a company's business cycle, leveraging our knowledge of supply chain dynamics and product cycles to pursue the best investment opportunities. Our research process carefully examines a product's life cycle: from concept to development, raw materials to finished product, and the translation into revenue generation and cash flow. We believe analysis of the underlying fundamentals driving the business leads to greater insight and discovery of untapped opportunities.

Unfortunately, good opportunities do not readily present themselves—they must be searched for actively. With literally thousands of potential candidates, investors must carefully sift through them to uncover the ones that warrant a more thorough look. Luckily there are methods to effectively generate a short list of investment ideas on which to focus.

With a list of prospects in mind, the determined investor must then delve further to accurately assess those opportunities. At this stage, we find that passive information gathering is often insufficient to obtain the full picture, and direct access to a company's management and other market players is warranted. We spend additional time cultivating contacts by attending industry trade shows, viewing product demos, and sharing information among the network we have developed over many years. Often one idea inspires us to look in the same direction to find another opportunity.

After speaking with the management team of a prospective investment, we develop an investment thesis that lays out a road map that can be independently verified with third party sources such as customers, suppliers, and distributors. The investment thesis provides a valuation model that we then assess against the FACTS (explained in detail later) and compare to our investment objectives. This approach provides us with a suitable pipeline of qualified prospects, not yet recognized by the general market, that can lead to strong risk-adjusted returns.

GENERATING THE IDEA

With so many possible stocks to look for, where does an investor begin to look for new ideas?

While each investor generally approaches idea generation from a different perspective, I will describe some of the tools and methodologies we have used at my firm to enhance our idea generation.

Stock Screens

With over 10,000 publicly traded companies, stock screens help to filter out the noise in order to find the names with the greatest likelihood for success. We look at the following criteria to help narrow our focus:

- *The company's 52-week highs and lows.* Companies make new highs and lows for a reason. A company that is beginning to consistently break new highs may attract new buyers due to the strong underlying fundamentals. Alternatively, if a company stabilizes after hitting a new low, it might indicate that the bad news is sufficiently reflected in its new low price. Both scenarios offer fertile ground for the investor to seek potential investment ideas.

- *Stocks between $5 and $10.* Most institutions are precluded from buying stocks below $5. When a company breaks the $5 mark for the first time, it might attract new institutional sponsorship. If we can confirm that this move is the result of solid fundamentals, we can capture the next phase of growth.
- *Price to earnings (P/E) multiple lower than earnings growth rate.* Earnings multiples reflect investors' perceptions of a company's expected future growth rate. When a company's earning multiple trades at a discount to its growth rate, it implies that investors do not believe that the growth rate is sustainable. Over time, as a company executes, that discount will shrink, which makes this screen quite effective as a source of new ideas.
- *Companies with expanding margins.* Analysts often underestimate the impact of operating leverage in a company's business model. A company that can consistently increase its gross margin will see strong operating leverage as its revenues accelerate. Often turnarounds will fit this category as management finds ways to reduce costs.
- *Companies with financial flexibility.* Companies with high cash balances and no debt have the financial flexibility to execute their business plans.
- *Market capitalization between $50 million and $5 billion.* Microcap and small-cap companies are usually underfollowed by Wall Street analysts, allowing the astute investor to get an early look before they are discovered by the larger institutional funds. From a practical standpoint, it is often easier to do trade checks on micro- and small-cap companies because they tend to have fewer product categories and concentrate more on domestic business, making it easier to independently verify management's story by channel-checking with a few distributors.

Earnings Reports

A company's earnings report provides a quarterly report card as to the health of its business. On a daily basis, we actively scan the press releases of companies that are reporting earnings. These earnings reports provide a snapshot as to the past execution and future direction of a company's business strategy.

We look specifically for key themes such as new products, new management, and expanding margins. We pay attention to anything reported that reflects a change from the status quo. We look for major balance sheet changes, quarter over quarter. Has there been a financial restructuring or write-off that may impact the company's prospects down the road?

We examine management's tone, noting whether they appear cautious or bullish, and especially the reasons behind it. We are extremely interested in companies that exceed or miss consensus estimates by greater than 5 percent. When a company is able to exceed consensus estimates by more than 5 percent, it implies that analysts may have underestimated how the leverage in the company's business model would benefit as the revenues accelerated. Contrast that with a company that misses a consensus estimate due to the temporary slippage of a deal from the current quarter to the next. Analysts may have underestimated the impact the loss of revenues would have over the fixed costs of the business. Both cases imply misunderstood opportunities that can be capitalized on. Later I illustrate an example that shows how an investor can take advantage of a misunderstood story to maximize profits.

Conference Calls

Company conference calls provide additional information that earnings press releases may not fully disclose. Although we encourage investors to participate in real-time earnings calls, the reality is that conference calls are time consuming.

Fortunately, there are two useful transcript services that allow investors to cover a broader universe efficiently: Thompson Street Events (www.streetevents.com) and Call Street (www.callstreet.com). These services cover 80 percent of all earnings call webcasts, allowing investors to save time and jump directly to the highlights.

Publications and Journals

The best ideas can be derived from simply reading a diverse set of publications. Reading these journals provides an overview of industry dynamics that may inspire or confirm an investment thesis. Depending on your interests, there is probably a trade journal, or specialized publication that focuses on one sector. *Purchasing Magazine* is one source that is quite helpful. This industry journal, for chief procurement officers and supply chain executives, provides a good overall picture of various inputs that make up the U.S. economy.

Trade organizations often do informal surveys among their members on the various moving parts that affect their industry. They are waiting for you to pick up the phone and call them to let them voice their views about a particular issue or company.

Today the prevalence of online tools simplifies an investor's information gathering abilities. Investors can directly subscribe online to local and regional newspapers as well as use information aggregators such as LexisNexis and HighBeam Research to scan for news. Often the most interesting section of these papers is where they profile new promotions and executive movements for companies you may be interested in. It only takes a few minutes of your time to call the executive and congratulate him or her on their new position, but that may give you an important lead that may confirm your investment thesis.

Insider Activity

While insiders may have various reasons to sell stock, they have only one reason to buy: to make money! The following are a few web sites that provide data feeds and filtering for insider activity:

www.insider-transactions.com

www.insidersignal.com

www.form4oracle.com

www.insiderbuying.com

www.realtimeinsider.com

www.secform4.com

finance.yahoo.com

When looking at insider activity, we give more credence to companies that have a variety of executives buying at the same time. Often you will see the chairman of the board or the president of the company buying shares that are only a small percentage of their overall shareholdings, making the purchase less meaningful. However, when we observe vice presidents and lower-level executives committing their hard-earned cash to open market purchases, or when we see an executive's purchase exceed 10 percent of his or her current shareholdings, it becomes quite valuable to note.

Interviewing Management Teams

Once a list of prospective names is created, we begin setting up half-hour phone interviews with either the company's chief financial officer or the director of investor relations. The purpose of these interviews is to gauge whether it is worth doing more fundamental work on the company. In today's world of Regulation FD (Fair Disclosure), management teams cannot disclose any new information that has not been previously disclosed in a public forum without violating the law. Therefore, one cannot simply ask questions like "How is the company doing?" or "How much are you going to beat the quarter by?"

It is important to develop an interactive relationship with management so that the conversation becomes an exchange of ideas rather than one-sided question-and-answer sessions. While there is no one direct checklist of questions to ask, we generally frame our questions so that we can understand what inputs will drive success in the business. The following are some examples:

- Please give us an overview of your strategic plan for this current year and what are some of the internal and external factors you will watch for in order to be successful in its execution.
- At this point last year, when you drew up your business plan, were you tackling the same issues as you experienced this year, and if so, what ultimately changed the most between what you planned for and the final result?
- Who are the most knowledgeable analysts who cover your company and what distinguishes them from their peers?
- If you were to beat the consensus numbers, what would be the primary sources—would it come from revenue acceleration or operating leverage?
- Are there any revenue opportunities that have not been factored in guidance that could potentially be realized in the next 12 to 18 months?
- Can you give us a few customer references who can speak to why they have a positive relationship with your company?
- Has there been any major turnover in key employees over the past 18 months?
- How does management communicate its story with investors? Is the company active in participating in sell-side analyst conferences?
- How are both lower-level and senior-level management compensated? What metrics does the company use to judge an employee's success/productivity?
- Which competitors in your industry do you respect the most and what have you learned from them?
- Talk about a deal that you have won recently and what factors allowed you to win. Did you beat a competitor out for the deal, or was it single sourced?
- Talk about a deal you have lost versus the competition and what factors led to its failure.
- When will you walk away from a deal?

- Describe the seasonality in your business.
- At what rate are you growing relative to the marketplace you participate in? Is the opportunity great enough to sustain multiple competitors, or will growth come solely from market share gains?
- Help us understand the inputs that comprise your business. What are the most important raw materials and costs you need to secure in order to maintain a healthy operating margin?
- What is the impact of currency fluctuation and energy costs on your earnings?

Be prepared for the fact that for every 25 interviews you conduct, only one company might ultimately fit into the portfolio.

UNDERSTAND WHAT TYPE OF STOCK YOU ARE INVESTING IN

Different stocks attract different investors based on their profiles. We group our stocks into three categories: growth, value, and turnarounds.

A *growth* company typically exhibits strong revenue acceleration as a result of a new product cycle. Growth investors are willing to pay a premium for companies that consistently execute to the strength of their product cycle. Often these are new businesses that experience significant margin expansion as their business model develops. For these companies, seasonality plays less of a role, as they are growing from a small revenue base. Instead, sequential quarterly revenue growth is more important in maintaining a premium growth multiple.

A *value* company typically trades at a discount to liquidation value. This may be comprised of a strong cash position, low debt, assets carried at book value, or a discounted earnings multiple, relative to its growth rate. It is often said that value is in the eyes of the beholder, so we must bear in mind that cheap companies may remain cheap for many years if there is no spark to help others recognize their value.

It is entirely possible that companies that were once value stories can turn into growth stories if the right catalysts are in place. A good example of such a *turnaround* company is Apple Computer. Back in 2002, Apple was trading close to the value of its cash on its balance sheet. The company had no debt and was clearly cheap by every traditional valuation metric. Yet investors continued to sell shares due to the perception that Apple would continue to lose its diminishing market share to the Windows-Intel (Wintel) PC platform. Despite new products like the iPod digital music players, Apple's PC market share continued to decline. A leading PC manufacturer's executives even suggested at an industry conference that the best thing Apple could do would be to liquidate and shut itself down before the market would do it for them.

In 2003, Apple opened the iTunes online music store. Without the success of the iTunes online store, investors who bought Apple because of its balance sheet value would have owned a company that remained cheap due to a lack of growth prospects. Apple's market value might still be languishing at cash if not for iTunes.

The success of the iTunes music downloading service was the catalyst necessary to generate iPod sales and reignite Apple's revenue growth. The same investors who abandoned Apple when it was trading at cash were now willing to pay a premium growth multiple once revenues accelerated again. Indeed, things change rapidly in the market based on perceived reality. While the E of an earnings ratio can be controlled by a company's fundamental execution, the P reflects the price multiple investors are willing to pay for that growth. It is the P that fluctuates constantly when perceptions change.

When timed correctly, a value company with a turnaround profile is the most successful investment. But before investing in a turnaround stock, investors must first understand the reasons behind why a company became cheap and out of favor in the first place.

As previously discussed, growth investors had abandoned Apple as its market share continued to decline versus the Wintel juggernaut. Today everyone knows what an iPod is, but in 2001, the initial release of the iPod was considered unsuccessful. Despite this, Steve Jobs, Apple's visionary leader, was busy negotiating with music labels to provide a legalized form of online downloads for songs, to combat against the widespread piracy caused by file sharing services such as Napster and Kazaa.

When the iTunes online music store was introduced, it became the first legalized online music store to allow users to download individualized music tracks and burn their own CDs. Analysts were initially skeptical about the prospects for iTunes, wondering out loud what a computer manufacturer would know about the music business. To facilitate the market's understanding of its business model, Apple regularly published updates on the number of songs sold through iTunes on its web site. Fundamental investors who called Apple stores also noticed that there was an increasing acceleration to the number of iPods purchased, which was commensurate with the growth in popularity of the iTunes store.

Subsequent quarterly updates demonstrated an increasing positive correlation between tracks sold on iTunes and the amount of iPods sold. The success of iPod stemmed the decline in revenues that had caused previous growth investors to sell down Apple to its cash value. With each quarter of increasing revenue growth, investors returned to Apple, rewarding the patient value buyers and marking a successful product-driven turnaround.

Developing an Investment Thesis

After you have investigated a potential investment idea and taken the time to speak with company management, the next step is to develop a workable investment thesis. This includes determining the current profile of the stock and identifying the key points that will attract the corresponding type of investor to the company.

The market valuation of a company fluctuates daily based on the perceived prospects of a company's future earnings. Inefficiencies occur when those future prospects are either too pessimistic or too optimistic relative to fundamental realities. Therefore it is equally important to find out what the consensus earnings and revenue expectations are for the company. Once you know what the consensus viewpoint is, assess the possibilities for variations.

The investment thesis should include a model based on management interviews to determine where the possible leverage points are that are not factored into consensus expectations. It is also important to independently confirm management's strategy by speaking with competitors, consultants, customers, and suppliers to support your investment thesis. Finally, compare that thesis with consensus perception and determine whether the potential upside meets your return objectives and time frames.

Assessing the FACTS: Financial, Accounting, Credibility, Timing, Sector

The following is a worksheet we call the FACTS which will help support the investment thesis you have developed. Figure 6.1 provides a summary guide to this text describing the components of the FACTS.

Financial   Comparable company analysis allows you to assess the company by financial metrics and see how it compares to competitors in the same industry. Such metrics include:

- Price-to-earnings (P/E) ratio (or multiple)—price divided by earnings.
- Enterprise multiple—enterprise value divided by EBITDA.
- Price-to-sales ratio—price divided by sales.
- Multiple of book value.
- Return of capital versus cost of capital.
- Discounted cash flow valuation.
- Market value of assets held on balance sheet.

Financial	Accounting	Credibility	Timing	Sector
P/E ratio	Earnings quality	Reputation and track record of management team	What is the catalyst that will drive the stock price appreciation?	Barriers to entry
Enterprise value/EBITDA	Conservative or aggressive accounting	How is Management rewarded/ compensated?	Multiple expansion	Market opportunity
Does return of capital exceed cost of capital	Are expenses capitalized?	Do they have a history of under promising and over-delivering?	Contract wins	Pricing power
Price/sales	Change in auditors		Earnings announcements	Growth rate
Discounted cash flows	Deferred revenues rising or declining?	Are they shareholder friendly?	Seasonality of the business	Fragmented or consolidated? Supply chain
Real asset value of the business	FIFO/LIFO	Insider ownership- Does management invest their savings with shareholders?	How is the company perceived by Wall Street	
Comparable company analysis	Revenue recognition			
	Off balance sheet items?	Communication- Does management have an effective communication strategy with the investment comunity?	Product roadmap	
	Cash earnings vs. GAAP earnings			

FIGURE 6.1 FACTS: What We Look for When Evaluating Potential Investments

Accounting This section relates to earnings quality. It is important to examine the quality of earnings to determine whether they are solid and sustainable. A strong company should achieve its growth without resorting to overly aggressive accounting. Here are some things to watch for.

- Check whether expenses are recognized immediately or capitalized over time.
- Track deferred revenue to see whether it is increasing or declining.
- Understand a company's revenue recognition policy as compared to current industry practices.
- Highlight any off-balance-sheet items and partnerships. For example, Enron's problems became fully exposed when the off-balance-sheet partnerships unraveled.
- Ask about any recent auditor changes.
- Distinguish between cash earnings and generally accepted accounting principles (GAAP) earnings, as well as any pro-forma projections.
- Inventory valuation done by first in, first out (FIFO) or last in, first out (LIFO). In an inflationary environment, FIFO will artificially expand gross margins whereas LIFO will more accurately reflect current market conditions.

Credibility Ultimately, the reputation and successful execution by the management team determine whether a company can attract institutional sponsorship. Many investors like to follow companies that have a history of underpromising and overdelivering. We prefer to invest in management teams whose interests are aligned with their shareholders. Therefore, we track the percentage of insider ownership relative to their compensation.

It is also important to understand what metrics are used to reward management. For example, if bonuses are calculated based on sales increases versus profitability, it might encourage management to take on unprofitable business deals in order to make their sales targets and achieve their bonus at the expense of overall profitability.

We also look for companies that have a clearly defined communication strategy with the investment community. Management teams that are accessible in both good and bad times give investors comfort by acknowledging the issues and factors that lead to their successes and failures.

Timing   Formulate an action plan by creating a time line for your investment thesis to develop. This helps minimize the emotions caused by a stock's volatility and fosters a focus on the fundamentals rather than short-term gyrations.

- Map out the possible catalysts that will drive stock appreciation.
- Be aware of any public forum presentations, including earnings conference calls, sell-side conferences, or industry trade shows, that might lead to new information being disclosed.
- Understand the seasonality of the business and compare it to consensus expectations.
- Scale into the position by taking into account the daily trading liquidity. For more liquid stocks, you have the luxury of waiting until closer to the targeted time period before accumulating a position.
- For new product cycles, understand the ramp-up schedule and road map. Also understand the key inputs and outputs of the company's operations and look for leading indicators of change.
- Factor in the significance of new contract wins and how they impact the business model.
- Review your expectations of market growth and the business cycle. Identify the appropriate signals and triggers for entering, holding, and exiting the investment.

Sector   Sector analysis provides a foundation for evaluating how a prospective portfolio company fits within the public markets. On a basic level, we seek to understand what the underlying market opportunity is. Important questions to ask include:

- Is there pricing power in the industry?
- Is the sector currently in favor or out of favor?

- What is the long-term industry growth rate?
- What are the barriers of entry for new competitors in the business?
- Is the sector fragmented or consolidated?
- Who has the largest market share in the industry?
- Who is adding or shrinking capacity in the industry and how does it affect pricing?
- Are there any disruptive technologies (e.g., digital music) or events (e.g., legislation) that may substantially change the market?

An investor who can predetermine where an industry is, relative to its business cycle, has the advantage of being the first to spot and take advantage of potential inflection points that may change consensus perceptions.

CASE STUDY

The best way to understand our investment process is to utilize a successful investment, BE Aerospace, as a case study. BE Aerospace (NASDAQ: BEAV) is a manufacturer of interior products for commercial and general aviation aircraft cabins. Historically, BE Aerospace's management had been quite astute at identifying key inflection points in the business cycle. Broad insider selling in early 2001, when the company was trading between $20 and $25, foretold the peak of the cycle. The 9/11 tragedy exacerbated the slowdown in the aerospace industry as many airlines canceled new plane orders due to falling traffic. By 2003, BE Aerospace had reached a low of $1.50 a share, which was lower than the $2.00 a share the company had earned in 1999. At that time, sell-side analysts were unanimously negative, rating BE Aerospace a strong sell and predicting impending bankruptcy.

Our insider buying screen alerted us that management began buying shares around the $6 level in 2004 (idea generation: insider buying). Intrigued, we looked at BE Aerospace's June 2004 10-Q SEC Filing, under the "Management's Discussion of Operating Results" section. All dollars mentioned in the filing reflect millions. The filing reads as follows:

> *This rapid decline in industry conditions caused us to implement a facility consolidation and integration plan designed to re-align our capacity and our cost structure with changed conditions in the airline industry. The facility consolidation and integration plan, which was completed as of December 31, 2003, included closing five facilities, relocating 12 major production lines and reducing workforce by approximately 1,500 employees, net of several hundred employees that were hired and trained to operate the relocated*

*production lines. We believe these initiatives will enable us to sig-
nificantly expand profit margins even at the current low level of revenues and even more so when industry conditions improve and
demand increases. The total cost of this program was approximately $174.9, including $73.7 of cash charges. We believe the annual cash savings arising from this consolidation program are
approximately $60.*

The June 2004 10-Q SEC Filing continues by discussing the financial
results:

*The net sales for the three months ended June 30, 2004, were
$185.3, an increase of $33.5 or 22.1% as compared to the same period in the prior year. Bookings for the quarter of approximately
$285 were a record for any quarter in our history and were about
$70 or 33% greater than the same period in the prior year. Backlog
at June 30, 2004, of approximately $615, was up 23% above the
June 30, 2003, backlog of $500. During 2004, we were selected by
Thai and Malaysia Airlines, Qantas Airways and Emirates Airline
to design, manufacture and install luxurious first class cabin inte-
riors for their wide-body aircraft. The combined initial value of
these four awards, which aggregate over $225, exclusive of option
aircraft, and for which initial product deliveries are scheduled to
begin in the second half of 2005, were the principal reasons for the
backlog growth.*

Analysts had been negative on BE Aerospace because of the financial
troubles of the domestic airlines (consensus expectation). However, our
research determined that the investment opportunity was in the international airlines that were upgrading their internal cabins as they purchased
new models of Airbus and Boeing aircraft (investment thesis).

Our conversations with airlines such as Emirates Air and Singapore
Airlines confirmed that financially healthy international airlines were willing to invest the money necessary to upgrade their first class cabins as "air
suites." These suites resemble a private hotel room and would make long-
haul travel more bearable for the frequent business traveler (third party
confirmation).

In addition, management's attention to cost control, as highlighted in
their June 2004 10-Q, prepared the company for the next aerospace up cycle. Our earnings model projected that the company could earn 55 cents in
2005 and $1.00 in 2006, through a combination of revenue growth and
margin improvement (operating leverage).

Remarkably, investors had the same chance to buy with insiders at $6, a price which was only six times the 2006 projected earnings of $1.00, despite an implied growth rate of 50 percent (price inefficiency equals opportunity).

As of March 2006, BE Aerospace is trading at over $20, a gain of 230 percent over a 24-month period.

CONCLUSION

Fundamental investing consists of common sense and the dedication to dig for the facts and go where others fail to tread. In the end, there are multiple paths one can take to find a good stock. Each additional conversation or third party contact an investor has with a prospective investment is one step closer toward potentially finding out whether that stock might be the next BE Aerospace.

The art form of efficiently screening and finding the best companies takes time and experience to determine what works best for you. However, if you are willing to put in the extra effort, a wealth of tools and information awaits to help you identify, investigate, and evaluate investment opportunities.

In summary:

- Look for investment ideas beyond earnings reports and what Wall Street analysts propose.
- Evaluate opportunities not only by leveraging online information sources but also speaking with management teams and third party sources.
- Be aware of whether the stock you own is a growth or value stock, and create a suitable investment action plan accordingly.
- Formulate your investment thesis by careful research, and then use it to have the conviction to ride out the volatility from short-term price fluctuations.
- Utilize the FACTS as a framework to back up your investment thesis.
- Remember that value is often in the eyes of the beholder, so focus on the type of catalysts that will swing consensus sentiment to accept your investment thesis.
- Know your responses to signals and triggers for entering, holding, and exiting at the opportune time.

Most importantly, have fun and enjoy the hunt.

PART III

Sentiment

CHAPTER 7

The Secret Messages of Equity and Options Markets

Fari Hamzei

We Shall Never Surrender . . .
—Sir Winston Churchill,
in his speech before the
House of Commons,
June 4, 1940

From 1996 through 1998, I was a futures trader on a mission: to find a better method that would significantly differ from all the usual indicators that were being widely used to predict and capture the short-term moves of the market. At the time, I was a member of the Los Angeles Chapter of Omega Research Users Group, known as OUGA. Omega Research is the developer of a trading software platform called TradeStation, a real-time decision support system popular among sophisticated retail and institutional traders. Back then, I was exclusively using TradeStation. Its main charting interface looks a lot like a 747 cockpit, with many switches to flip during preparation for takeoff; but once it is airborne, for a disciplined technical trader, it is the Rolls-Royce of all platforms.

A number of my local trading buddies and I looked for various tools to improve our trading prowess. We were diligent and rigorous in our search, meeting every third Saturday of the month for breakfast, followed by a presentation from a great speaker, usually an active derivatives trader. The hard-core traders sat in the back, and each guest speaker's words, charts, and presentation were dissected for any possible clues. In this business, few presenters will share their steaks with you. All you are permitted to see or hear is the sizzle.

In this chapter, I'm going to give a good-sized serving of the steak—and I am going to let you into the kitchen to see how the indicators I have developed and utilized came together and are put to use. Specifically, these tools include:

- Dollar-weighted put/call ratios for indexes, exchange-traded funds (ETFs), and stocks that show—in real time—what the smart money as well as the ill-informed herd mentality is doing in a particular market.
- A new variant of the tried and true support, pivot, and resistance (SPR) levels used for projecting short-term optimal entry, money management, and profit target prices.

For years, as a technical trader, I used charts. Price, volume, moving averages, trend lines, oscillators, channel breakouts, and support/resistance levels ruled in my battle space. One thing was clear from the onset: Much like our primal instincts—fear and greed—the markets are also driven by nonlinear systems. Still there was a fundamental void: I was looking at what everyone else was looking at—and it was all rearview mirror stuff. Once the price and volume made it to the charts, everyone else was looking at basically the same indicators, and this was very unsettling.

I was trading the "Beast," which is what traders affectionately call the large S&P futures contract traded at the Chicago Mercantile Exchange (MERC). Back then each S&P futures contract had a notional value of the S&P Index times $500. I had some early success but, make no mistake, the S&P contract, traded in the pit, had a well-earned reputation for eradicating off-the-floor traders like me, usually within six months.

In late 1994, I had finished developing a "neural oscillator" based trading system that in the summer of 1995 went through a fairly exhaustive review by Morgan Stanley & Co. Proprietary Trading Division in New York, as well as a cursory review by Goldman Sachs. Morgan had a massive mechanical system that traded some 26 futures markets—every futures market except the S&P futures. The year before, it had made a killing in coffee futures and, as the head of proprietary trading proudly put it, "The system paid the rent around here." We are talking tens of floors of prime midtown Manhattan real estate, located at 1251 Avenue of the Americas in Rockefeller Center. You do the math.

I recognized that the task of devising a robust mechanical system to successfully trade the S&P futures was a tall order, but I was also inspired by the cherished words of my freshman lightweight crew coach at

Princeton: "I will never cut you from the boat, you will cut yourself." I wasn't going to cut myself out of the opportunity that was presented to me, no matter how daunting the challenge, and I was determined to better equip myself with the best tools as the battle with the Beast waged on day after day.

In the late 1990s, with the advances in high-speed communications, cheap DRAM memories, fast hard disks, and massive computing power on every desktop, we could monitor and observe the dynamics of the stock index futures compared to its underlying index. Specifically, the stock index futures traded ahead of its index, and the index traded ahead of its components. This in effect would pull or push individual stocks up and down throughout the trading day. Since U.S. markets are highly efficient, arbitrageurs no longer ruled, and any price disparity was neutralized in seconds. So how could I or any other off-the-floor trading warrior do battle and survive in this brave new world?

INVESTOR PSYCHOLOGY AND THE DOLLAR-WEIGHTED PUT/CALL RATIO

At one of the OUGA meetings, a couple of novel ideas were kicked around. The most promising concept warranting further research turned out to be taking an in-depth look into the S&P 100 Index (OEX) options activity, traded at the then busiest pit at the Chicago Board Options Exchange (CBOE). The OEX had a very high correlation to S&P Futures. Its options chain was very liquid and professional pit traders at the Chicago MERC kept an eye on the OEX value flashing every few seconds on the big board above the S&P pit. In the OEX pit at CBOE, the reverse was true. Everyone would have one eye fixed on S&P futures on the big board above the OEX pit.

One key premise of this research was that the majority of OEX retail players traded with their hearts rather than their minds by buying lots of calls at tops and lots of puts at bottoms. Given this underlying assumption, the majority would be wrong, especially at market extremes, due to the psychological aspects of fear and greed. And at market extremes, the dollar-weighted put/call ratio ($wPCR) of OEX would become significantly skewed.

In November 1998, I began to write the first lines of code to measure the OEX $wPCR, following a short feasibility study on the available hardware and software required for this daunting task. Many datafeeds were contacted, and the promising one turned out to be a specific "server package" offered by Townsend Analytics (TALnet), now a division of Lehman Brothers. The software platform selected was Microsoft Excel. Excel's extensive built-in math library, its real-time charting capabilities, and its Visual Basic Application (VBA) environment were the cornerstone of this project. After much trial and error, in the summer of 1999, the first beta version of software (a single-user application, not the internet-based one that we have now) was completed and released for beta-testing to Nestor Turczan, a fellow OUGA member who ran an actively managed portfolio at Prudential Securities (now Wachovia Securities) in Pasadena, California.

After several updates and internal timing improvements to deal with various potential market conditions, the winter of 2000 arrived and with it, the volatility in the markets slowly began to rise. April 4, 2000, was a day no market participant will ever forget. NASDAQ Composite dropped over 634 points, or 14.8 percent, on an intraday basis on volume of 2.8 billion shares, with the CBOE's OEX Volatility Index (VXO) rising to over 35 percent, a 15-month high.

Figure 7.1 depicts the April 4, 2000, market activity focusing on the

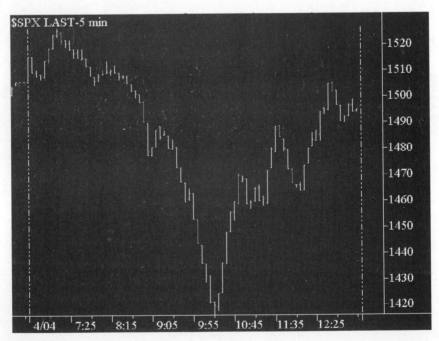

FIGURE 7.1 TradeStation 5-Minute Price Chart for SPX on April 4, 2000 (*Source:* TradeStation.)

price action in the S&P 500 Cash Index (SPX). Figure 7.2 shows the simple put/call ratio (PCR) versus the $wPCR for OEX on that same day, during which the S&P 500 Index and NASDAQ Composite experienced their highest intraday point drops to that date. Our put/call engine endured a massive stress test. It was baptism by fire. The reason I am showing the SPX cash prices here is to eliminate the noise of the S&P futures, which will better illustrate the power of the $wPCR versus the simple PCR.

It is worth noting that the dollar-weighted put/call ratio for OEX had exhibited a very high signal-to-noise ratio vis-à-vis the simple put/call ratio, and it properly identified the intraday reversal point.

Before we go further, we need to examine the forces that are doing fierce battle with each other every trading day in the six U.S. options exchanges. I would separate option trading activity into two camps: *smart money* and the *herd mentality*.

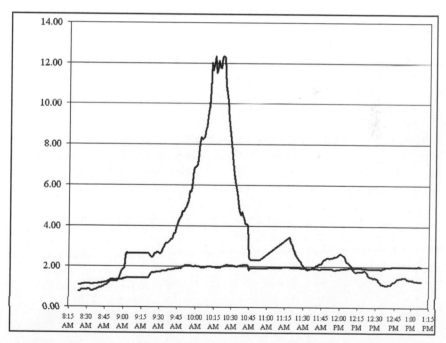

FIGURE 7.2 Simple Put/Call Ratio (bottom line) versus Dollar-Weighted Put/Call Ratio for OEX (top line) on April 4, 2000 (Courtesy of HamzeiAnalytics.com.)

THE SMART MONEY AND THE HERD MENTALITY

Smart money generally refers to investors in the know. These are the professional traders and institutions that use sophisticated options pricing and statistical models as a basis for their strategies as they take highly leveraged positions in certain stocks and indexes ahead of key macroeconomic or stock-specific event risks. For example, when there is reason to believe a company is going to have positive news such as an upside earnings surprise, you will notice that the smart money will begin to go long calls or short puts, such as in a hot name like Apple Computer (AAPL). The opposite will happen when negative news is expected; smart money will go long puts or short calls, and in volume. And of course, at certain times, the $wPCR indicates possible insider trading activity in these names, legal or otherwise.

A *change* in market sentiment is often an early indication of a trend change for a particular stock or narrow-based sector. Therefore, trending put/call ratios are reinforcing indicators of price direction. This type of activity has to be monitored closely and blended with exogenous inputs, such as technical analysis tools. At the outset, the true reasons are hidden. What is clear is that the market participants vote with their pockets for a number of reasons.

Once sentiment picks up in the market, it spreads like wildfire from the institutions to retail. This brings us to the *herd mentality*, which is usually late—and almost always wrong. For that reason, the movements of the herd are contrarian indicators (i.e., OEX put/call). For example, if a particular company is receiving a lot of positive attention in the mainstream financial media, the call activity will increase and so will the premiums paid. The smart money bought these calls when they were inexpensive and started the trend that can sometimes turn into hysteria. The herd will keep thundering into the calls, pushing the options sales volume—and the premiums—even higher. That's when a stock is likely to be in an overbought condition, reflected in an excessive swing in its put/call ratio. Alternatively, negative news on a company may prompt massive buying of puts until the stock is oversold.

PUT/CALL RATIOS: SIMPLE AND DOLLAR-WEIGHTED

The first distinction that must be made is the difference between a simple PCR and the $wPCR. The simple PCR, first introduced by Dr. Marty

Zwieg, one of the original elves on PBS's *Wall Street Week with Louis Rukeyser*, measures the ratio of the total number of all put contracts to the total number of all call contracts for CBOE, which back then dominated listed options trading. It assigns equal weight to every contract. For example, if one day only 300 IBM puts and 600 IBM calls are traded at CBOE, just for the sake of simplicity of the argument, then the simple PCR would be 0.5. This is not a totally accurate reflection of the options activity, however, since options premiums vary greatly for different strike prices and different expirations. And, of course, there is no fund flow consideration. Why? The processing cost was just too enormous. In today's world, cheaper semiconductors and high-speed communications allow us to compute the dollar-weighted put/call ratios and decipher a better signal from its complex behavior.

Indeed, we wanted to leverage the high technology available today to follow the money trail. The reason for going to the $wPCR model was that not all options contracts were valued and/or traded equally. Rather, each has a discrete premium paid value, which leads to the conclusion that each should be weighted according to its real dollar value.

Dollar-weighted put/call ratios calculate the total dollar value of premiums paid for all the put contracts divided by the total value of premiums paid for all the call contracts. This is computed for the complete options chain, including long-term equity anticipation securities (LEAPS). As more data became available, we stored this information into a vast SQL database for future reference and data mining. For the 500 root symbols that we now cover in our universe of 500 stocks, ETFs, and indexes (aka HA500), we had to marry the necessary hardware and software systems along with the requisite telecommunications infrastructure. This enabled us to fetch and crunch the data, in real time, using approximately 62,500 unique options contracts, including LEAPS, all of which is appended after each trading day to our historical database. In order to track the internals of these 500 options chains in real time, we needed to have 2,000 accumulators at work from the open: one accumulator each to keep track of call contracts, call dollars, put contracts, and put dollars per root symbol.

Table 7.1 shows one of my favorite put/call screens. It is sorted by total premiums paid, displayed in the far right-hand column. It is our best measure of options liquidity. Notice GM, closing that day at 19.54, is sporting a 23.6 $wPCR. This is very bearish. Our put/call engine has been bearish on GM since December 15, 2004, when GM (closing on 38.96), carried a 68.3 $wPCR. This signal was again featured on March 16, 2005, in Dan Fitzpatrick's column on RealMoney.com.

TABLE 7.1 Dollar-Weighted Put/Call Ratios for April 4, 2006, Sorted by Highest Liquidity

Symbol	Call Volume	Put Volume	Call $wVol	Put $wVol	Simple P/C Ratio	Dollar W P/C Ratio	Total Volume	Total $wVol
SPX	99,215	108,609	262,348	154,428	1.09	0.59	207,824	416,776
GOOG	84,471	56,131	161,236	78,000	0.66	0.48	140,602	239,236
GM	48,967	262,549	5,450	128,582	5.36	23.59	311,516	134,032
AAPL	58,809	57,079	13,541	52,587	0.97	3.88	115,888	66,128
NDX	11,880	20,355	18,068	40,320	1.71	2.23	32,235	58,388
IWM	36,117	166,028	11,510	21,867	4.60	1.90	202,145	33,377
SPY	29,362	111,884	8,593	15,573	3.81	1.81	141,246	24,166
AMZN	2,719	21,363	478	21,233	7.86	44.42	24,082	21,711
BMY	80,652	1,968	19,947	292	0.02	0.01	82,620	20,239
MO	26,611	14,894	15,563	4,229	0.56	0.27	41,505	19,792
SNDK	18,634	20,323	6,703	12,912	1.09	1.93	38,957	19,615
QQQQ	46,912	183,062	5,930	10,724	3.90	1.81	229,974	16,654
RIMM	31,709	22,087	10,980	3,781	0.70	0.34	53,796	14,761
OIH	11,396	13,623	8,614	5,039	1.20	0.58	25,019	13,653
OEX	29,291	33,296	6,539	6,647	1.14	1.02	62,587	13,186
AMD	24,800	14,171	5,629	7,308	0.57	1.30	38,971	12,937
NYX	8,646	4,698	6,518	6,134	0.54	0.94	13,344	12,652
JPM	25,103	3,773	11,591	743	0.15	0.06	28,876	12,334
PD	9,544	13,806	7,566	4,517	1.45	0.60	23,350	12,083
NVDA	12,373	22,589	8,027	4,015	1.83	0.50	34,962	12,042

Courtesy of HamzeiAnalytics.com.

ADVANTAGES OF REAL-TIME DOLLAR-WEIGHTED PUT/CALL RATIOS

The advantage of a real-time $wPCR is that it enables you to view changes in investor sentiment as they occur. The real-time $wPCRs are dynamically updated throughout the day and reflect changes in both volume and options premiums paid. Measuring the real-time changes in sentiment is critical, and as the recent expansion in options volume attests, many retail and institutional investors are playing equity options as a surrogate for trading the stocks, but often with a short-term horizon.

Another tool to better monitor the intricate sentiment changes is to keep an eye on the $wPCR baskets. They provide us with clues on where the options activity is concentrating within an index or a sector and where it is not. Our $wPCR baskets include big-cap and high-beta stocks, Dow Jones Industrial Average, S&P 500, NASDAQ-100, oil service, techs (which includes computer hardware, software, Internet, and semiconductor companies), consumer, retail, utilities, health care, basic materials, energy, and financials. The baskets allow a trader, at a glance, to spot an anomaly during the trading day.

A good, simple case study is Microsoft Corporation (MSFT), the giant computer software developer. Without getting into all the pertinent details of the decade-long legal wrangling between the Department of Justice (DOJ) and MSFT, we fast-forward to April 1, 2000, when U.S. Court of Appeals Chief Judge Richard Posner ended efforts to mediate the trial. On April 3, the U.S. District Court Judge Thomas Penfield Jackson ruled that the software giant violated antitrust laws and consistently acted to hold on to its power over industry competitors. Microsoft appealed Judge Jackson's ruling immediately. On June 7, 2000, U.S. District Court Judge Thomas Penfield Jackson ordered the breakup of Microsoft into two companies. On September 26, 2000, the U.S. Supreme Court refused to hear the case. On February 27, 2001, a federal appeals court heard Microsoft's appeal of Judge Jackson's decision. On June 28, 2001, a federal appeals court reversed the breakup order.

Table 7.2 depicts our $wPCR readings and the stock prices immediately before the reversal of the breakup order for MSFT. All through June, the $wPCR for MSFT was very bullish, except on June 21 and 26, when it was in a neutral (higher than 0.50) zone. The day before the final ruling, it dropped precipitously to a massive bullish reading of 0.11. The very next day, the ruling became public and the stock hit an intraday high of 34.26. Given the huge number of outstanding shares MSFT has and its high market cap, it took a large inflow of cash into the stock for a move of this size to occur.

For a couple of weeks preceding June 28, 2001, I spoke almost every

TABLE 7.2	Dollar-Weighted P/C Ratio Readings for MSFT and High/Low for the Stock, June 2001		
Date	**$wPCR**	**High**	**Low**
6-Jun	0.10	33.06	32.19
7-Jun	0.09	33.17	32.43
8-Jun	0.22	33.18	32.42
12-Jun	0.41	32.58	31.86
14-Jun	0.45	32.58	31.86
15-Jun	0.48	30.73	29.88
18-Jun	0.45	30.58	29.70
19-Jun	0.34	30.98	30.08
20-Jun	0.32	31.31	30.19
21-Jun	0.64	31.74	31.01
25-Jun	0.51	31.41	30.49
26-Jun	0.83	31.59	30.46
27-Jun	0.11	32.18	31.21
28-Jun	0.20	34.26	31.73

Courtesy of HamzeiAnalytics.com.

morning with Tom Costello, the senior correspondent for CNBC who often reported from the NASDAQ MarketSite from Times Square. In every conversation where MSFT came up, he immediately discounted the divestiture reversal order as another "rumor" by the bulls and expected that even if it were true, the event was probably "priced in." But by the early morning of June 28, 2001, the news of the reversal order was out and Tom called to congratulate me. It was a great feeling. Those who know Tom and have worked with him know that he is a thorough and respected financial journalist. He just wished he had gone on the air with this data as he had with our previous put/call signals for stocks and indexes.

Moving to another example, Table 7.3 shows a snapshot of our historical database for Amgen (AMGN). On July 10, 2003, the simple PCR was 2.02, which on the surface appears to give a bearish reading. However, the $wPCR was 0.55 and on the previous day it was 0.27. This paints a far more bullish picture than the simple PCR does, since it reveals that significantly more money was being diverted to the call options. As Figure 7.3 shows, AMGN closed at 69.51 on July 10 and hit a high of 72.37 on July 15. As this example shows, what we look for is an

TABLE 7.3 Internal Options Chain Metrics for AMGN, July 9–11, 2003

AMGN	Call Volume	Put Volume	Call $wVol (000)	Put $wVol (000)	Simple P/C Ratio	$ W P/C Ratio	Total Volume (000)	Total $wVol (000)
07/09/03	18562	11688	18931	5197	0.63	0.27	30250	24128
07/10/03	8070	16270	3660	2028	2.02	0.55	24340	5688
07/11/03	10457	7871	6362	1860	0.75	0.29	18328	8222

Courtesy of HamzeiAnalytics.com.

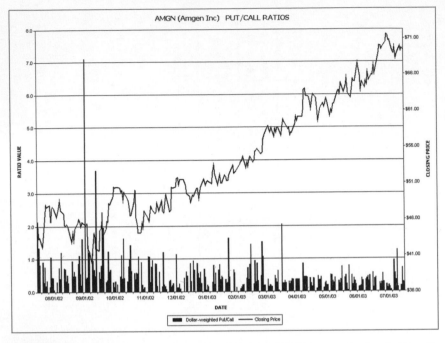

FIGURE 7.3   Dollar-Weighted Put/Call Ratio of AMGN versus Its Stock Price for 52 Weeks Ending July 31, 2003 (Courtesy of HamzeiAnalytics.com.)

extreme reading accompanied by high liquidity as measured by recent dollar-weighted options volume.

AN INDEX EXAMPLE

On June 3, 2003, around 11:40 CST, with the NASDAQ-100 Index (NDX) hovering around 1,192, our $wPCR engine flashed a 16.5 reading with some 7,400 options contracts, representing some $45 million in premiums traded. A reading of this level is very bullish.

As noted earlier, unlike single stocks or narrow-based ETF and indexes, the wide-based indexes provide contrarian signals. The key is to monitor the ratios as orders come in and dollar volume accumulates in the put and call contracts throughout the trading day. Extreme readings are often unsustainable and are ripe for a snapback sharp reversal caused by a domino effect of short covering and a buying frenzy.

We alerted our subscribers in our online trading room, then we

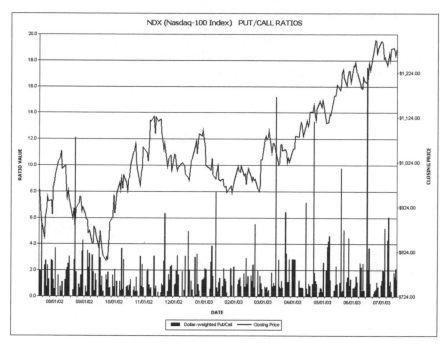

FIGURE 7.4 Dollar-Weighted Put/Call Ratio of NDX versus Its Price for 52 Weeks Ending July 31, 2003 (Courtesy of HamzeiAnalytics.com.)

contacted Aaron Task, the senior writer for RealMoney.com, who reported to his readers that the ratio was at levels that had augured explosive bullish moves in the past. This indicator generally leads the market by a few hours to three days. These levels don't occur very often, but when they do, they can provide an excellent opportunity for the short-term trader.

The NDX proceeded to close at 1,198 the same day and hit a high of 1,265 three days later (see Figure 7.4). One can trade this signal in two different ways, either using at-the-money NDX or QQQQ call options, which defines and limits your downside risk to actual premiums paid for the options; or if you prefer a bit more leverage and are ready for spin in a Lamborghini Diablo, try going long the NDX E-mini futures (NQ) contract on Globex. A big player may want to fly the U.S. Navy F-18E SuperHornet by going long the large NDX futures (ND) contract at the MERC. But beware, in the case of the NASDAQ futures, the large contract, or the E-mini, you have unlimited downside potential, and you'd better be strapped in tight and ready for the ride of your life. Magic Mountain has *not* built a roller coaster this fast or this furious.

Market Sentiment Can Change Rapidly

Signals from our dollar-weighted put/call engine are actionable from a few hours up to three days. This empirical observation puzzled me for months. And then, first in spring of 2001 and next in fall of 2003, I had the privilege of visiting with Jon "Doctor J" Najarian, the founder of Mercury Trading, the huge Designated Primary Market Maker (DPM) at CBOE. He explained what he went through with his traders on the floor of CBOE every trading day. As orders came in, his mandate as a DPM was to create and manage an orderly market, for which his firm and other DPMs are paid handsomely. This means buying at the bid (that is, you and I are *selling* to a DPM at the bid) and selling at the ask (that is, you and I are *buying* from a DPM at the ask). In this fashion he filled the call and put options orders from retail and institutional customers alike, much like the specialists on the floor of NYSE. In effect he was matching buy (long) and sell (short) orders for calls or puts while locking in, on the fly, the bid and the ask spreads for his own account.

But in reality the buy and sell orders never perfectly match. There are simply too many trading opportunities, as evidenced by the depth of options chain per root symbol. There is always an imbalance. Many times in the day, his firm was on the other side of trades with the public. This further meant he was taking an enormous risk at the end of each trading day for his net out-of-balance positions held on his books. Well, market makers are not in the risk business. Rather, they are in the risk *transfer* business between two interested parties, no matter what strategies the interested parties are deploying or why. DPMs have to go home delta-neutral. That means he needs to transfer *his net risk* every day in the cash market, like NYSE or NASDAQ, and lay off its inherent risk there.

Typically a DPM the size of Mercury may trade 100,000 contracts a day with up to 3,000,000 shares in the cash market. And the DPM needs to stay in the trade until the expiration of each distinct option contract! How does a large DPM finance this? That is where the market maker's warehousing line of credit comes into the picture. Margins are thin and the bankers are pretty strict about the loan covenants attached to that line of credit. Those strict covenants force the market maker to stay delta-neutral at the end of each trading day.

Now let's talk settlements. Derivatives for exchange-listed instruments, like options and futures, settle daily, while stocks have a three-day settlement rule. And since trading options and futures is a far more efficient method of holding a position, the DPMs will try every conceivable option strategy, so they are not forced to go the cash market and finance a large stock transaction and pay for it in three days. Now, keep in mind, there are six options exchanges in the United States. So, in effect, an extreme reading on $wPCR for a given root symbol is flashing the *aggregate net pressure* on all DPMs for that root symbol. But if the extreme pressure is not mitigated, in three days or less, we have a move on our hands as predicted by the $wPCR as the DPMs are forced to neutralize their books.

Let's recap: The $wPCR is only a sentiment indicator, albeit a very sophisticated one. Comparing current readings of $wPCR with historical $wPCR values gives you the proper perspective. It is not a buy or sell mechanical system in itself. You must employ other technical tools from your toolbox to navigate the equity names you are trading in. What it does for you is provide a sentiment signal that is indicating either *bearish, neutral,* or *bullish.*

What Are the Parameters to Look For?

We have observed empirically that $wPCR is an excellent forward-looking sentiment indicator. For single stocks and narrow-based indexes or ETFs, the signal is directional. For wide-based indexes or ETFs, the signal is contrarian. In both cases the shelf life of the signal is from one to three days. The key is the *changes* in $wPCR—that gives us the real-time heads up.

Today's market environment is more challenging than ever. Traders are constantly striving to improve their results and their trading edge. The value of noncorrelated data cannot be overemphasized. As shown in numerous examples, both in this chapter and in our trading, $wPCR has an enormous impact on alerting traders to profitable opportunities. We feel that this is an invaluable trading tool and belongs in every trader's arsenal. One key principle that all leveraged traders must adhere to, whether utilizing derivatives or not, is to be constantly vigilant of their money management theory and practice. This takes us to our next quantitative trading tool for your toolbox.

A VARIANT OF SUPPORT, PIVOT, AND RESISTANCE LEVELS

Once a short-term trade is identified and plans are made to undertake it, it is important for the trader to identify the optimal entry points, stop-loss levels, and the profit target prices. One tool that has helped us manage our trades very objectively is a variant of the tried-and-true support, pivot, and resistance (SPR) levels.

First let's go through a bit of background. Everyone is familiar with the traditional methods of estimating support and resistance prices by spotting accumulation distribution patterns on a price chart. The SPR levels that we are discussing here are quite different. These levels are computed by fixed formulas using the previous period's open, high, low, and close prices, and by their clever design, they will have volatility data imbedded in them. These formulas have been handed down from old experienced traders to the young turks on the floor of exchanges in Chicago and New York. Some call them simply *pivots* as they have a tendency to pinpoint key reversal prices.

First let me give you the formulas. By the way, they apply to any bar interval that is daily, weekly, or monthly. In this section, our focus is on using the weekly SPR levels on 60-minute bar (hourly) charts, which in our firm we call the "HotSpots."

There are seven distinct price levels. The center price level is called *pivot*. Here is how it is computed:

$$Pivot = (High + Low + Close)/3$$

The inputs are the high, low, and close prices from the immediately preceding period of the same length. For example, if you are computing the weekly SPR levels, then your inputs are weekly high, weekly low, and weekly close.

A variant formula for the pivot that is dear to many experienced traders is when the open is also used in calculating the pivot. Then the formula for the pivot becomes:

$$Pivot = (Open + High + Low + Close)/4$$

The main issue we object to is the variant formula for the pivot is the accuracy of the daily open as posted by many data vendors. We usually employ three or four different data vendors. Invariably, we observe different opening prices on many issues on any given day, especially on stock index futures. That is when the variant pivot formula creates further debate. For the sake of simplicity here, we will stay with the original formula without the opening price as the fourth input.

The next two levels we need to compute are resistance one (R1) and support one (S1). Once we have the pivot, it is easy to compute R1 and S1. Here are the formulas for this step:

$$R1 = (2 \times Pivot) - Low$$

$$S1 = (2 \times Pivot) - High$$

The area between R1 and S1 (as you will see, it always envelopes the pivot), in my trading style, is considered the "neutral zone."

The next levels we are interested in computing are resistance two (R2) and support two (S2). To compute R2 and S2 levels, the R1 and S1 values have to be known. Here are our next formulas:

$$R2 = \text{Pivot} + (R1 - S1)$$

$$S2 = \text{Pivot} - (R1 - S1)$$

As you will see, what is significant here is that once the price moves above the daily R1 or below the daily S1 levels, the underlying is "in play"—it is out of the neutral zone. You will then see the R2 or S2 levels as the next price levels trying to pull up or push down the price action until one of those objectives is achieved. One has to keep an eye on the volume (intraday or daily) but a surge will generally accompany such movement as the R2 or S2 price objective nears. And then, often, you will witness a pause in the price action by the sideways movement of the asset.

Let's go through the formulas for the next price objectives. They are:

$$R3 = (2 \times R1) - S1$$

$$S3 = (2 \times S1) - R1$$

Ideally, if you are day trading, pay attention to the daily SPR levels and plot the price of the asset using 15-minute or 30-minute bars (see Figure 7.5). This is very useful for trading any stock index futures, and highly

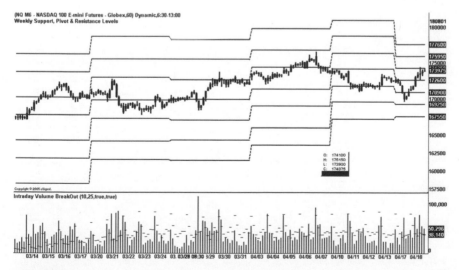

FIGURE 7.5　Daily SPR Levels for NASDAQ E-mini Futures June 2006 Contract (NQ M6) Plotted Using 15-minute Bars (*Source:* eSignal. www.esignal.com.)

recommended for trading the Beast or any high-beta stock like Google (GOOG), Broadcom Corp (BRCM), or Nvidia Corp (NVDA).

If you are swing-trading stocks—that is, holding to a position for at least one to two weeks—by all means, plot the weekly SPR levels on a chart with the hourly or daily bars (see Figure 7.6). You will not believe your own eyes. Usually when I lecture, I have the audience pick the underlying instrument and then I will provide the analysis right there and then. You have to be there to see the reaction of the audience in person.

I have not utilized the monthly SPR levels to a great extent, but of course, it is intuitively clear that this indicator is reserved for the buy and hold or the sell and hold crowd.

I am always asked why these SPR levels work so well, and honestly, we simply do not know! But empirically, the picture is very compelling. It tells us these are very important price levels to many market participants out there, as evidenced by the surge in volume as we approach the next key level. Often we also witness the price hugging that next level just like a magnet, going sideways for a period before zooming to the next level. We can only surmise that since a majority of professional traders and investors are swing traders with a keen sense of volatility cycles, they often time their trades patiently and enter and exit at key volatility levels.

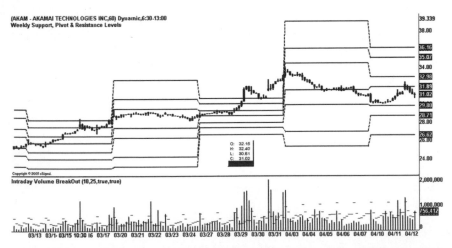

FIGURE 7.6 Weekly SPR Levels for AKAM Plotted Using 60-minute Bars (HotSpots) (*Source:* eSignal. www.esignal.com.)

CONCLUSION

In the 10 years since I began my search for better real-time indicators, I have been immersed in options, both as a derivative instrument to trade and as advance indicators of sentiment for specific issues and the market in general. Throughout this time, I have experienced the power of using the two tools introduced in this chapter: the dollar-weighted put/call ratio and the support, pivot, and resistance (SPR) levels.

I believe that, based on the overview of this chapter, traders will see the potential for using these two tools as a means to improve the identification and execution of their trades. First, traders can decode the secret messages of the options market using the put/call engine—seeking out bullish or bearish themes and names ahead of the herd and then picking the correct instrument that best meets their risk/reward objectives. Second, after identifying the opportunities, traders must wait patiently, just like a great deer hunter, and pursue the target using the SPR levels with total confidence.

As a student of the market, I never stop learning from the indicators I use, from other traders, and from the market itself. While all trading systems evolve over time, put/call ratios and SPR levels will be major factors in how I view, analyze, and execute trades now and in the foreseeable future.

CHAPTER 8

Trading Seasonality

Phil Erlanger

O f all the methods and techniques that traders and investors use to analyze and interpret the market, one of the most misunderstood and least used is seasonality. Over the years, however, the more we have used seasonality at my research firm, the more we have come to value it as a primary factor in our decision-making. Seasonality is the tendency toward repeatability as a financial instrument moves in relation to a particular influencing factor. That factor could be the time of year, interest rate changes, inflation, the rise or fall in energy prices, or a dozen other influences. The essence of seasonality is that the ebb and flow of a market can be observed and predicted with a high degree of confidence based on the repeatability of certain patterns.

Now contrast this with the proverbial quest for some magical set of indicators that will guarantee a steady return. This is the desire of many traders: to have a technique or set of techniques that will produce the equivalent of planetary alignment. Truth be told, however, some of these indicators add some value, some add only a little value, and some add no value at all. The reason is that the stock market is a nonlinear environment in which myriad complex influences exert forces—sometimes in concert and other times in opposition—on market prices. Looking at *all* these forces in total leads to the possibility of there being countless end results. This leaves the trader having to determine which factor or factors merit the most attention in the decision-making process. This selection, if you will, is also what makes the market nonlinear. Some traders are focused on certain factors and projecting one outcome, while at the same time another group of traders emphasize other factors that lead to another conclusion.

In this nonlinear marketplace, however, most Wall Street research indicators are linear in nature. This further complicates matters. One factor becomes the sole focus of a methodology to the point that it becomes a science. Other approaches are inhibited by the fact that they take into account so many factors that it becomes more and more difficult to arrive at an informed opinion. The best approach is for a trader to look at the universe of all possible factors and decide which are the most valuable. The obvious choices are those that are independent of other factors, have a reasonable degree of correlation to price action, and have a successful track record of repeating over time.

Seasonality meets all of these requirements. In particular, we focus on the influence of seasonal cycles derived from the time of the calendar year on stock prices. Seasonal cycles do not *cause* prices to move a certain way. Rather, they reflect a measure of the *tendency* of prices to move a certain way. Keep in mind that ongoing price action continues to be influenced by many factors, and only some of them will occur on a regular and repeatable basis. In addition, the factors that regularly cause a stock to rise or fall at a particular time of year may or may not be known. Nonetheless, their combined seasonal influence will be reflected in seasonal indicators. Moreover, this seasonal influence can be qualified by several techniques that measure the breadth and consistency of a stock's seasonal pattern.

When entering into a trade, there are two basic types of indicators: setups and triggers. Seasonality is a setup indicator. *Setup* indicators are designed as filters that steer the trader to moments when making a trade will result in greater success than at other times. Examples of setup indicators other than seasonality include sentiment (often a contrary setup indicator), industry group relative performance, fundamental information (e.g., earnings momentum) and price, volume, or other divergence oscillators (e.g. relative strength index or RSI, moving average convergence-divergence or MACD, or Erlanger Volume Swing). Oscillators are used as setups most often when they begin to diverge from price action. For instance, if price is rising to a new reaction high unconfirmed by the RSI oscillator, a setup for a potential short sale exists.

Triggers are designed to tell the trader the exact moment to execute a trade by measuring when price begins to move in the direction indicated by setup indicators. Examples of triggers include moving average crossovers, price moving through a displaced moving average (DMA) channel, or a change in status of a trend direction indicator. Some indicators, like the MACD, are used as both setup and triggers (setup when the MACD diverges with price, trigger when the MACD crosses its signal line).

The prelude to the trading process is one or more signals generated by the setup criteria. When the market then moves sufficiently in the anticipated direction, setting off a trigger indicator, a trade is made. After the trade is entered, *monitoring* indicators are used until the trade is exited. These monitoring indicators can in some instances be the same indicators used for setup or trigger events, or they can be a completely different set of indicators or indicator criteria. For instance, one can trigger a long position if price moves above the 10-day moving average, but monitor the position and sell only if price falls below the 21-day average. The indicators and criteria are up to the individual trader's style and preference.

Stock price changes are what the trader tries to exploit. In the end, a successful trader either buys at a lower price than sold, or sells short at a higher price than covered (buying to close out a short position). Setup and trigger indicators therefore generate information for either direction of an opening trade (long or short). The contribution that seasonality makes is that it uncovers those moments when the market or stock tends to rise (a setup for long trades) or fall (a setup for short trades).

What makes seasonality so unique is that it is known far in advance, and yet it still is valuable as a timing mechanism. We know of no other stock market factor that has this feature. Let's step through the process of developing seasonal statistics for stocks, and examine how effective they can be for trading purposes.

THE YEARLY SEASONAL CYCLE

Seasonal cycles can be created using any of a number of different time periods. In reality, cycle analysis is really only an effort to measure seasonality. Therefore, we could look at 20-year, 10-year, monthly, weekly, daily, or even hourly periods in an effort to uncover repeating patterns. For the purposes of this exercise, we will focus on uncovering seasonal patterns associated with daily closing price action over the calendar year.

Figure 8.1 shows the first step in preparing a seasonal cycle. We have chopped up the 15-year history of Bausch & Lomb (BOL) and plotted each year, January 1 through the end of December. At first brush it looks like spaghetti, or for the more imaginative it might serve as some sort of Rorschach inkblot test. However, by compositing these years into

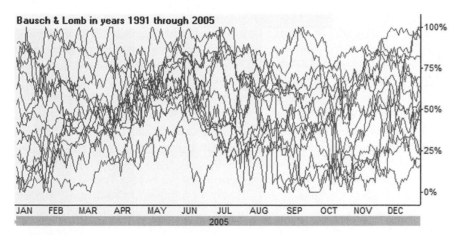

FIGURE 8.1 Bausch & Lomb (BOL), 1991–2005, Spliced into Yearly Lines

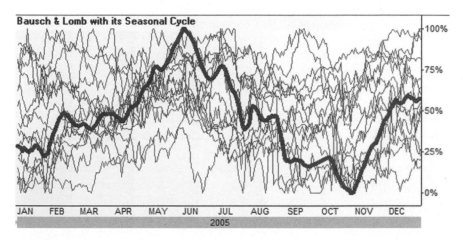

FIGURE 8.2 Bausch & Lomb with Its Seasonal Cycle

one linear curve, a seasonal cycle is born. Figure 8.2 shows Bausch & Lomb with each year and the composite seasonal cycle derived from those years.

The number of years used to create a seasonal cycle is subjective. Enough years are needed to establish a statistically valuable pattern, but too many years could add old and possibly outdated information. We look back 15 years as a default, and then do a moderate process of optimization to find the best, most recent period of data to use. Optimization can be injurious to good results when testing for signals in stock data indicators. This is especially true if criteria or parameters are set as a result of excessive optimization techniques. The danger is one of curve fitting, where the indicators are parameterized to work well with a specific body of data, but are ineffective outside in the real trading world. However, here we are doing something a bit different.

In any sample of data there is going to be a composite cycle. The key is to find a composite cycle that is a repeating pattern. We do this by taking a large enough sample (up to 15 years). We then split this sample in half and create two additional composite cycles—one from the first half and one from the second half. If these two mini cycles are somewhat correlated, then we have greater confidence that the original cycle represents true seasonality. Optimization comes in by adjusting the original sample size to maximize the correlation of that sample's mini cycle halves. Let's look at an example.

In Figure 8.3, does the seasonal pattern reflect tendencies throughout the 13-year history of Trident Microsystems (TRID), or is it a random cycle? To answer this question, we create the two mini seasonal composites, one from the first half of TRID's 13-year history (1993 to 1998—the thin line in Figure 8.3), and one from the second half of TRID's 13-year history (1999 to 2005—the dotted line in Figure 8.3). We only use complete years in constructing seasonal cycles. If the sample size is an odd number of years, we add the median year to the latest mini cycle composition. The thick line is the seasonal cycle based on all 13 years of TRID price history. All these cycles bear similarities, especially at certain times of the year (the high points in late January and early December and the low point in mid-April, for instance).

We use a correlation statistic called *Pearson's R*, which is a statistical expression of linear relationship between two variables. It ranges from +1 to −1, with a reading of +1 being a perfect match between two variables. A reading of −1 indicates a perfectly inverse relationship between two variables, while a reading of 0 implies no relationship or correlation at all between the two variables. In the lower portion of Figure 8.3 a *Cycle r* statistic is listed. This is the Pearson's R of two variables, the seasonal cycle for TRID based on years 1993 through 1998 (thin line) and the seasonal cycle for TRID based on years 1999 through 2005 (dotted line). In this case the Cycle r equals −0.02, implying no correlation.

Our conclusion from this is that the yearly cycle derived from the entire 13-year history has too much noise in it to be very effective. *Noise* in the data reflects price action that is random and obscures the clarity of the seasonal pattern we are looking for. However, many of the turning points of the 13-year cycle do seem to match well with the price action in

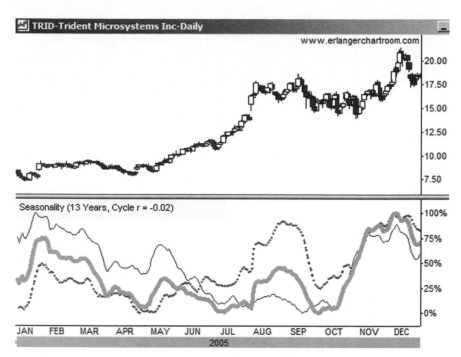

FIGURE 8.3 Trident Microsystems (TRID) with its mini cycles, 13-Year Sample

2005. We have observed that cycles with a Cycle r statistic around zero have some worth when looking for turning points. We eschew cycles whose Cycle r statistic correlations are negative. These indicate a composite where conflicting patterns exist: There is too much noise in the data to expect future price action to follow the cycle.

Faced with a Cycle r statistic of –0.02 for our 13-year sample cycle for TRID, we can decide to look at shorter sample periods to find a higher Cycle r statistic, and perhaps a more significant seasonal pattern. The sample with the highest Cycle r statistic turns out to be of 5 years duration. Because this is a shorter sample period, the persistence of this seasonal pattern is considered to be statistically local—that is, less representative of longer-term cycles. Nevertheless, the trade-off is a much higher Cycle r statistic of 0.90 (see Figure 8.4). In this 5-year pattern, the mini cycles are highly correlated. Interestingly, the key turning points found in the 13-year cycle (the high points in late January and early December and the low point in mid-April) clearly remain in the 5-year cycle.

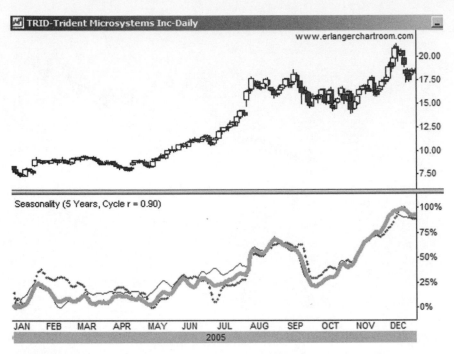

FIGURE 8.4 Trident Microsystems (TRID) with its mini cycles, 5-Year Sample

SEASONALITY ZONES

At this point, let's focus on those 14-day (or longer) periods in the seasonal cycle that are the strongest zones and also highlight those 14-day (or longer) periods in the seasonal cycle that are the weakest zones.

These zones are plotted in Figure 8.5 for Bausch & Lomb (BOL). In this chart, the seasonal cycle uses a 14-year sample from 1991 to 2004. This particular cycle was created on January 1, 2005, and was not changed in any way as 2005 actually transpired. In other words, the seasonal cycle you see below Bausch & Lomb's 2005 price action was created using data prior to 2005, and it was up to the price of Bausch & Lomb to follow it or not to follow it. The computer program has added shading to highlight the seasonality zones. Shadings *above* the seasonal cycle represent the strongest seasonal periods of 14 days or longer. Shadings *below* the seasonal cycle represent the weakest seasonal periods of 14 days or longer. Note how the price of Bausch & Lomb moved during 2005 relative to these zones.

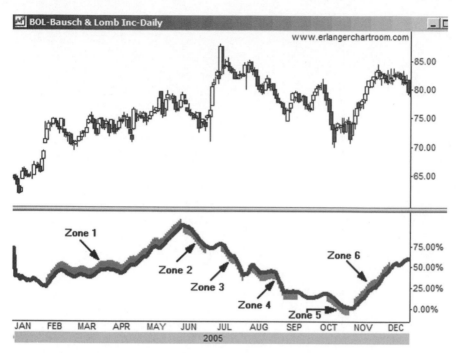

FIGURE 8.5 Bausch & Lomb (BOL) Seasonal Cycle with Seasonality Zones

Table 8.1 contains the data for all the seasonality zones for Bausch & Lomb in 2005. There were six zones in 2005—two strong zones and four weak zones. Remember that these zones were identified with data ending in 2004. The price action of Bausch & Lomb in 2005 remarkably followed the paths of these zones in all six instances. Not including commissions, the cumulative return in Bausch & Lomb's stock price during these zones was 45.94 percent. For 2005 as a whole, Bausch & Lomb's stock price rose 3.44 points, or 5.34 percent. For Bausch & Lomb in 2005, trading the seasonality zones outperformed a buy and hold strategy by 40.60 percent (45.94 minus 5.34.)

Table 8.2 contains the data for all the seasonality zones for Disney (DIS) in 2005. There were seven zones in 2005—four strong zones and three weak zones. Again, please note that these zones were identified with data ending in 2004. Not including commissions, the cumulative return in Disney's stock price during these zones was 36.51 percent. For 2005 as a whole, Disney's stock price fell 3.83 points, or –13.78 percent. For Disney in 2005, trading the seasonality zones outperformed a buy and hold strategy by 50.29 percent (36.51 minus –13.78).

TABLE 8.1 Bausch & Lomb (BOL) Seasonality Zone Trades in 2005

Year 2005

Company	Zone Trades	Type of Zone	Opening Date	Closing Date	Opening Price	Closing Price	Net	Net %	P/L	Winner/ Loser	Cumulative Return[a]
Bausch & Lomb (BOL)											
	1	Strong	01/31/05	06/01/05	$72.89	$78.95	6.06	8.31%	8.31%	Winner	8.31%
	2	Weak	06/01/05	06/21/05	$78.95	$73.58	−5.37	−6.80%	6.80%	Winner	15.12%
	3	Weak	07/05/05	07/25/05	$87.50	$82.21	−5.29	−6.05%	6.05%	Winner	21.16%
	4	Weak	08/01/05	09/12/05	$83.53	$79.24	−4.29	−5.14%	5.14%	Winner	26.30%
	5	Weak	10/06/05	10/27/05	$78.17	$71.36	−6.81	−8.71%	8.71%	Winner	35.01%
	6	Strong	10/31/05	12/01/05	$74.19	$82.30	8.11	10.93%	10.93%	Winner	45.94%
								Wins:		6	
								Losses:		0	

[a]Brokerage charges not taken into account.

Source: Phil Erlanger Research Co., Inc.

TABLE 8.2 Disney Corp. (DIS) Seasonality Zone Trades in 2005

Year 2005

Company	Zone Trades	Type of Zone	Opening Date	Closing Date	Opening Price	Closing Price	Net	Net %	P/L	Winner/ Loser	Cumulative Return[a]
Disney (DIS)											
	1	Strong	01/05/05	02/14/05	$27.40	$29.39	1.99	7.26%	7.26%	Winner	7.26%
	2	Weak	02/17/05	03/31/05	$29.35	$28.73	-0.62	-2.11%	2.11%	Winner	9.38%
	3	Strong	05/11/05	06/01/05	$26.67	$27.58	0.91	3.41%	3.41%	Winner	12.79%
	4	Weak	06/10/05	07/11/05	$27.53	$25.18	-2.35	-8.54%	8.54%	Winner	21.32%
	5	Weak	08/01/05	09/21/05	$25.61	$23.33	-2.28	-8.90%	8.90%	Winner	30.23%
	6	Strong	09/26/05	11/07/05	$23.26	$25.16	1.90	8.17%	8.17%	Winner	38.39%
	7	Strong	11/14/05	12/06/05	$26.01	$25.52	-0.49	-1.88%	-1.88%	Loser	36.51%

Wins: 6
Losses: 1
Win/Loss Ratio: 6
Avg. Win: 6.40%
Avg. Loss: -1.88%
Avg. Win/Avg. Loss Ratio: 3.40

[a]Brokerage charges not taken into account.

Source: Phil Erlanger Research Co., Inc.

SEASONAL HEAT

Seasonal cycles are simple guidelines to past behavior during specific periods. They are composed of past price action, and as such they hide measures of seasonal consistency throughout the price action's history. We can adjust the historical look-back period to optimize for Cycle r as discussed previously, but this optimization process tells us more about the *validity* of the seasonal pattern than it does about the pattern's *consistency*. To measure seasonal consistency, we need another process, which we call *seasonal heat*.

At the start of each new year, the seasonal cycle is updated with new seasonality zones, incorporating data from the prior year's action. Because this new data is used and in some cases old data is discarded, these seasonality zones do not appear precisely at the same time intervals each year; however, they do not generally deviate greatly from past years. This is at least the case for stocks that have strong seasonal tendencies.

The objective is to identify when seasonality zones most often occurred in prior years. The more frequently a seasonality zone occurs in *past* years, the greater the seasonal heat for the current years. (In our charts, seasonal heat is greatest when the background shading is lightest.) Seasonal heat can be either positive or negative. Positive seasonal heat is a greater number (lighter background above the 50 percent line in the charts). Negative seasonal heat is a greater negative number (lighter background below the 50 percent line in the charts.)

Figure 8.6 shows the Disney chart with its seasonality zones and its seasonal heat map added. Positive seasonal heat is shown above the 50 percent line; negative seasonal heat is shown below the 50 percent line. Looking at the heat map above the 50 percent line, the brightest sections correspond to those periods most frequented by strong seasonal zones in prior years. This illustrates the consistency of seasonality. The more a seasonal pattern repeats, the more likely it is to occur in the future. This is true for both strong and weak seasonal patterns. Moreover, those periods in a seasonal map during which the positive seasonal heat is absent (darkest) are potentially riskier moments for Disney than other times of the year. This was certainly true in 2005, as Figure 8.6 demonstrates.

Taking the concept of seasonal heat further, let's examine all the Dow Jones Industrial Average 30 component issues during 2005. We will confine our long strategy to buying these issues only during the strongest seasonality zones that have the most positive seasonal heat. In a case where there are two strong seasonal zones with similar extremes in seasonal

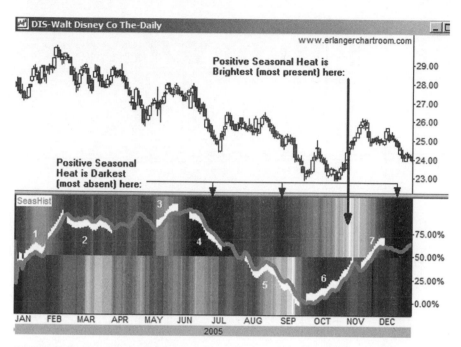

FIGURE 8.6 Disney (DIS) with Seasonality Zones and Seasonal Heat Map

heat, we will count both as trades. We will confine our short-selling strategy to shorting issues only during weak seasonal zones that have the most
negative seasonal heat. In the case where there are two weak seasonal
zones with similar peaks in seasonal heat, we will count both as trades.
Table 8.3 shows the results.

The results for 2005 are remarkable. Out of 69 trades, 55 were profitable, resulting in a win/loss ratio of 4:1, an average win to average loss
ratio of 1.97:1, with average wins equal to 7.05 percent and average loss
equal to –3.57 percent. The average trade yielded a 4.90 percent gain. The
maximum gain was 22.50 percent, and the maximum loss was –7.94 percent. For the year of 2005 as a whole, the Dow Jones Industrial Average itself lost by –0.61 percent.

SEASONALITY AND OTHER INSTRUMENTS

Seasonality analysis need not be confined only to stocks. Any instrument
that has enough price history can be the subject of seasonal analysis. For

TABLE 8.3 Dow Jones 30 Issues Seasonality Zone Trades in 2005

Year 2005

Company	Zone Trades	Type of Zone	Opening Date	Closing Date	Opening Price	Closing Price	Net	Net %	P/L	Winner/ Loser	Cumulative Return[a]
Alcoa	1	Weak	08/02/05	09/28/05	$28.76	$24.07	-4.69	-16.31%	16.31%	Winner	16.31%
(AA)	2	Strong	09/28/05	12/07/05	$24.07	$28.59	4.52	18.78%	18.78%	Winner	35.09%
Amer Intl Grp	1	Weak	02/15/05	03/14/05	$71.85	$63.85	-8.00	-11.13%	11.13%	Winner	11.13%
(AIG)	2	Weak	08/02/05	09/02/05	$60.75	$59.33	-1.42	-2.34%	2.34%	Winner	13.47%
	3	Strong	10/11/05	11/02/05	$61.71	$66.22	4.51	7.31%	7.31%	Winner	20.78%
Amer Express	1	Weak	08/02/05	09/14/05	$48.63	$50.01	1.38	2.84%	-2.84%	Loser	-2.84%
AXP)	2	Strong	10/14/05	11/15/05	$47.95	$50.93	2.98	6.21%	6.21%	Winner	3.38%
Boeing	1	Strong	03/16/05	06/15/05	$56.77	$64.41	7.64	13.46%	13.46%	Winner	13.46%
(BA)	2	Weak	06/17/05	10/13/05	$64.62	$66.49	1.87	2.89%	-2.89%	Loser	10.56%
Citigroup	1	Strong	09/26/05	11/09/05	$45.09	$46.82	1.73	3.84%	3.84%	Winner	3.84%
(C)	2	Weak	04/18/05	05/10/05	$46.21	$46.38	0.17	0.37%	-0.37%	Loser	3.47%
Caterpillar	1	Weak	01/04/05	01/26/05	$47.01	$45.56	-1.45	-3.08%	3.08%	Winner	3.08%
(CAT)	2	Strong	01/26/05	03/08/05	$45.56	$49.50	3.94	8.65%	8.65%	Winner	11.73%
DuPont	1	Weak	06/10/05	09/27/05	$47.25	$38.43	-8.82	-18.67%	18.67%	Winner	18.67%
(DD)	2	Strong	11/16/05	12/06/05	$41.89	$43.48	1.59	3.80%	3.80%	Winner	22.46%
Disney	1	Weak	08/01/05	09/20/05	$25.61	$23.75	-1.86	-7.26%	7.26%	Winner	7.26%
(DIS)	2	Strong	09/26/05	11/07/05	$23.26	$25.16	1.90	8.17%	8.17%	Winner	15.43%
General Electric (GE)	2	Strong	10/13/05	12/29/05	$34.02	$35.19	1.17	3.44%	3.44%	Winner	3.44%
		Weak	07/20/05	08/08/05	$35.30	$33.76	-1.54	-4.36%	4.36%	Winner	7.80%
General Motors (GM)	1	Weak	08/30/05	10/12/05	$34.45	$26.70	-7.75	-22.50%	22.50%	Winner	22.50%
	2	Strong	01/31/05	03/10/05	$36.81	$34.61	-2.20	-5.98%	-5.98%	Loser	16.52%

Company	#		Date 1	Date 2	Price 1	Price 2					
Hewlett-Packard (HPQ)	1	Weak	07/18/05	10/10/05	$24.92	$26.67	1.75	7.02%	-7.02%	Loser	-7.02%
	2	Strong	10/12/05	11/07/05	$27.30	$28.73	1.43	5.24%	5.24%	Winner	-1.78%
Home Depot (HD)	1	Weak	08/26/05	10/13/05	$39.81	$37.95	-1.86	-4.67%	4.67%	Winner	4.67%
	2	Strong	10/13/05	11/17/05	$37.95	$42.51	4.56	12.02%	12.02%	Winner	16.69%
Honeywell (HON)	1	Strong	10/04/05	11/07/05	$36.78	$35.90	-0.88	-2.39%	-2.39%	Loser	-2.39%
	2	Weak	08/02/05	09/30/05	$39.26	$37.50	-1.76	-4.48%	4.48%	Winner	2.09%
Intl Bus Mach (IBM)	1	Weak	09/14/05	10/04/05	$80.48	$80.11	-0.37	-0.46%	-0.46%	Winner	0.46%
	2	Strong	04/18/05	05/19/05	$76.65	$77.16	0.51	0.67%	0.67%	Winner	1.13%
	3	Weak	02/16/05	04/18/05	$94.62	$76.65	-17.97	-18.99%	18.99%	Winner	20.12%
	4	Strong	10/27/05	11/29/05	$82.31	$89.10	6.79	8.25%	8.25%	Winner	28.37%
Intel (INTC)	1	Weak	03/21/05	04/15/05	$23.50	$22.12	-1.38	-5.87%	-5.87%	Winner	5.87%
	2	Weak	08/18/05	10/06/05	$25.83	$23.76	-2.12	-8.19%	-8.19%	Winner	14.06%
	3	Strong	06/24/05	07/18/05	$26.10	$28.23	2.13	8.16%	8.16%	Winner	22.22%
	4	Strong	10/12/05	11/08/05	$23.24	$24.55	1.31	5.64%	5.64%	Winner	27.86%
Johnson & Johnson (JNJ)	1	Strong	04/01/05	04/22/05	$66.85	$68.49	1.64	2.45%	2.45%	Winner	2.45%
	2	Weak	01/03/05	01/24/05	$62.90	$61.49	-1.41	-2.24%	-2.24%	Winner	4.69%
JP Morgan (JPM)	1	Strong	01/04/05	02/11/05	$38.41	$37.48	-0.93	-2.42%	-2.42%	Loser	-2.42%
	2	Weak	06/08/05	10/13/05	$35.67	$33.75	-1.92	-5.38%	5.38%	Winner	2.96%
Coca-Cola (KO)	1	Strong	04/13/05	06/01/05	$42.10	$44.59	2.49	5.91%	5.91%	Winner	5.91%
	2	Weak	08/18/05	09/23/05	$43.53	$42.35	-1.18	-2.71%	-2.71%	Winner	8.63%
McDonald's (MCD)	1	Strong	09/23/05	11/17/05	$32.64	$33.19	0.55	1.69%	1.69%	Winner	1.69%
	2	Weak	06/13/05	09/21/05	$29.11	$31.42	2.31	7.94%	-7.94%	Loser	-6.25%
3M (MMM)	1	Strong	01/31/05	02/16/05	$84.36	$86.80	2.44	2.89%	2.89%	Winner	2.89%
	2	Weak	08/16/05	09/02/05	$71.66	$71.50	-0.16	-0.22%	0.22%	Winner	3.12%
	3	Strong	09/26/05	11/21/05	$73.13	$79.23	6.10	8.34%	8.34%	Winner	11.46%

(Continued)

171

TABLE 8.3 *(Continued)*

Year 2005

Company	Zone Trades	Type of Zone	Opening Date	Closing Date	Opening Price	Closing Price	Net	Net %	P/L	Winner/ Loser	Cumulative Return[a]
Altria (MO)	1	Weak	03/07/05	04/12/05	$65.65	$65.19	-0.46	-0.70%	0.70%	Winner	0.70%
Merck (MRK)	2	Strong	09/30/05	11/18/05	$73.71	$71.25	-2.46	-3.34%	-3.34%	Loser	-2.64%
Merck (MRK)	1	Weak	01/03/05	01/25/05	$31.26	$30.95	-0.31	-0.99%	0.99%	Winner	0.99%
Microsoft (MSFT)	2	Strong	10/12/05	11/25/05	$26.78	$30.98	4.20	15.68%	15.68%	Winner	16.68%
Microsoft (MSFT)	1	Strong	05/02/05	05/27/05	$25.23	$26.07	0.84	3.33%	3.33%	Winner	3.33%
Microsoft (MSFT)	2	Weak	07/18/05	08/03/05	$26.16	$27.25	1.09	4.17%	-4.17%	Loser	-0.84%
Pfizer (PFE)	3	Strong	10/11/05	11/15/05	$24.41	$27.50	3.09	12.66%	12.66%	Winner	11.82%
Pfizer (PFE)	1	Strong	01/21/05	06/21/05	$24.48	$28.61	4.13	16.87%	16.87%	Winner	16.87%
Procter & Gamble (PG)	2	Weak	07/14/05	09/15/05	$27.60	$25.70	-1.90	-6.88%	6.88%	Winner	23.75%
Procter & Gamble (PG)	1	Strong	08/10/05	11/18/05	$53.71	$57.45	3.74	6.96%	6.96%	Winner	6.96%
AT&T (T)	2	Weak	06/07/05	06/27/05	$55.45	$52.67	-2.78	-5.01%	5.01%	Winner	11.98%
AT&T (T)	1	Strong	05/26/05	06/15/05	$23.65	$24.01	0.36	1.52%	1.52%	Winner	1.52%
United Technologies (UTX)	2	Weak	01/03/05	01/28/05	$25.59	$23.62	-1.97	-7.70%	7.70%	Winner	9.22%
United Technologies (UTX)	1	Strong	01/18/05	02/02/05	$51.10	$49.81	-1.29	-2.52%	-2.52%	Loser	-2.52%
United Technologies (UTX)	2	Strong	11/15/05	12/06/05	$53.41	$54.97	1.56	2.92%	2.92%	Winner	0.40%
United Technologies (UTX)	3	Weak	08/01/05	09/26/05	$50.02	$51.79	1.77	3.54%	-3.54%	Loser	-3.14%

Verizon	1	Weak	06/22/05	07/26/05	$35.03	$34.13	-0.90	-2.57%	2.57%	Winner	2.57%
(VZ)	2	Strong	05/27/05	06/16/05	$35.46	$34.94	-0.52	-1.47%	-1.47%	Loser	1.10%
Wal-Mart	1	Strong	11/01/05	11/18/05	$46.59	$49.50	2.51	5.34%	5.34%	Winner	5.34%
(WMT)	2	Weak	08/18/05	09/29/05	$47.24	$43.54	-3.70	-7.83%	7.83%	Winner	13.17%
Exxon-Mobil	1	Strong	01/31/05	04/25/05	$51.60	$59.96	8.36	16.20%	16.20%	Winner	16.20%
(XOM)	2	Strong	11/11/03	12/23/05	$56.52	$57.10	0.58	1.03%	1.03%	Winner	17.23%
	3	Weak	10/21/05	11/07/05	$55.37	$57.10	1.73	3.12%	-3.12%	Loser	14.10%

Wins:	55
Losses:	14
Win/Loss Ratio:	4
Average P/L:	4.90%
Max Win:	22.50%
Max Loss:	-7.94%
Avg. Win:	7.05%
Avg. Loss:	-3.57%
Avg. Win/Avg. Loss Ratio:	1.97

[a]Brokerage charges not taken into account.

Source: Phil Erlanger Research Co., Inc.

instance, the price action of one stock relative to another stock (called pairs trading) can exhibit seasonal patterns. Let's examine the Pepsi (PEP) versus Coca-Cola (KO) pair.

The seasonal cycle for the Pepsi/Coca-Cola pair in Figure 8.7 is relatively flat until September, when it rises sharply with maximum positive seasonal heat. The pair itself rises when the stock price of Pepsi outperforms the stock price of Coca-Cola. Since the seasonal pattern favors a rise in the paired trade starting in September, traders would expect a long Pepsi/short Coca-Cola trade to be set up at this time. Indeed, in 2005 the Pepsi/Coca-Cola pair did rise from 1.24 on September 7, 2005, to 1.39 on October 19, 2005, when the seasonal cycle flattened out just prior to a weak seasonal zone.

Seasonal analysis can be performed on other indexes. Industry group, sector, and market indexes are prime examples. Many professional money managers believe that the influence of groups, sectors, and the stock market itself play a large role in the path taken by individual stocks. We agree, and constantly apply our seasonal microscope to such indexes.

Figure 8.8 shows the seasonal pattern of the retail sector. The retail

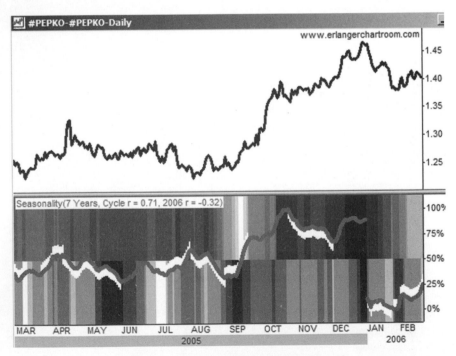

FIGURE 8.7 Pepsi/Coca-Cola Pair with Seasonal Patterns

FIGURE 8.8 Retail Sector Seasonal Patterns

sector is a composite of many industry groups related to retail sales, including building material chains, catalog and specialty chains, clothing/shoe/accessory chains, computer/video chains, department stores, discount chains, drug store chains, food chains, and other miscellaneous retail chains. These diverse retail industries are reflected in the one retail sector index. As Figure 8.8 shows, the 11-year seasonal cycle of the retail sector has a high Cycle r statistic of 0.68, indicating the presence of a valid seasonal pattern throughout the past 11 years. There are also moments of strong seasonal heat, indicating consistency of seasonal zones appearing at the same time in prior years. This information is invaluable to professional portfolio managers who often make sector and industry group money management decisions.

In Figure 8.8, we see a seasonal pattern of weakness for the retail sector in September, followed by strength in October and November. As it turns out, this is similar to the seasonal pattern of the market as a whole, but the task now becomes one of finding retail industry groups and particular stocks that strongly follow the seasonal pattern of the retail sector. In general, most of the retail groups follow this pattern, but

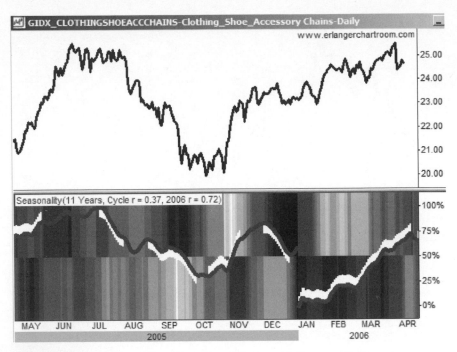

FIGURE 8.9 Clothing/Shoe/Accessory Chains with Seasonal Patterns

the clothing/shoe/accessory chains appear to most suitably mirror the September through November retail sector seasonal setup.

In a similar fashion to the seasonal data derived from the retail sector index, Figure 8.9 shows a weak seasonal curve in September for clothing/shoe/accessory chains, with a large degree of negative seasonal heat. This turns around in the October and November period, with November showing a large degree of positive seasonal heat for clothing/shoe/accessory chains. As it turned out, the 2005 price action of the clothing/shoe/accessory chains followed this pattern closely. The task now becomes finding stocks that show comparable seasonal tendencies.

Figure 8.10 shows the seasonal pattern for Limited Brands (LTD), a major retail stock from the clothing/shoe/accessory chains industry group. This is a good candidate because its seasonal curve follows the path taken by its group and sector (and of course the market as a whole), and also because its seasonal heat patterns of the current seasonal zones show great consistency with seasonal zones of the past. Moreover, the Cycle r statistic over the past 15 years is a highly correlated 0.69, which means the seasonal pattern is valid over the 15-year look-back period. In truth, there are a number of individual retail issues that qualify as portfo-

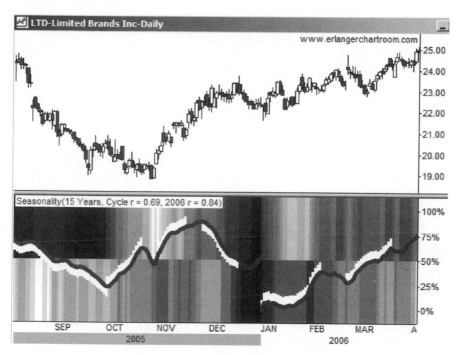

FIGURE 8.10 Limited Brands (LTD) with Seasonal Patterns

lio candidates using such seasonal criteria. It is the job of the portfolio manager to sift through the candidates and select those that meet seasonal and other criteria as befits the manager's style.

DEPLOYING SEASONALITY AS PART OF AN OVERALL STRATEGY

Seasonality is a powerful technique that portfolio managers should employ. However, no one factor should dictate strategy. A sound strategy uses setup indicators and trigger indicators, and follows up with a reliable monitoring mechanism to aid in exiting trades. Seasonality is primarily a setup mechanism. Other setup mechanisms include (but certainly are not confined to) measures of sentiment. For instance, the observation of short sellers can uncover moments in time when either the bulls or the bears are particularly at risk from contrary moves— hence the setup. A great example (Amgen) that we took advantage of in 2005 illustrates the point.

Figure 8.11 highlights two factors that show Amgen may be set up for a third-quarter buying opportunity. The seasonal curve turns up on June 24, initiating a positive seasonal zone. Seasonal heat is also very positive. In addition, the short interest ratio has swelled significantly during 2005 heading into this positive seasonal period. Clearly these short sellers are either unaware of or are ignoring the seasonal tendencies of Amgen.

In a matter of days from the strong seasonal zone that started on June 24, 2005, Amgen took off, activating any short-term trigger indicators one might employ. The ensuing short squeeze included a huge gap to the upside and peaked 87 days later on September 19, 2005, just days after the completion of the second strong seasonal zone. This action handed the bulls a 40.53 percent gain.

Of course it is wonderful when the market follows those factors we employ. The market, however, is not so easily tamed. Its nonlinear nature assures us of many moments when unforeseen factors rise up and bite us in tender places. Ironically, one of the most valuable observations that can

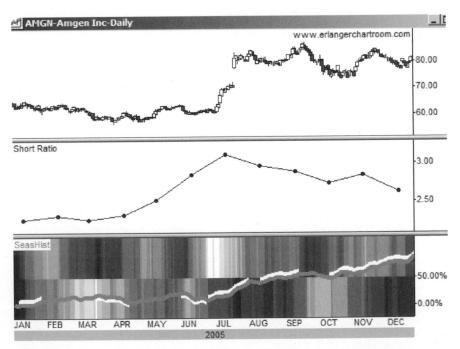

FIGURE 8.11   Amgen (AMGN) with Short Ratio and Seasonal Patterns

be made of setup indicators is to recognize when they fail to work. Such moments indicate an unforeseen factor is in play—a factor that is more meaningful to the marketplace. When indicators fail, it means another game is afoot; this is a clue to the portfolio manager that adjustments are needed. At the very least a failed indicator should taint the manager's bias (either long or short).

Consider the seasonal pattern of Alkermes in Figure 8.12. The June weak seasonal zone is accompanied with blazingly negative heat. Nevertheless, price action rallied during this period. (Incidentally, trigger indicators would have kept traders from shorting here, because price action was so positive.) Clearly something else is biasing the action in Alkermes price—a clue for portfolio managers to be biased to the long side. As it turned out, Alkermes was in the midst of a long-term uptrend peppered with only the briefest and most moderate of pullbacks. All three weak seasonal zones in Figure 8.12 did little to hurt price action. These failures were clues to expect more than average performances of the strong seasonal zones.

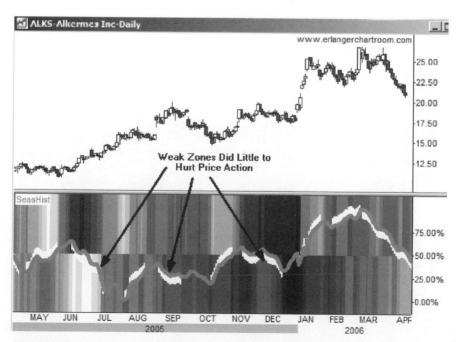

FIGURE 8.12 Alkermes (ALKS) with Its Seasonal Patterns

CONCLUSION

Seasonality can be measured, and as such provides valuable insights into the market. However, seasonal cycles do not cause the market to move. Rather, seasonality is a reflection of other factors—both known and unknown—that influence the direction of stock prices over and over again. The advantage to traders is to limit their trading to those periods when seasonal tendencies are consistent. At these times, improving one's chances of success requires diligence and continual study. As is true with most of the areas of Wall Street analysis, more research needs to be done in the areas of technical analysis in general and seasonality specifically. We hope this text encourages many to pursue their understanding and experience with seasonal trading.

PART IV

Derivatives

CHAPTER 9

Volatility and Its Importance to Option Investors

Alex Jacobson

T o anyone who actively trades options, an understanding of volatility can be as important as, if not more important than, an option user's view on the trend of the underlying instrument on which the option is based. In fact, a trading rule for all short-term option users is: If you're correct about trend, but wrong about volatility, your trade may underperform your expectation. If you're correct about volatility, but wrong about trend, your trade may outperform your expectation. My working definition of a short-term user is not based on time. Short-term can mean one day, one week, one month, one year, but a short-term user is anyone who trades out of the option prior to expiration.

Option traders are essentially making forecasts of three variables. Trends can be bullish, bearish, or neutral. It is important to recognize that options are the only equity tool that allows users to benefit from a totally unchanged underlying. Options traders use a forecast of time to help select the expiration chosen and a forecast of the volatility they expect to experience over the life of their trade.

Options have value for two core reasons. Think about a stock trading at $100 a share. For the moment assume the stock pays no dividend. If the rate at which I could invest the $100 strike risk-free is 4 percent—then the stock has a $4.00 carry. In other words, if you bought the stock at $100 and held it for one year and it remained unchanged, you would incur an opportunity loss of $4.00. On a 100-share round lot, which is what options are based on, you could view that $4.00 of option premium. If the stock paid a $2.00 dividend over the one-year life of your option, your carry would decline to the 4 percent costs of money minus the 2 percent dividend for a net carry of $2.

How this would actually be priced into the cost of the option would depend on the option's exercise style. Options can be one of two styles—American or European. American style options can be exercised early. Essentially they can be retired early by their owners. This right to early exercise should be thought of as the right to convert the call option to the stock or, similarly, use the put option to convert stock to cash. This right to early exercise has value and as such American style options are more valuable then their European cousins. Thus:

Stock price	$100
Strike price	$100
Dividend	0
Volatility	20%
Cost of money	4%
Days to expiration	365
Value of American call	About $10
Value of American put	About $6.45
Value of European call	About $9.90
Value of European put	About $6.00

European options can be traded all day like their American counterparts, but they cannot be exercised early. They can only be exercised on the last Friday of their particular expiration month. You'll notice that the $4.00 carry translates into the almost exact difference between the European call and put options. As this is a chapter on volatility and not one on pricing options, I won't get into a lot of detail about the carry components of options. Suffice it to say that the $4.00 carry in the stock amounts to about $2.00 of the value of the call and a minus $2.00 in the value of the put. Why is carry positive in calls and negative in puts? Simply, calls are a surrogate for stock ownership and as such they incur part of this cost of money. Puts are a surrogate for shorting stock, and when stock is shorted a credit balance is created. The interest earned on this credit balance is rebated back into the creation of the put option. One way to view this would be to set the interest rate to zero on the European options.

Stock price	$100
Strike price	$100
Dividend	0
Volatility	20%
Cost of money	0%
Days to expiration	365

Value of European Call   About $7.90
Value of European Put   About $7.90

The reason it's important to understand the carry function is that when I eliminate it, an option's value becomes determined solely by volatility. Time and strike are still a consideration, but we are now looking at values determined by volatility. We have, in a sense, removed the noise of the carry function.

Volatility is often discussed as a measure of expected price distribution. It is important to understand that this is not the definition of volatility; it is, rather, a method of translating it. So the $100 dollar stock with 50 volatility would have an expected range of $50 to $200 two-thirds of the time (plus or minus one standard deviation) over the next year. This is not the definition of volatility, although that is how it is commonly understood.

Volatility is the cost of hedging, in effect the cost of transferring risk. This cost is a function of a number of factors. It is a measure of the liquidity of the underlying asset, the liquidity of the market makers creating options, the competition among the competing dealers, the time of day, the day of the week, and the costs involved in hedging. Volatility is in effect the cost of transferring risk—the costs that the market makers incur when manufacturing option positions.

THE ELEMENTS OF VOLATILITY

Let's examine each of the components. Liquidity of the underlying is a measure of how easy (or hard) it is to acquire a long position or create a short position in the underlying. If we are trading options on a stock like IBM, Microsoft, or Intel, we can easily buy and sell shares without impacting the stock price. The easier it is to accomplish trades in the underlying, the lower the volatility. In the examples of companies like IBM, Microsoft, and Intel, market makers might choose to hedge with an index or futures instrument that is correlated to their option. So instead of buying IBM shares to hedge an IBM options trade, a market maker might choose to hedge by holding S&P options or futures, and hedge by holding the correlation between an individual company and its relationship to a well-known benchmark.

The key benefit here to market makers is they may now be able to hedge wholesale instead of retail. In effect, if a market maker hedges IBM options by buying IBM shares to hedge calls, the market maker must buy IBM at the stock's ask price and sell it at the stock's bid price. The market maker would effectively lose the cost of the stock's bid/offer spread. Market makers trading millions of shares a day to hedge their options would see this as a large expense in the cost-of-hedging equation.

Instead, a market maker making markets in multiple companies might choose to create a book of option risk correlated to an easily traded index benchmark. Large market making firms will actually run books of options correlated to others, so that a market making firm making markets in companies like IBM, GE, Dow Chemical, and other blue chip big-caps might also be market making in the options of the S&P 500 ETF, the well-known Spider. By correlating the risks in their IBM, GE, and Dow positions with those companies' correlation to the S&P 500, they could net their risks and only need to hedge the balance. In this fashion much of the risk is laid off internally in their market making organization. This minimizes both their costs and the market impact of their hedging activity. The easier this is to accomplish, the lower the volatility of the traded options. The easier it is to create these correlations, the easier it is to hedge. The easier to hedge, the lower the cost. And the lower the cost, the lower the volatility.

This innovation of pairs trading of options was pioneered by Blair Hull, who founded Hull trading, which grew into one of the largest market making organizations in the world. In the mid1980s when Hull began pairs market making, they actually ran a dedicated PC for each option's name in which they made markets. I remember visiting their offices and seeing the racks and racks of PCs driving their market making operation.

They networked these PCs down to the floor of the CBOE. In trading pits with Hull traders they located coded PCs. These PCs showed a matrix of colors that had meaning to the Hull traders but were a mystery to other members of the trading crowd. These coded PCs helped the traders define their appetite for the puts and calls trading in their crowd. To simplify their trading technique, let's say they had just bought a lot of IBM calls. Their trader would communicate that by hitting coded color squares on the touch screen of the Hull PC in their crowd. All the traders who had products that were well correlated to the price of IBM would see their screens change to reflect the new firmwide inventory. In effect their markets in S&P 500 futures, S&P 500 futures options, S&P 500 cash options, and S&P 100 cash options and other IBM options would reprice.

Not every option listing will be well correlated to an index benchmark. Options on companies like Cisco, Microsoft, and Intel would correlate well to a NASDAQ or a QQQQ benchmark. Clearly some companies don't correlate well to any broad benchmark and they will be harder to trade. Harder to trade means harder to hedge, which means higher volatility.

Options in U.S. security markets currently trade on six exchanges. Some listings trade on all six exchanges. Competition is good for liquidity. Each exchange has a unique model for how trades are allocated among their market making community. Generally the more exchanges and market makers that are trading in a name the better the market quality. Some option listings trade on only one exchange, some trade on a few exchanges. Investors should be cautious when trading in options that are single-listing companies. Options trade on one exchange for one of two reasons: Either the other exchanges have chosen not to list the company or they are license-protected products. In either case the lack of competition could lead to periods of higher volatility than competitively traded products.

IMPLIED VOLATILITY

The ability to trade options against their correlation to a benchmark index is also what keeps relative volatility in line. If volatility on stocks like Cisco, Microsoft, and Intel were vastly different than volatility on QQQQ options, market makers would create a portfolio of options on the individual stocks and offset against options on the QQQQ. Generally volatilities on the individual company options are higher than volatility on the index. If this relationship were to become inverted, market makers would sell index volatility and buy individual company volatility. A classic example of this was the October 1987 crash when index volatility got well out of line to individual stock volatility. Market makers would sell index volatility by selling puts and calls in the index and hedge their trading by buying puts and calls on the major index components. This condition is much rarer today because of the ease of the arbitrage.

This cost-of-hedging is simply market volatility. In the options world we define this as implied volatility. This volatility is deemed to be implied because the only way to capture it is by reverse-engineering the price of an option. Essentially we take an option model and back-solve for volatility. We take a pricing model and fill in the strike price, underlying price, days to expiration, and the net carry. Normally a user would fill in an estimate of volatility and generate an option price. To calculate volatility we fill in the last sale of the option and solve for the volatility. Implied volatility is the volatility implied by the traded price of the option—that volatility that the option's price implies.

Implied volatility is the current consensus view of volatility because it represents the actual last price at which a trade was done. As I outlined earlier, this imbedded volatility which we term the implied volatility measures the cost of hedging. As there is no formula for this volatility, the only way to observe its value is by back-solving from the price. Are there days and times when volatility is altered by the variable of day and time? Let's think about hedging at the opening of the trading day, near the close of the trading day, and when approaching expiration. Options begin trading moments after the opening in the underlying security. So if IBM closes at \$86.15 on Tuesday and opens at \$86.16 on Wednesday, IBM options are pretty easy to price and the opening price will be easy to establish. Even if it has a tendency to open a few cents either side of its close, it will be easy to establish an opening price.

Trading gaps are one of the key sources of volatility. Option hedging works best when market makers are presented with a continuous price stream. Market participants, both market makers and option users, will develop a sense of how common trading gaps are. A stock that demonstrates a tendency toward overnight gaps—gaps between close and open—is very challenging to price from an options market making standpoint. This tendency to gap will translate into extra volatility at the opening. Entering market orders preopening on these kinds of names is ill advised.

When thinking about volatility, think about how market makers will hedge their trading. One of the most challenging times to hedge is in put options on down days late in the day. To hedge puts market makers will need to have an offsetting short position. If it's a few minutes prior to the close and you are looking to purchase some puts on a stock that was being hammered down all day, keep in mind that market makers will most likely have to short the stock to hedge. Bear in mind the market impact of shorting a weak stock very near the close. Market makers know that if they can get the short accomplished it can very easily drive a weak stock lower. In effect the options will be priced with the extra uncertainty of the market impact the trade could have. Volatility in the puts could represent the extra cost of the expected market impact the hedging could have that late in the day. I often get asked if this would be a better time for put sellers. It is important to recognize that any trade decision should be driven by an expected view of trend in the underlying. If an investor is a put seller to begin with, he is effectively a seller of volatility and could easily receive the highest volatility of the day under those circumstances.

Expiration volatility can also be a material factor in the overall calculation. Movement in the underlying at or near expiration can move options in or out of the money with very little time to hedge. An option \$.50 out of the money prior to expiration requires very little hedging. Move that stock into an in-the-money position and it needs to be rehedged quickly. Both the end-of-day concern and the expiration concern will translate into additional volatility. This will show up in one of two ways—in the actual price of the option, and/or in the width of the bid/ask spread. Think about the bid/ask spread in any option as a real measure of the sell/buy volatility.

So we have defined implied volatility as measuring the cost of hedging. We observe that implied volatility is not constant across different option strike prices and different expirations. Minor variations are pretty common and can occur for any of a number of reasons. Variations can occur because of simple rounding, short-term supply/demand considerations, or structural conditions in the options market. Prior to the 1987 market crash, volatilities were relatively constant across strikes and no long-dated options were trading (we currently trade LEAPS with expirations approaching three years).

Post 1987, many instruments began trading with what we term in the options market as skew. Simply put, skew occurs when different expirations or different strikes trade at volatilities different from one another. Skew is most commonly observed in out-of-the-money puts and their strike partner, in-the-money calls. Skew is also common in out-of-the-money calls and their strike partner, in-the-money puts. It is generally not as pronounced in the out-of-the-money calls as in the out-of-the-money puts.

In the Google example in Table 9.1, we observe that the $400 puts, which are about at the money, are trading a 37.00 percent volatility at the offer. The $350 puts are trading at a 44.70 percent volatility at the offer. Essentially the 350s are trading with almost 20 percent more volatility than the 400s. This volatility snapshot was taken on February 6, 2006, the day of Google's earnings release.

Volatility information is readily available via the Internet from brokerage house sites, exchange web sites, and volatility services. In fact an Internet web search for volatility information will bring back more data than any one investor can use.

Figure 9.1 shows Google volatilities taken from the International

TABLE 9.1 Google Puts on February 6, 2006

Google	Put	Options	Google at 402.53	16 Days to Expiration
400 Puts	10.7	10.9	36.50%	37.00%
390 Puts	6.8	7	37.00%	37.75%
380 Puts	4.1	4.3	38.00%	38.75%
370 Puts	2.45	2.6	39.50%	40.25%
360 Puts	1.5	1.6	41.50%	42.30%
350 Puts	0.95	1	44.20%	44.70%

GOOG All data at least 15 minutes delayed.
Last update 18:28:11 PM ET on 24 Feb 2006.

BID	ASK	LAST	VOLUME	CHANGE
377.00	377.25	377.40	6,486,245	-0.18 %

HISTORICAL VOLATILITY

30	60	90	120
54.71 %	44.21 %	43.85 %	39.68 %

IMPLIED VOLATILITY

30	60	90	120
37.62 %	41.56 %	40.22 %	39.17 %

FIGURE 9.1   Volatilities on Google Options on February 6, 2006 (*Source:* International Securities Exchange. Used by permission.)

Securities Exchange (ISE) web site at www.iseoptions.com. This data is available for free on every instrument traded at the ISE. Volatilities by strike and expiration are also available free. Your broker's web site may also be a good source for volatility information.

HISTORICAL VOLATILITY

Historical volatility, unlike implied volatility, is drawn from the price action of the underlying security. In essence we draw historical volatility from the daily high, low, and close of the stock. Option practitioners will debate forever the relationship between implied and historical volatility. They will debate and defend the concept of implied volatility reverting to the mean value of historical volatility. I will do nothing to settle that debate except to showcase a couple of valuation ideas.

Options are always priced correctly, which is to say implied volatility is the correct volatility right at this moment. Can options users disagree about volatility? Of course they can, and an informed user often will disagree, but that disagreement should not be based simply on a comparison between historical and implied. When I started in the options industry I was taught that if implied volatility was greater than historical, then options were overpriced. Conversely I was taught that if historical volatility was greater than implied, options were cheap. Many people are still being taught this concept. Here's the problem: Options are only expensive or cheap if you have a view of future volatility, which should be based on an option user's view of future volatility. This view is something that will differentiate between an informed option user and a novice. To be an informed option user requires a perception of expected volatility. This view of expected volatility requires the user to develop an intuitive sense of what the correct volatility should be for their underlying. It's what I call the Goldilocks decision-making process: Is implied volatility too high, too low, or just right?

What is the best way for an option investor to develop this intuitive sense of volatility? There is no better tool than an investor's intuitive thought process. I would encourage any investor who wants to become a better-informed option trader to look at the implied volatility of the at-the-money options every week, and more frequently if they are trading something with lots of volatility swings. (At the time of this writing, a prime example would be options on Google). Record the number; if you are good at spreadsheets, create one.

Some general thoughts on volatility: Volatility and price are generally inversely related, so if your view is that a stock is in an uptrend, that should be happening with implied volatility trending lower. Large trading gaps will almost always be accompanied by spikes up in volatility. Stocks trending lower and stocks that crater will almost always do so in an increasing volatility environment. The classic novice trader's mistake is to not take into account the impact of volatility.

Imagine a stock you've been following for a while. The company misses earnings estimates and the stock craters from $60 dollars to $51. Prior to the earnings report the stock was trading with the options at a 30 percent implied volatility. The day it craters $9.00, implied volatility climbs to 45 percent. So you figure this $9.00 correction was an overreaction. You step in and buy some short-term $55 calls, looking for a quick trade. You don't bother to check volatility; you just buy the $55 calls:

Stock price	$51
Strike price	$55
Volatility	45%
Cost of money	4%
Days to expiration	20
Call valuation	$.85

The next day, the stock rallies back up to $53.50—a $2.50 jump. Volatility on the rally drops back into the 30 percent range:

Stock price	$53.50
Strike price	$55.00
Volatility	30%
Cost of money	4%
Days to expiration	19
Call valuation	$.90

Ouch. A move of almost 5 percent in the stock is almost totally lost to the decline in volatility.

Changes in volatility impact options in different ways. A change in volatility will have the largest nominal impact on at-the-money options:

Stock price	$50
Strike price	$50
Volatility	16%
Cost of money	4%
Days to expiration	30
Call valuation	$1.00

If I double the volatility:

Stock price	$50
Strike price	$50
Volatility	32%
Cost of money	4%
Days to expiration	30
Call valuation	$1.92

A doubling of volatility almost doubles the value of the at-the-money option. This will be the largest nominal price change. If the interest rate component was eliminated the option would have doubled in price.

Now let's value an option that is 5 percent out of the money:

Stock price	$50
Strike price	$52.50
Volatility	16%
Cost of money	4%
Days to expiration	30
Call valuation	$.20

If I double volatility:

Stock price	$50
Strike price	$52.50
Volatility	32%
Cost of money	4%
Days to expiration	$.93

Doubling the volatility of a call 5 percent out of the money gives us a price change of $.73—not as big of a nominal move as with the at-the-money call, but a 365 percent change in price.

This concept needs to be clear in every option trader's mind. Changes in implied volatility can have a huge impact on out-of-the-money options. In high-volatility environments novice users will look for cheap options. As I outlined earlier, options are never expensive or cheap until you overlay your view of what tomorrow will look like. If your forecast is that volatility will be lower going forward, then out-of-the-money options may not prove to be your best choice.

The in-the-money option will have the smallest nominal price change and the smallest percentage change as well:

Stock price	$50
Strike price	$47.50
Volatility	16%
Cost of money	4%
Days to expiration	30
Call valuation	$2.78

With volatility doubled:

Stock price	$50
Strike price	$47.30
Volatility	32%
Cost of money	4%
Days to expiration	30
Call valuation	$3.41

In our previous example, if I thought the stock was going to rally and the rally was expected to accompany a decline in volatility, I would not have bought the out-of-the-money call. In fact, some option traders might have considered that a poor trade right out of the box.

FORECAST VOLATILITY

Back to the issue of expensive or cheap options. If I believe that options are always fairly priced, then let's establish a benchmark for setting expectations about volatility. Investors looking to benefit from option erosion (notice I didn't say premium sellers—there are premium buying strategies that benefit from erosion and, as I demonstrate later, these strategies often offer a better risk/reward ratio) are hoping that volatility is constant or declining. Option buyers are hoping that volatility expands over the life of their trade. This brings me to the introduction of a third kind of volatility: forecast volatility.

We've now identified six different kinds of volatility: implied, historical, forecast, opening, closing, and expiration volatility. Sounds like a lot of work and effort to manage, but it won't be. Here is why. You'll find for most of the things you trade that after a few months of observing volatility you will develop an intuitive sense of the correct volatility of your options. Like Goldilocks, sometimes it will seem too high and you'll want to adjust your trades so that they benefit from the expected decline in volatility. Sometimes it will seem too low and you'll want to adjust your trades so that they benefit from the expected increase in volatility. and sometimes they will feel just right.

Trades you would avoid if your view was that volatility was high would be trades where you are not long out-of-the-money options. Credit spread trades where an out-of-the-money option is purchased to hedge are also at a disadvantage when you expect volatilities to decline. That does not mean you should totally avoid the strategies. Rather, what it means is that there might be a better way to achieve the same objective, or that your actual performance might be less than what you expect for a given move in the underlying security.

ALL OPTION STRATEGIES WORK

An option strategy is a trade based on an expectation of trend (bullish, bearish, or neutral), an expectation of time, and an expectation of volatility. This third dimension of volatility is what separates the well-informed trader from the less-informed. (There are also option strategies that could be based on expectations of changes in the cost of carry component— they are not discussed here as the focus is volatility.) There is also a parity factor in option trades. By parity I mean that there are trades that are exact mirror images of other trades. The popular buy-write strategy, buying a stock and selling covered calls against it, has a parity cousin in the cash-secured put transaction. So in effect, covered call writing and uncovered put sales have the same economics. What if the calls and puts are not at the same volatility? This would change parity and result in a bias of one strategy over another. These differences may be minor or at other times may be larger and more significant.

Going back to the Google example, let's compare two identical trades and look at how differences in volatility can impact them. A popular strategy among individual investors is credit put spreading. Individuals like the strategy because they get a credit deposited into their account as opposed to having a debit taken out of it.

With Google at $402.53 an investor with a relatively neutral view of Google might consider a credit put spread. So we are going to examine a 400/350 put spread: The $400 put is trading at $10.70 bid, $10.90 ask. The $350 put is trading at $ .95 bid, $1.00 ask. So the spread is trading for a credit of $9.70—selling the $400 at $10.70 bid and buying the $350 at $1.00 ask. The math is pretty straightforward: it's a $50 spread with a credit of $9.70

The parity trade to this 400/350 put spread is a debit in-the-money call spread. They are in effect the same trade: a $350 call with $53.50 bid, $54.00 ask; and a $400 call with $14.10 bid, $14.30 ask. So the call spread is trading for a debit of $39.90. Buy the $350 call at $54.00 and sell the $400 call for $14.10.

Let's examine both trades to prove out the parity claim. The $50 debit put spread has a maximum risk of $50. It gets traded for a credit of $9.70. So the maximum possible profit of the credit put spread is $9.70 and the maximum risk is $50.00 minus $9.70, or $40.30. The debit call spread has a maximum risk of the $39.90 debit and a maximum upside of $10.10. Thus, the debit call spread is $.40 better overall.

Some important points to make:

- These spread prices reflect the current bid/ask differentials in the market.
- Options are being bought at the ask price and sold at the bid price.

There are a few other important considerations. These are prices during the trading day, and Google is a very volatile stock. The debit call spread is $.40 better. Shouldn't the market makers have arbitraged that difference away? The answer here is both yes and no. Will differences like this eventually be arbitraged away? Eventually yes, but options don't exist in a static environment. A static environment would imply no volatility. Many options trade on multiple exchanges among multiple market makers. Small differences in pricing are in effect small differences in volatility, and on many instruments traders can observe these differences in the prices quoted. Should an investor who has always been one style of trader change to attempt to benefit from these pricing differences? The answer here is really up to you, the investor. If you've been successful with a specific style of trading and you have a high comfort level with that style of trading, then there is no reason to change.

Another concern I hear a lot is a time management issue. Is it really worth the extra time to do the extra research in an effort to create a trade that might be better? Again, this is a question that only you, the investor, can answer. Often, having a better understanding of volatility will allow you to identify a trade that is a few ticks better. Sometimes all the research will just prove to demonstrate parity, and one trade or its mirror parity component will have exactly the same risk/reward. This implies that all the option volatilities are either uniform or are out of line in the same places. Sometimes, understanding volatility will keep you out of a bad trade.

Let's further examine this issue of volatility skew. As I mentioned earlier, we didn't see a great deal of skew in the U.S. markets until the 1987 market break. Post 1987, much of the option community set about readjusting its view of risk. Some participants, primarily index option put sellers, were greatly reduced in number. In effect, before 1987 there were natural sellers of puts and calls as well as natural buyers of puts and call. Post 1987, some of that community left the market. So what one began to observe post 1987 was a skewed volatility picture. It became most evident in out-of-the-money American-style index puts.

For much of the next decade this skew continued to exist. Index options as much as 20 percent out of the money had generous premiums. In fact we, the options industry, named this phenomenon the crash premium. Again the question arises as to why the market making community simply didn't arbitrage away these differences. Why didn't they buy the low-volatility instruments and sell the high-volatility instruments?

Simply put, the arbitrage in this case is not going to be a perfect arbitrage. Selling out-of-the-money puts and hedging them with at- or in-the-money puts leaves the market maker's portfolio at what we term gamma risk. In fact, if you look at market maker portfolios in the post-1987 environment, you would observe that market makers' bias would be to own out-of-the-money puts. I know a number of market makers who will begin every trading month by buying an out-of-the-money strangle. They buy some far out-of-the-money puts and far out-of-the-money calls as a hedge on their market making business. They effectively buy insurance on their own business of market making, recognizing that very frequently this insurance will go unused. I know of a couple of retired market makers who used to insist that the traders who worked for them not include these out-of-the-money strangles in their daily profit/loss calculation. They took them off their inventory so as not to create a sense of overconfidence in their market making operation.

Do market makers manufacture skew? They are the engines creating the quotes and often they will all have similar skew imbedded in their market making operations. Why don't they trade with one another and eliminate these variances? Well once again, in the last few years, market making has become more competitive and some of these variances in competitively traded products have gotten smaller. Trading in INTC, MSFT, CSCO, IBM, SPY, DIA, and QQQQ options, just to name a few, has gotten very competitive with lots of available size and competitive pricing. Not all instruments are as competitive as these, and not all instruments are as easy to hedge as these.

Let's justify skew under a less efficient market model. The text-book case for skew relates to a lack of natural trades, but let's create another case.

Let's say the market making community has just absorbed a large call seller. The market makers have all just bought calls. Their inventory consists of lots of put and call positions and hundreds of thousands of shares of stock. Their inventory has become unbalanced. They have gotten too long in this particular stock. This stock is a thinly traded stock and they are holding lots of it. In market maker terminology they are long a lot of delta. (Delta is a measure of options share equivalency. An at-the-money call is about 50 delta; 100 shares of stock is 100 delta.) They would like to rebalance and get their deltas down.

Their first reaction would be to sell some of the stock. Back to my premise that this is a thinly traded stock. If they hit the market with a block of shares, they move the stock lower. Keep in mind they don't just move the block that they sell lower, but rather they reprice their inventory down. If selling 10,000 shares moves the stock down $.20 and their inventory is hundreds of thousands of shares, they would revalue their entire inventory. Assuming I don't want to do that and I still have an appetite to rebalance, what other avenues are available to me?

To get delta out of my position I would need to sell calls or buy puts. Great idea, but to whom? I'm the market maker. I need to advertise for put sellers—so I could become a put buyer—or for call buyers, so I could become a call seller.

Advertise? What is the market maker advertising? The quotes. If I'm looking to manufacture put sellers I raise put volatility—that is, I raise the premiums. If I want to manufacture call buyers I lower the premium. No pricing algorithm is bigger than supply and demand in the short run. Can skew be an effort to create the hedges I need to rebalance my market making operation? Can it really be this simple? Skew has many factors imbedded in it. In some ways skew is probably representative of a market making community with an unbalanced or uncomfortable inventory.

It's 2006 and volatility is about as low as we've seen it in 33 years of options trading. What are the factors influencing this, and how does an investor benefit from this? Well first, back to our definition of volatility as a measure of the cost of hedging. Why may hedging be cheaper today than it was in years past?

First and foremost are the events of 9/11. When the markets reopened the week after the horrible events of 9/11, we in the options industry observed a strange situation. Much of the post-1987 crash premium had vanished. Now instead of observing premium 20 percent out-of-the-money, these options reopened as almost worthless and premium could really only be observed down to about 10 percent out-of-the-money on broad indexes. What has happened to our markets in these last few years that has led to the draining of volatility? I can suggest eight factors:

1. The crash premium is gone—I'm tempted to qualify this by saying something like "for now," but it is gone.

2. Market making is done by much larger and better-capitalized organizations. The days of independent market makers trading with $50,000 in their trading accounts is gone. Today's market making firms are the household names of the brokerage community with great technology and very large balance sheets.

3. There is greater competition in the options market. Many options now trade on all six exchanges with multiple market makers on each exchange. Exchange algorithms reward both market quality and liquidity provided. The country clubs that were the trading floors have lost out to robust electronic exchanges.

4. Opening gaps in the broad market have become rare. It has been more than five years since we've had an opening gap of more than 2 percent to the downside.

5. Costs are lower. The proliferation of electronic brokerage platforms and the competition among them have brought costs for individual investors down to below the costs commonly charged in the institutional community.

6. Information distribution gets better and better every day.

7. Investors look at volatility more. Exchanges have established and quote benchmark volatility measures and the industry will create products that will allow investors to directly benefit from changes in volatility.

8. Geopolitical events post-9/11 and risk have not had much impact on the overall volatility picture.

So one question that comes up a lot is, when will volatility return? The retired investors who live off of the option premiums from their covered writing against GE, AT&T, and XOM are seeing premiums that are a fraction of what they were 5 and 10 years ago. What will bring volatility back? Will it be a market event, a geopolitical event, technology innovation, or some other factor? No one knows. And many of the reasons for lower volatility that I've noted are structural changes, which I think means that the conditions that gave us volatility in the past will give us less volatility today. We are experiencing this effect now and should be in this environment going forward.

Volatility lows often occur prior to large events in markets or stocks. The 1987 crash came off of a volatility in the S&P 500 of under 8 percent. It got to over 150 percent during the day on October 19, 1987. The 1989 market break came off of low volatility. The August 1982 rally that began the bull market of the 1980s came off of low volatility. Other volatility lows have occurred with nothing happening, so you can draw your own conclusions, but I want to own some premium in low-volatility markets.

Volatility is a part of all option trading—securities options, futures options, commodity options, all options. Any risk transference instrument with a nonlinear payoff will have a volatility component and a volatility value. Stocks and futures are linear payoff instruments. Prior to the advent of listing trading in April of 1973, you were presented with three investment choices: long, short, and not at all. Futures are just leveraged long, short, or not at all. Options opened up an entire pantry of choices. The new generation of option users is using a broader array of option products and strategies. Years back, spread trading was a tiny fraction of investors' participation, but today it is commonplace. Brokers promote electronic spread order entry. Some have spread commission schedules that bring costs down.

VOLATILITY THOUGHTS

Let's recap what we have learned about volatility. It is the market's current view of the cost of transferring risk. The best place to observe it is in the market. We reverse-engineer it back out of option prices to understand it. It represents a lot of information. It impacts different options in different ways. It has the greatest percentage impact on

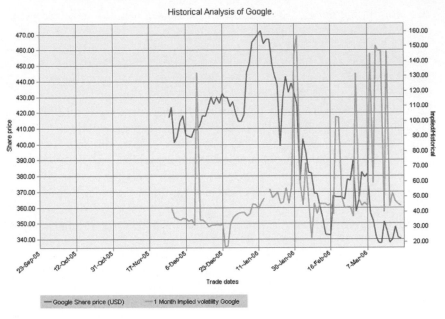

FIGURE 9.2 Google Price Volatility Action (Courtesy of SuperDerivatives, Inc.)

out-of-the-money positions and could be the most important component of a trade's profitability.

Traders entering and leaving the options market prior to expiration have an imbedded volatility component in the value of their option. At expiration this component washes out. At actual expiration, options are either in the money and trading very close to parity or they are worthless. Ten minutes before expiration, one day before expiration, one month before expiration, a volatility component exists. It is important to informed option traders to have an understanding of how volatility affects their trades.

Volatility and price are generally inversely related. When stocks or indexes trend up, implied volatility trends down. When stocks trend down, implied volatility trends up. (See Figure 9.2.)

There are exceptions to this, and the most common is when a stock or index has experienced a big gap higher, which is commonly associated with an increase in volatility. In fact, any gap in pricing will result in an increase in volatility, no matter which direction. (See Figure 9.3.)

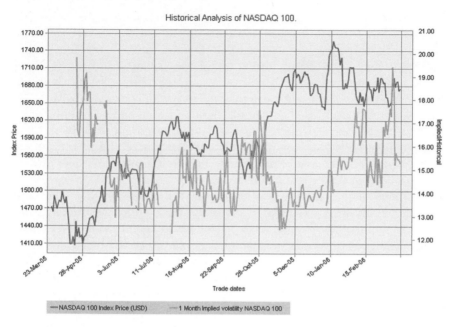

FIGURE 9.3 Volatility Action in the NASDAQ 100 (Courtesy of SuperDerivatives, Inc.)

PREMIUM HARVESTING STRATEGIES

Now that we understand volatility, let's establish a framework for successful options trading. Traders net long option premium are hoping that volatility expands over the life of their trade. Effectively option buyers are hoping that actual volatility—the volatility they experience over the life of their trade—exceeds implied volatility, the volatility they bought. Option users who sell premium, as well as income or hedge traders, are hoping volatility remains constant or even declines.

There are four core premium harvesting strategies. The most widely used option strategy is the covered call write. Covered call writing is the sale of a call option against an existing stock position or done simultaneously with the purchase of a stock. From a perspective of volatility, the premium received from the call that is sold will be directly related to the implied volatility of the underlying. Higher volatility stocks mean higher premiums.

This raises the question as to whether higher premiums are better. An investor should be thinking about the risk-adjusted rate of return here. If I sell covered calls on General Electric or Dow Chemical, the premiums will be lower than if I sell covered calls on Google. The better or worse equation is really based on the risk tolerance of the investor. What is important to take away is that option premiums, because they are volatility based, offer a risk-adjusted rate of return. Stocks with more risk will generate higher premiums. The best analogy here is the cost of insurance for two different drivers. The 45-year-old driver pays an annual premium of a $1,000. The 16-year-old driver pays an annual premium of $2,000. If you were an insurance company underwriting risk, you would be a premium seller. Which driver would an insurer choose to insure—driver A at a $1,000 a year, or driver B at $2,000 a year?

An insurance company would choose to insure both. It would view both as equally attractive risks by charging the different premiums. Insurance companies underwrite risks. When listed option trading began in 1973, selling covered calls was called overwriting, and selling put options was called underwriting. They are effectively the same trade. The economics of selling a covered are identical to the economics of selling a cash-secured put. They are what we term parity trades for one another. They give the investor identical performance in either form. Can one be better than the other?

Here comes the issue of volatility again. If skew exists and the puts are trading with an implied volatility higher than their parity covered call match, then the put sale would be superior. Again, as in the previous examples, this difference may only amount to a nickel or dime. From the standpoint of transaction costs the put sale would also involve less trading and lower transaction costs, so it would also be cheaper from a commissions standpoint.

Covered call writing and put selling are income-oriented strategies that afford the user a partial hedge from the option premium received. For some investors this may still be more risk than they want, so an alternative preferred by many is credit spread trading. In credit spread trading an option is sold—say a put if the investor has a bullish bias—and another put is purchased to hedge the risk of the original short option. Bullish credit spreads involve the sale of put options; bearish credit spreads involve the sale of call options.

As with the covered write and put sale parity example, there is a debit spread trade that gives the same economics as any credit spread trade. I previously outlined a Google parity example and found that the debit spread trade is often superior to the credit spread trade. This is kind of like beating a dead horse, but investors tend to have a strong bias for credit spreads when in fact frequently the debit spread trade can be anywhere from a little better to many cents better, especially on days when stocks make big moves.

Regarding volatility events, how do I position myself if I expect a big move in a stock or in the market? This is my favorite option trading environment. Traditionally, when investors wanted to benefit from an expectation of a big move, they would purchase an option straddle (a put and call with the same expiration and same strike price) or an option combination (a put and call with different strike prices). So if I were looking at an underlying trading at $100 and I expected a big move, but I didn't have a strong view as to direction, I could buy the $100 straddle by buying the $100 put and the $100 call. Sounds okay, but buying two options on an underlying with a high expectation of price change can start to get expensive (see Table 9.2).

Let's look at the economics of buying the straddle first. Buying the $100 straddle would cost $12.10 ($6.50 + $5.60). The breakeven of the straddle at expiration would be $112.10 or $87.90. A more important consideration is that if the stock doesn't move from its current $100 price, the straddle loses $12.10. If the stock goes to $150 or to $50, the straddle has total symmetry and the trade would earn $38.90 if held to expiration. Many investors consider buying the straddle as pure buy of volatility, as profit is made on the move without regard for direction.

Let's examine buying a call backspread and a put backspread. Now instead of buying the $100 straddle I'm going to sell it. It sells for a credit of $11.90. I'm selling at the bid prices. I'm now going to buy two of the $110 calls for a total of $5.60 ($2.80 times 2) and I'm going to buy two of the $90 puts for $3.70 ($1.85 times 2). So I'm long two $110 calls and two $90 puts, and I'm short the $100 straddle. I actually have a net credit of $2.60.

Let's look at the dynamics of the backspreads. The absolute risk of the overall position is lowered. The straddle had a maximum risk of $12.10. The backspreads have a maximum risk of $7.40 ($10.00 minus $2.60) and this would occur at either $110 or $90; again, symmetry exists. So they make or lose money at different prices, but at no time is the backspread as risky as the straddle. The straddle works great if a big move actually does occur. In our volatility example, a $50 move in either direction nets the straddle a profit of $38.90. A $50 move in the backspread nets $32.60, less than the straddle, but again with lower overall risk. Do the

TABLE 9.2 Data for Sample Straddle and Backspreads

100 Stock	90-Day Options		30% Implied Volatility
$110 Calls	$ 2.70–$ 2.80	$110 Puts	$11.80–$12.00
$100 Calls	$ 6.40–$ 6.50	$100 Puts	$ 5.50–$ 5.60
$ 90 Calls	$12.60–$12.80	$ 90 Puts	$ 1.80–$ 1.85

math at all the possible prices and you'll start to clearly see the benefit of these kinds of volatility trades.

The options market is a place for clever, well-informed traders. You quickly begin to see that solutions exist in options that cannot be created anywhere else. One of the keys to bettering your performance will be your understanding of volatility. Understanding how it changes and how those changes impact option prices can make you a better options trader.

CHAPTER 10

A New Options Game: The Market Taker

Jon "Doctor J" Najarian

The options market is a new game with an entirely different playbook. Multiple listings of options across six exchanges, increased activity by large funds with huge capitalization, and dramatic gains in connectivity to the market have led to greater liquidity and transparency in options trading. This, in turn, has resulted in better trading opportunities for investors and speculators, as well as institutional participants such as hedge funds.

As a 24-year veteran of the options market, including on the floor of the Chicago Board Options Exchange (CBOE) where I was a market maker, I have witnessed—and experienced—the dramatic change in the option market. The new dynamics have effectively squeezed out some players, namely many of the market makers on the floor who found it difficult, if not virtually impossible, to compete in a market dominated by huge players taking positions amounting to thousands of contracts. Aggressive trading by these monster players resulted in a narrowing of bid/ask spreads that negated much of the profit margin for independent market makers to the point of a no-win situation.

The new options game, however, has opened up opportunities for a different kind of player, whom I call the *market taker*. The market takers—myself and my brother and trading partner, Pete Najarian, included—are a specific kind of options market speculator. Market takers are opportunists and, in that, are the mirror opposite of the market makers who are obliged to trade a range of calls and puts on specific stocks. Further, market takers move swiftly and decisively, not scaling into and out of large positions as the funds do. Nor are market takers day trading, flipping in and out of positions intraday. Rather, they are looking for short-term trading opportunities that are based on smart-money intelligence, which can be gleaned from market insights, including specific types of block trades, discussed later in this chapter.

THE NEW OPTIONS DYNAMICS

Opportunities for market takers in options have been born of new dynamics. Today, options are trading on six exchanges: the CBOE, the American Stock Exchange (AMEX), Boston Stock Exchange (BOX), International Securities Exchange (ISE), Pacific Stock Exchange (PCX), and the Philadelphia Stock Exchange (PHLX).

According to the Options Clearing Corporation (OCC), total options trading volume for 2005 will well surpass the 1 billion contract mark for a second year in a row. In fact, the OCC said total options volume for year-to-date 2005 was 1,184,267,123 on October 24, 2005—surpassing the previous year's same-date record volume of 1,182,040,096 contracts. (For a breakdown of options trading volume by exchange and in total, see Table 10.1.) By comparison, in 2004, options trading volume on all six exchanges amounted to 907,858,655.

When my book *How I Trade Options* (New York: John Wiley & Sons, 2000) was published, options volume on five exchanges (AMEX, CBOE, ISE, PCX, PHLX) amounted to about 726.7 million contracts (of which nearly half, 326.4 million, were traded on the CBOE). In 1973, when options trading first started, there was only one exchange: the CBOE.

The increase in options trading volume is directly linked to wider hedge fund, mutual fund, and other institutional trading activity. For

TABLE 10.1 Option Volume by Exchange	
OCC Total Options Contracts	1,182,040,096
Equity (91.68%)	1,083,649,226
Index (8.30%)	98,160,091
Foreign Currency (0.02%)	230,779
Option Volume on Six Exchanges	
AMEX	202,692,231
BOX	20,741,271
CBOE	361,086,774
ISE	360,852,519
PCX	103,262,458
PHLX	133,404,843

Source: Options Clearing Corporation.

example, when I started my trading career at the CBOE in 1981, there was probably only one firm with a market capitalization of $100 million active in options. In 2000, there was perhaps one firm with $1 billion in market capitalization. Today, there are at least five or six multibillion-dollar firms active in options. Among the biggest players is Citadel Investment Group, the world's largest options trading firm with an estimated capitalization of some $12 billion to $14 billion. (In 2004, *Crain's Chicago Business* listed Citadel as a $10 billion hedge fund.) When large firms commit billions to a market, it's great for liquidity and trading volumes, which makes for better trading opportunities for investors and speculators who are looking to follow the smart money. Smaller players going head-on with the larger funds, however, face some serious competition.

The key to this competition is understanding how these funds trade, given their traditional "2 and 20" management fee structure. (Two percent annual management fee and 20 percent of the upside versus the performance of a given index benchmark, such as the Standard & Poor's 500.) Let's take the example of a smaller fund with $500 million under management. A 2 percent fee would amount to $10 million a year, amortized over 12 months. The fund's goal would be to meet or beat the benchmark and collect the 20 percent performance fee. Thus, if the S&P is up 8 to 10 percent on the year, the fund would stand to make its 20 percent fee if it can return at least 10 percent, or $50 million on the $500 million under management. To make that 10 percent return, a fund is going to trade large positions quickly and aggressively. Since it's not trying to eke out every possible profit on a trade, the fund is less concerned about the bid/ask spread; instead, the object is to get the trade on and off profitably.

As a result of this high-volume trading activity by the funds, independent market makers have felt the pinch when it comes to the bid/ask spread. Back in what now seems like the good old days of being a market maker on the CBOE floor, just a few years ago, if the bid was at 2.00 the offer was at 2.20, or (in the days before decimalization) when the bid was 4, the offer was $4\frac{1}{4}$. Those were the days when market makers on the floor had the ability to make sizeable profits.

With the bid/ask spread narrowed to a nickel in many cases, the profit margins are just not the same. Consider, too, that individual traders and smaller trading firms have, on average, $200,000 to $500,000 in available capital for trading. To cover the cost of seat leases, commissions, and other expenses (and hopefully turn a profit) they need to make a 100 percent return on their money—not the 10 or maybe 15 percent that the hedge funds are aiming for to earn their fees. Plus, those independent traders may find themselves unfavorably on the other side of the trades from the monster players who are flinging around a huge volume of contracts.

These trade imbalances occur because the bid and ask quotes are now changing more quickly than ever before, thanks to the trading actions of the large funds. Even for floor traders with supposedly instant access to the options market, there can be times when stock quotes are delayed a fraction of a second. Such a seemingly miniscule delay can spell disaster.

Consider the scenario of a trader on the floor of an exchange, making a market for options in stocks such as eBay or Cisco Systems. As a market maker, that trader is constantly updating bids and asks on eBay or Cisco options at a variety of strike prices above and below the current price of the stock. Now let's say an institutional investor comes in to buy eBay calls. The market makers sell the calls and immediately hedge the upside risk of those short calls by buying shares of the underlying stock. Depending on how deep in the money the calls are, the market makers buy some portion of 100 shares per call they sell. Since the market makers don't have the benefit of a crystal ball, the next trade they make could just as likely be to sell to another buyer of those calls, or buy from a seller, so they need to constantly move their bids and offers and hedge accordingly. This process goes on continuously throughout the trading day.

The market maker is depending on live, up-to-the-second quotes in the stock market on which to base the bid/ask quotes on the options *and* to enter orders to buy or sell the underlying stock. For most investors, the delay of a second or a fraction of a second wouldn't make a difference. But when a monster is getting into or out of the market—generating *hundreds of orders per second*—a fraction of a second can be the margin between success and disaster. If the real-time quotes traders rely on to make markets in options and buy or sell the underlying stock are a heartbeat behind, the quotes are just plain wrong. A few pennies off on a price quote multiplied over hundreds of contracts and hundreds of positions adds up to some serious money.

Why? Because if a market marker is just a few cents off the rest of the market, with a higher bid or a lower ask, even for a few seconds, that anomaly is going to be picked up by the computer-generated trading systems of these mammoth players. The computer is going to send massive orders to that market maker at *every* strike price in puts and calls. While not every stock has $400 call and put strikes like Google, even the dullest stock has an in-the-money call, at-the-money call, an out-of-the-money call, and corresponding puts, in the front month, second month, outer months, and long-term equity anticipation securities (LEAPS). In other words, we could see 50 different strikes. The market makers will soon find themselves on the other side of thousands of options contracts at a price that was stale by a second—and more times than not, the advantage will be to the computerized trading program and not to the market maker.

It wasn't that the floor traders needed better real-time quotes. They were trading with prices that were more accurate than most real-time investors use. The problem was the monster players in the market were generating orders so fast and furiously that the bandwidth just couldn't keep up. The delay was in the transmission of stock prices to the market maker on the floor. Technology, as good as it is, just isn't always good enough. (As an aside, I saw this in Frankfurt where banks and other institutions were physically moving their trading operations closer to the marketplace where quotes were disseminated to cut down on the delay, or latency, in price quotes, which may be only a fraction of a second but it adds up in terms of volume and money.)

Consider that a two-cent difference on 200,000 shares (2,000 options contracts) is $4,000. You won't even see it go—not even a flicker on your screen. It's like the ultimate bad marriage to someone with a gambling addiction or a serious shopping problem; you never see the money, it's just gone.

The moral of this story is *not* to pursue options trading as a market marker; that ship has sailed! As a market *taker*, however, a new game is unfolding for short-term directional trades, employing the best and latest tools of the trade.

GREATER LIQUIDITY AND TRANSPARENCY

Today's option market offers greater liquidity and increased transparency thanks to multiple listing of options, with both bid/ask price quotes *and* the number of contracts offered visible. Liquidity and transparency give some distinct advantages to being a market taker. Now, it needs to be said that whenever a market taker (meaning a professional or serious investor speculator) lines up against a market maker on an ultra short-term day-trade, the market taker will lose. In this matchup, the market makers have too many advantages on their side, including time and place (especially being on the options floor where the market is being made), being able to execute multiple trades in a second, and a different margin requirement as mandated by the Securities and Exchange Commission (SEC) that is up to 200 times better than that enjoyed by the public.

However, given the increased liquidity and transparency, market takers have a distinct advantage with directional, position trades lasting a day or a few days. For example, since my brother, Pete, and I sold our floor-trading firm, Mercury Trading, in October 2004, we have dramatically changed our investment/trading time frame. Instead of holding positions that could be out nine months to two years (because of the amount of inventory in stocks and options that we would have to carry as market makers), we're making trades that average two to three days. As market takers, we're usually in several trades spanning several days at a time. With the liquidity and narrowing of the bid/ask spread, we're not giving up much of an edge to get into or out of the trade. In other words, if the bid on an option is $2.10 and the ask is $2.15, and we execute within that spread, the maximum five-cent difference is not going to have a huge impact on our profitability per trade. Our objective is to make directional options trades that we predetermine to have the potential to make a run. Usually, this involves buying calls on the expectation that a stock will move to the upside, increasing the value of the option on that stock.

One of the major advantages for the market taker today is the increased transparency in the market. A glance at an options trader's screen clearly illustrates this factor. Screens display not only the bid and ask at each strike price, but also the number of options contracts available at every exchange at which the options are listed.

The result is instant transparency of the market, allowing traders with sophisticated trading programs to sweep the market when they execute a trade, scooping up the most advantageous bids or offers available across multiple exchanges. By sweeping bids and offers, the trade is executed at a blended price, based on the lowest possible offers and the highest possible bids.

For example, consider eBay, whose options are traded on all six major exchanges. Let's say call options at the $45 strike price are bid as follows: 200 options at PHLX at a premium of $2.10; 400 at PCX at $2.10; 200 at ISE at $2.15; 1,000 at BOX at $2.05; 700 at CBOE at $2.00; and 500 at AMEX at $2.10. As a seller with 1,000 options to execute, looking for the highest bid, you'd pick off the 200 at ISE at $2.15, leaving 800. Sweeping the PHLX at $2.10 and the PCX at $2.10, you'd sell another 600, and the remaining 200 would be executed at the AMEX at $2.10 (leaving 200 bid there). This entire sweep would take no more than seconds with a blended price of $2.15 to $2.10. In the old days when I started trading on the floor, market takers would pay Goldman, Morgan, Merrill, and others for their ability to provide or find the liquidity that is now readily available.

Most large firms that provide options execution, such as Spear, Leeds & Kellogg or Remote Dynamics Inc (REDI), both of which are owned by Goldman Sachs, and even some upstart brokerages allow sweeps across multiple exchanges. This strategy is not for the casual customer looking to buy or sell 5 or 10 options contracts. For professional traders and investors with hundreds of options contracts to execute, sweeping offers a significant advantage.

LOOKING FOR TRADING OPPORTUNITIES

As a market taker, there are a few basic ground rules to consider. Among them are these five:

1. *Focus on well-known and highly liquid shares.* With a little research, you can easily determine the average trading volume in a company's shares. (Just plugging in a stock symbol like eBay on a public web site such as Yahoo! Finance will quickly show you the average volume, in this case about 17 million shares daily.)

2. *Stay away from the roach motels*—the thinly traded, illiquid stocks where once you get in you can't get out. If the average volume is 250,000 shares or less per day, I'd generally avoid it. If you're still not convinced, consider who is going to be on the other side of that trade if you decide to buy or sell options on a thinly traded stock: a few moderately capitalized market makers rather than dozens of multimillion- or multibillion-dollar firms. You won't be playing in the same pond as the big funds that are throwing around size in options on a well-known stock, which are listed on multiple exchanges. You'll be up against a few market makers who are going to be able to maintain a comparatively wide bid/ask spread in order to make their money. With fewer players, liquidity is going to be horrific, as well.

3. *Look for options that are listed on at least three, but preferably four, five, or even all six options exchanges.* If an option only trades on one or two exchanges, don't trade it, because it lacks the inherent advantages of breadth, liquidity, and depth of market. Keep in mind that options on the stocks that investors generally want to trade—amounting to the high-80 percent of the total average daily trading volume—have robust markets being made for them. In other words, if the spread between the bid and offer is $.20 and the option we're trading is $1.00 offered at $1.20, then you're giving up 20 percent on entry by paying $1.20 and you'll probably get the same bad treatment on the way out, which may be another 20 percent. That is a pretty tough headwind to fly against!

4. *Be cognizant of the new market dynamics.* It's not just the assembly-line workers who can become obsolete with the advent of robotics; traders have faced their share of obsolescence due to the boom in derivative volume, the narrowing of the bid/ask spread, and a decrease in the potential profitability per trade. In these kinds of conditions, there are basically two alternatives: Be a market maker (either on the floor or electronically) and trade a lot more volume in hopes of making enough money to cover your expenses through

sheer volume of trades, or "go upstairs" and trade at a computer screen as a market taker.

5. *Follow the money.* Market intelligence, whether you subscribe to a service or you do it on your own, will help identify opportunities to trade when the big players are showing interest in the options on a particular stock. (At www.insideoptions.com, we utilize two proprietary systems to identify these stocks, which I discuss in trading examples in the next section of this chapter.)

FOLLOWING THE SMART MONEY

As of this writing in early 2006, the options market is a low-volatility environment. With relatively low volatility, the premium paid on options is fairly reasonable, giving market takers favorable conditions in which to trade. Why is that, Doc? Because in high-volatility conditions you need really extraordinary events to make money as the premium in the option is insanely high. Thus, low-volatility environments mean a market taker can buy options (often calls), and if he's right, there is the potential to make a profit faster with less volatility risk.

It goes without saying that market conditions are never static forever. Unfortunately, the trading world is rife with stories of people who believed that a particular event or scenario would never occur—until it does. Most legendary is the failure of Long Term Capital Management (LTCM), which believed that it was perfectly hedged and that *nothing* could possibly derail its strategy—until the seemingly impossible happened: Russia defaulted on its domestic debt and the markets closed for days. This disconnect meant firms like LTCM couldn't continue dynamically hedging their portfolios of illiquid debt securities. In fact, in October 1998, LTCM's losses were so vast, the Federal Reserve Bank of New York forced the Wall Street's bulge bracket banks—the triple-A counterparties on LTCM trades—to forgive the derivative obligations and take LTCM private stock as settlement instead, in effect engineering an overnight bailout of LTCM's "Dream Team."

That being said, many hedge fund managers in options are convinced that with so much money being devoted to derivative trading these days—thanks to the likes of large hedge funds and global trading entities such as Citadel, Timber Hill Group, Wolverine Trading, and Susquehanna International Group—volume will not decline. They are also convinced that these big players will keep hammering at the bid/ask spreads, keeping them in line as well.

Of course, one of these days, a fund could conceivably face a liquidation panic as its investors try to go into cash, and the impact will be felt in the market. For now, however, this is not the case, and until the dynamics change, options are a high-volume, relatively low-volatility game. In this kind of environment, I have found plenty of opportunities to be a buyer of calls in directional trades by following the smart money.

The smart money leaves a trail of its activity in the form of block trades and buying on the offer. With a direct feed from the Options Price Reporting Authority (OPRA), a high-speed, real-time option feed, I can look at activity in some 4,000 option classes, with hundreds of prices in each of those classes. Our computerized systems screen for specific kinds of trades, which I believe provide insight into the activity of large in-the-know players—also known as the smart money. The two systems we have developed are Distant Thunder™, a kind of early warning system that picks up potential moves in the future, and Heat Seeker™, which pin-points more short-term trading opportunities.

What I am looking for specifically are large block trades of options, usually calls, that are traded on the offer. Consider that an option can trade at one of three price points: at the bid, at the midpoint, or at the of-fer. If an option, for example, is bid at $2.10 and offered at $2.20, a trade could be executed at $2.10, $2.15, or $2.20. The ones I care about are large volume trades to buy calls at the offer. What this tells me is the player was so eager to get into a position and establish it in a major way, it didn't mat-ter what the price was—even buying at the offer. The trade needed to be executed quickly because the buyer expected either a pending news event, an expected announcement, or some other trigger that was seen as likely propelling this stock and the options on the stock.

People trade options in many different ways and for many different reasons. For example, if a trader sells 500 IBM calls (equivalent to 50,000 shares) with a strike price of $85 per share on the bid, then it's very possible that this person owns the stock and is selling the calls to collect the premium. This type of a trade provides cash and also estab-lishes a hedge against a $4 million position in 50,000 shares of IBM. If someone buys or sells a large block of calls at the midprice, it tells me very little. The same thing can usually be said for options trades involv-ing puts, which generally are used as insurance to hedge a physical po-sition in the stock.

When someone is buying a large number of call contracts—usually several hundred or several thousand contracts—at the asking price, then they're anxious to get in the market *regardless of price*. Most likely they know, or they think they know, something that is going to happen in a rel-atively short time frame, and they need to get into the market *now*.

Think about this for a moment: If someone had been studying a par-ticular stock, say XYZ Corporation, and they decided that the fundamental or technical analysis favored an upward move, how would that person behave? Most likely that trader or speculator would scale into a position over time, buying a few contracts at a time at what he perceived to be favorable prices until the position is established. If the goal were a 200-contract position, there would be no need to buy all 200 at once. By scaling in, the trade is executed at a range of prices.

Now, say that someone else hears—either legitimately and legally, or through some nefarious means—of an event that will likely spark an upward move in XYZ Corp. Perhaps this person works at a large hedge fund and has generated hundreds of thousands of dollars in commissions for its broker. In return, the person has been given the courtesy (all legal, by the way) of a one-day advance notice that the brokerage firm's research department is going to raise its rating on XYZ from hold to a strong buy. This person also surmises that other hedge funds may be similarly alerted by the same brokerage firm. With this kind of time-sensitive information, how would that person establish a position by buying 200 calls on XYZ (representing a 20,000 share position)?

I believe that person would buy the options *now* before bidding activity picked up, taking the value of the option along with it. It doesn't matter if the 200 option contracts are purchased at the offer with a bid/ask spread of $2.10 at $2.20. A nickel or even a dime difference won't matter if XYZ makes a major move. (Nor would that hedge fund trader want to be in the position of not moving aggressively and having the market take off without being on board. If that happens, that trader is not likely to stay employed at that fund for very long.)

Our criteria for scanning block trades have proved to be about 77 to 80 percent accurate in terms of putting us into profitable trades as of this writing. Our target is blocks of 200 option contracts or larger. A block trade of that magnitude indicates that someone is serious about establishing a position and most probably an institutional investor. Add to that a block trade of 200 contracts or larger bought *at the offer*, and that person is both serious and eager to get into the market immediately. This is a far different scenario than a 10-lot investor who is dabbling. With 200 contracts or more in a block trade, this is most likely a large firm with some knowledge or insight. We do not know the nature of this information. We're not privy to the name of the fund or other player executing the trade. All we know is that someone—and sometimes a few players—is buying large blocks of calls on the offer.

To illustrate how we use block trade information, here are some recent examples from our trading archives. (We archive our market commentary and trades on our web site, www.insideoptions.com. Our trade commentary for CBOE-TV is also archived on the CBOE's web site at www.cboe.com.)

Laserscope, July 2005

On July 27, 2005, we reported unusual option activity in Laserscope (LSCP). As we reported, Laserscope's earnings were due August 2 and the Street was looking for $0.19 a share. The stock had been upgraded recently to hold from underperform, which had helped propel it to $32.25 a share from $29.32. As of our July 27 report, the stock was trading at $31.03, and our option trading system had just identified unusual buying activity in the August $30 calls, with 85 percent of the trades executed by what we saw as aggressive buyers paying the offer. In addition, 146 percent of the imbalance against the open interest had turned over. The calls at the time were up $0.40 to $2.80, meaning this trade wouldn't be an inexpensive one, but we saw the potential for the stock to run to $35 and then potentially $40 a share. Laserscope's stock did indeed make a run. From the close on July 27, 2005, at $30.31, the stock moved up by $4 a share to close August 2 (the day of its earnings release) at $34.34. (See Figure 10.1.)

Avid Technology (AVID), October 2005

Avid Technology hit our radar screen on October 27, 2005, with shares up 2.7 percent as of the midsession and buyers accumulating the November

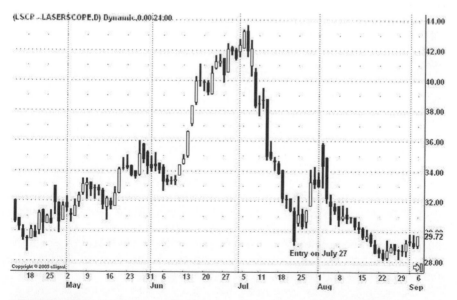

FIGURE 10.1 Laserscope Chart (*Source:* eSignal. www.esignal.com.)

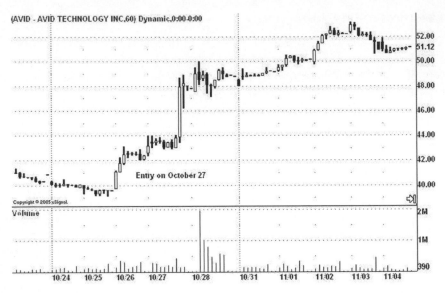

FIGURE 10.2   Avid Technology Chart (*Source:* eSignal. www.esignal.com.)

$45 calls. By the next day, the November $45 calls had traded up to $2.55, closing the session at $2.40. While we did not know what was behind that buying activity at the time, clearly it was linked to Avid's earnings, which surpassed expectations, pushing the shares and the option premium up strongly. (See Figure 10.2.)

Evergreen Solar (ESLR), November 2005

We watched Evergreen Solar closely in early November 2005, anticipating that this solar panel and systems manufacturer's quarterly results would show a narrower loss than expected. In the wake of Hurricanes Katrina and Rita, the stock was at $9.65, and our target was $14.50 for the stock, which could go up to as much as $17 a share depending on earnings or guidance. On November 3, the stock was up $1.30 to $10.90 on triple the normal trading volume—and November $10 and $12.50 calls were also attracting buyers in larger than usual volume. To illustrate, the prior week, only 826 calls on the shares traded. On November 3 alone, however, volume for the November $10 and November $12.50 calls totaled 1,300 and 1,100, respectively. Further, our system picked up block-trade activity in the November $12.50 calls, which traded 752 percent of the imbalance versus the open interest. Evergreen did report record product revenues, which were double the year-ago third quarter. (See Figure 10.3.)

FIGURE 10.3 Evergreen Solar Chart (*Source:* eSignal. www.esignal.com.)

Harrah's Entertainment (HET), October 2005

On October 31, 2005, our computers showed total volume of 5,700 of the November $60 calls on Harrah's Entertainment shares. Action in the November $65 calls was even more bullish—trading up 200 percent to $1.00 with 8,243 contracts changing. Even more telling, more than 86 percent of those contracts were bought on the offer. Harrah's earnings were due out November 3, with expectations of $1.02 per share and the possibility (at least based on the option activity) of some positive guidance. On November 3, Harrah's beat earnings estimates and posted a 78.2 percent increase in revenues of $2.3 billion. The Harrah's November $65 calls moved up from $1.00 to $5.00 in two weeks as the stock ran from $58 to $70! As is often the case, the action in the leveraged derivatives foretold positive action in the underlying security. (See Figure 10.4.)

Netflix (NFLX), November 2005

This stock came back to life after Netflix jumped all over rival Blockbuster in the DVD rental industry. As we noted in our November 8, 2005, report, Netflix was scheduled to present at the Pacific Growth Equities Top Pick in Tech Conference the following week. Ahead of that conference, our system detected both short covering and outright buying of the

FIGURE 10.4 Harrah's Entertainment Chart (*Source:* eSignal. www.esignal.com.)

November $30 calls—with buyers paying as much as $0.85 for out-of-the-money calls and 90 percent of those were bought on the offer. Then, as we noted in our November 10 report, a bullish story in the *Wall Street Journal* sent Netflix shares up 7 percent to a new 52-week high of $30.25. The November $30 calls were trading up 90 percent from the previous night's close on volume of 4,700 contracts. (See Figure 10.5.)

FIGURE 10.5 Netflix Chart (*Source:* eSignal. www.esignal.com.)

CONCLUSION

As these trading examples illustrate, our short-term directional trades in options are almost exclusively buying calls to capitalize on what may very well turn out to be an increase in the options value and the underlying stock. Certainly someone could use the insight gleaned from the options market to buy the stock, and many people do watch options activity as an indicator. I prefer buying the options because of the leverage and the ability to limit risk. This is particularly the case when buying call options that are near expiration.

For example, one of our trades in mid-November 2005 in Countrywide Financial (CFC) involved expiring options that were trading for around $0.30 per share. With every option contract representing 100 shares of stock, that $30 option was controlling $3,430 worth of stock. Consider taking a position of 10,000 shares in this stock. At the prevailing price of $34.30 per share that would tie up $343,000 of your capital. Compare that with spending $3,000 for 100 calls and controlling *the same position*. The downside, of course, was that these expiring options had a very limited life span. In the case of the Countrywide Financial trade, we purchased the calls just five days before expiration, and were able to reap a profit when the premium advanced as the stock price rose.

As these examples also show, these trades only last a few days. It reflects the old trading adage, "Buy the rumor, sell the news." In other words, we are looking to take a position in line with large volume block trades and exit when the news or event occurs. The trigger could be an earnings release, a new product announcement, even an acquisition. We saw this type of options activity before recent stock-moving events, including when Allergan Inc. (AGN) made a $3.2 billion bid for Inamed Corp. (IMDC), and when Apple unveiled its video iPod sooner than anticipated.

Typically when our systems pick up unusual options activity, the first place we go is to the news services to see what the company has been announcing, what it is expected to announce, or if there is a conference or analyst meeting on the horizon. Sometimes there is an obvious link, such as earnings to be released, while at other times it's not as clear. When large block trades of call options trade at the offer, however, it's a pretty good assumption that some people know something—or think they know something. Options traders looking to follow the smart money need to at least pay attention to this kind of activity, analyze it, and consider taking action.

Keep in mind that these are short-term trades, lasting a day or two, sometimes a few days. Buy-and-hold for the options speculator is dead and buried. Potentially lower risk, higher return trades can be made with a *disciplined* approach to short-term directional trades. As every serious investor or trader knows, the underpinning of one's discipline is the exit strategy. For short-term trades the rule we follow on a profitable trade is that when the premium value doubles, we take off at least half the trade. Then, with our initial investment of the premium recouped, we are only speculating with the rest (or playing with the "house money," as we say). If the premium should double again, we exit the trade. If it goes up some increment of that, we may also exit. Or if it starts to slip, we get out with a smaller profit, but a good return overall with limited risk.

The obvious question that is sometimes raised is, if the smart money gets you in, won't it get you out? The answer is an emphatic *no*. The smart money has several ways to exit that are not visible via options trading activity. Having established a large position in the options, these big players have the opportunity to exit on the stock side, which an options trader will never see. For instance, the option buyer could sell stock after the run and therefore stay undercover. Thus, it is essential to have one's own exit rules, separate from whatever the smart money may be doing.

Not every trade, of course, is profitable, and the discipline that applies to taking profits needs to be even stronger when it comes to cutting losses. We look at selling out of a losing position once the premium value declines by 20 to 40 percent, depending on the value of the option. Our belief is that the profits from taking off half or even all of a position when the premium value doubles will more than make up for the occasional loser when premium slips by 20 to 40 percent.

As a former market maker and floor trader, being a market taker and sitting upstairs at a computer terminal is a new game, requiring new skills. Like any professional in any business, I could not remain static for 24 years. I had to grow and change along with my industry. Led by the new dynamics of the market, I looked for opportunities off the floor, now as a market taker, with short-term directional trades as dictated by large volume block trades.

PART V

Trading Size

CHAPTER 11

Making Sense of Market Moves: Using Technical and Fundamental Analysis Together

Jeffrey Spotts

S tocks and, by confirmation, industry groups move well ahead of fundamental developments, even in the face of disbelief and faulty rationale by most market participants. For instance, very recently oil prices broke out of a multiyear base, clearing $30 per barrel and initiating a major uptrend. As crude prices broke through level after level—$40 per barrel, $50, and so on—more and more analysts came trotting out stating, "There is no fundamental supply/demand reason for this to be happening." Only through the $60-a-barrel price level did the consensus seem to point to the reasons for the move: demand for energy, particularly in the United States and Asia, lack of investment in capacity, and so forth.

As of this writing, the same situation is happening again, but this time in gold. The rationale of "there is little or no inflation" would discourage investors from participating in gold or in the underlying stocks. The stocks themselves are telling a different story—not that inflation is coming, but that it is already prevalent.

What these examples show is that one should look to anticipate scenarios that fit the stock action, such as the impact of high energy prices on the cost of goods and a development of systemic price inflation.

Technical analysis may not be able to tell you why something will happen, but it definitely assists the analyst in figuring out what will happen to varying degrees. The "why something will happen," as defined by fundamental information, usually occurs after the trend has already changed and been established. Equities are discounting indicators, after all, not just investments. Fundamentals, the way I manage a portfolio, become more important as the trend is already in effect. As developments with the company are revealed, we assess their impact. The fundamentals help the investor stay with the new trend.

INFLUENCES OF THINKING

Within this thinking, there are concepts that are undoubtedly familiar to many people. Personally, my greatest influence has been William O'Neil, a living legend who has figured out the ways to be in the best stocks. Steve Shobin, another money manager (and author of the Foreword to this book), is also an influence. His focus on the "big base" structure now permeates my thinking with regard to investment prospecting. Lastly, Bob Farrell, another legend in our time, was one of the only technicians who crossed over to the fundamental side with eerie accuracy.

Wanting to provide me with an example of crowd behavior, Bob gave me a book entitled *One-Way Pockets*, by Don Guyon (New York: Cosimo, 2005). It provides clear examples of faulty trading habits, mostly caused by misplaced fear, greed, disbelief, and euphoria. The entire book is only 64 pages long and is narrated by a manager at a brokerage firm. The story goes something like this: One of the manager's duties was to review all of the trading of the customers. During slow times in the market, as it was ebbing back and forth in a tight range, the customers traded back and forth with some success, making small profits from high to low and back again. Then, without warning, the market moved away to the upside, well beyond the previous range. Stocks were sold earlier in the range, leaving customers uninvested.

The thinking of the customer base was that there was no reason for the market to be moving that high and that it should come back down, as was the recent norm. After a short consolidation period, however, the market moved higher. The money chased it, and then the market would pull back, flushing out the customers again. There was no explanatory story to back up the rise in the market, other than some murmurings about the economy or some new technology. The air was full of caution. This continued for some time, and as the trend moved higher and higher to record levels, the reason for the price action was eventually known to all. Near the very top of the market, the customers and the investing public decided that trading was a waste of time, leading them only to missed opportunities. A buy-and-hold strategy to remain fully invested—instead of the foolhardy endeavor of trading—was the way to invest for the future, given the new, positive paradigm in place.

With the sideline buying dried up, the peak coincided with favorable fundamental developments, and a new downtrend was initiated. This sparked yet another cycle of disbelief, the waiting for a recovery to sell, and buying bargains that got cheaper and cheaper—until virtually everyone shied away from the market as the fundamental conditions worsened.

Does this scenario sound familiar? The Internet bubble, perhaps? No, the book was originally published in 1917, well before the crash of 1929.

USING TECHNICAL AND FUNDAMENTAL ANALYSIS

Clearly, when looking at market behavior, very little is new when it comes to the cyclical nature of markets and the irrationality of investors. The best way to proceed in this environment is with a combination of technical analysis and fundamental research to make sense of the market moves and identify opportunities.

My method of investing utilizes a heavy dose of technical analysis applied to more than 4,000 stocks and indexes. Through computer modeling that seeks certain trading signatures of stocks beginning new trends, we isolate the opportunities for our fundamental research efforts. This sequence—technical screening first and fundamental analysis second—allows us to be in some of the best stocks early before the story is out and the stocks have moved too far. This is an effective system of investment prospecting instead of haphazardly stumbling across a sector or stock whose story sounds good.

In my early days as a portfolio manager, fundamental analysis was the main thrust of the investment process. Upgrades, downgrades, opinion changes, and guidance were the perceived drivers of price action by most of the money managers. Hanging on to the words of an analyst on a squawk box was standard practice. Some equity salesmen would put the phone next to the speaker when the analyst was talking so that their institutional client could hear it firsthand. (Some of you are laughing, to be sure, but I have a good friend who still does this.) Arguments and opinions would be exchanged in circles of logic about what should happen next with a company.

Granted, fundamentals are important, but knowing when to buy or sell based on fundamentals is a very difficult task to do consistently. For that, you need to use technical analysis.

My clientele used to include a few CEOs, CFOs, board members, founders, and concentrated position holders of company stock. As I watched them tour through town, speaking at investment conferences, brokerage firm analysts would begin issuing reports on these companies. Most of the reports were just regurgitations from conference calls and symposiums. No gumshoe channel-checking or investigative techniques were applied. With most analysts covering better than 30 companies, I could sympathize with their task. Also, it is hard to go out on a limb when your legal department is now part of the investment process.

One major thing bothered me, though: Most of the upgrades were happening well into an uptrend, and most of the downgrades were happening as the stock had already broken down and was moving in a downtrend. The worst opinions always came after a stock had had a huge run and it was clearly topping out on a chart basis. On the first big price break, the analysts would emerge, defending the stock and their buy rating by spouting that the fundamentals had not changed. Too often, these were the proverbial "famous last words." It was clear to me that not only most analysts who publish, but also most of the ones investing real money, such as mutual funds and investment advisers, moved in packs like anyone else.

CROWD BEHAVIOR

As evidence that crowd behavior occurs quite rampantly in the mutual fund industry, consider the weekly equity charts in Figures 11.1 through 11.4, with the number of institutional holders reported that quarter. The important insight from these charts is the *trend of the number of institutional holders*, rather than an opinion applied to proper market valuation.

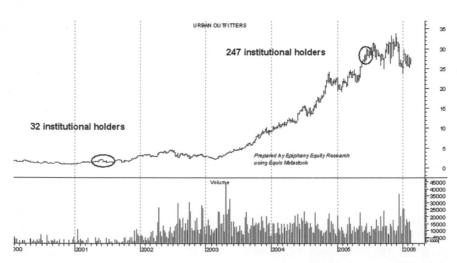

FIGURE 11.1   Urban Outfitters—Weekly Price and Volume Chart (*Source:* Chart provided by MetaStock.)

FIGURE 11.2 EBay—Weekly Price and Volume Chart (*Source:* Chart provided by MetaStock.)

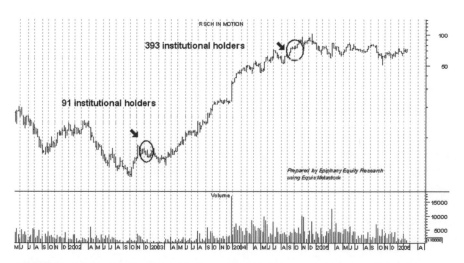

FIGURE 11.3 Research in Motion—Weekly Price and Volume Chart (*Source:* Chart provided by MetaStock.)

As these charts show, at major weekly bottoms, quarterly readings of institutional holders move to their lowest levels, while near their respective highs, holdings peak. This has to happen. Why else would a stock move other than buying or selling pressure? The reason for the actual price movement is actually technical; there are more or fewer buyers or sellers. At price peaks, the majority of participants recognize

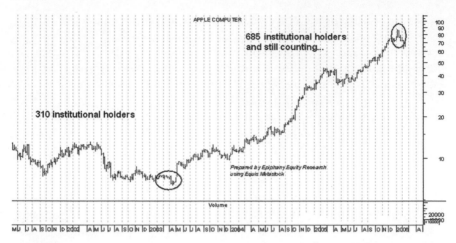

FIGURE 11.4 Apple Computer—Weekly Price and Volume Chart (*Source:* Chart provided by MetaStock.)

the fundamental story and become fully invested, and at price lows, they are all out.

I do believe that there are some brilliant fundamental investors out there. Stocks are accumulated by these players—usually a select few—when a fundamental change is beginning to be anticipated. Nothing is more professionally satisfying to a portfolio manager than making the correct call early, staying with the new trend, and riding it through all the disbelief until the position is ejected, on the last few buy or sell ratings as the rest of the market is recognizing the story. Doing this on a thematic basis in one or two industry groups can make the money manager's career.

UPGRADES AND DOWNGRADES AS ANECDOTAL SENTIMENT

Upgrades and downgrades of a stock or sector occur in usual positions, which taken together make up the anatomy of a trend. Depending on how far along a stock is on its trend, the strength of the fundamental theme, and the slant of the media coverage, upgrades or downgrades can be anecdotal sentiment. You don't trade on this information, but should be aware of the possibility that many participants have been pulled in or flushed out of the stock based on these analyst opinions. I am generalizing the faults of the equity research and investment industries, but have seen these shortcomings happen, firsthand, on a consistent basis.

These inefficiencies, however, allow smarter money managers advantages in the marketplace. Therefore, an investor or trader who is aware of the dynamics of upgrades and downgrades on the market has an advantageous position, in that there is ample room for significant profits by the market participant with the right set of disciplined processes.

A PROFITABLE, REPEATABLE PROCESS

At the end of 2005, we examined all of our trading during a grueling exercise overseen by a Six Sigma management consulting team. For those unfamiliar with the Six Sigma methodology, it is a statistical practice whereby the enterprise eliminates defects (losing trades) and duplicates effective processes (finding and making winning trades). One can eliminate defects in almost any process, from conducting spinal surgery to manufacturing semiconductors. Not only do you look at the trade style, you also look at the trade inputs. This is a time-consuming but rewarding process. Reviewing trades is often the most underappreciated and avoided but most effective method of revealing defects in trading. At the same time, it is very uncomfortable for anyone with high trading standards.

In our review, all trades were meticulously examined. Everything from market positions, source of ideas, mental attitudes, information flow, fundamental rankings, oscillation position, and so on, was reviewed at the time of trade, both entry and exit. As it turned out, our investment discipline utilized over 180 inputs with 54 trade types. By doing this exercise, we could extricate faulty or inert trading input. Removing or refining investment concepts can take years of experience, but with the Six Sigma process evaluation, it took only a few months to really hone down what makes money.

I liken the process to becoming a prima ballerina—not that I am a ballet dancer, but my wife was a serious one for many years and our daughters are also dancers. She explained to me that the best instructors constantly remind their students to study themselves in the mirror. The dancer may have felt the position or move was adequate but, on further review, could see that the body was not in proper position. Adjustment after adjustment is made, with the instructor physically moving the body into proper position, until the move is perfect and repeatable. At our trading firm we were not trying to achieve perfection; our goal is to eliminate defective trades to increase profitability. To achieve even greater performance, one must be able to duplicate the best winning trades.

The 80/20 rule applies to almost any process: 80 percent of your output is caused by about 20 percent of your input. As a result of the Six Sigma process, we have eliminated many of the relatively inferior inputs and trade types. Based on that experience, I would like to share some of the best trade inputs and signatures for the long and short equity player.

KEY TRADE SIGNATURES

As mentioned, we apply technical analysis first to find investment prospects. One note: Keep your analysis simple. All the indicators in technical analysis are derivations of two elements—price and volume. Most traders attempt to build screens utilizing a combination of all types of oscillators and systems, backtesting and optimizing, and pointing to trades that could have been. Create a weekly bar chart, put in 10-, 30-, and 120-week moving averages, and add volume. That's it. Nothing else is necessary for the initial prospecting phase. Overbought or oversold indicators can throw off your analysis, keeping you from investigating great stocks.

The best stocks remain in overbought readings for longer periods of time versus the underperformers of the market. Relative strength begets more relative strength. Secular or defining changes in price are looked over as being too extended, which is a grave mistake. Imagine a rocket blasting off from Earth. It requires a great deal of initial thrust and velocity to send it into orbit. Similarly, stocks need certain events or market occurrences to provide them with thrust and velocity for an uptrend. There are techniques to identify these issues before they begin their launch.

Often stocks begin to move off lows not because of a deluge of buying but because the sellers have all dried up. This is called *neglect*, a state in which a stock may trade back and forth, basing in a tightening range on low volume. These formations are often called bases and have several types. The *pencil base* tends to have the least volatility and lowest volume during the formation. Weekly base structures are attractive points of entry. Early in the stock's uptrend, base structures happen two or three times. After five or six, I would be wary of the base. Once a change in relative strength is detected, especially if it is occurring in more than one stock in the group, that is the signal to initiate positions and focus research in the industry and specific stocks.

The quest to determine why something will happen is really not that important in setting up the initial position. There is no rule in investing that you need to thoroughly know the fundamentals to buy a stock initially. I am more interested in how stocks move. Of course, if the "why" is coinciding with the price action, and it is not widely known and discounted, that is all the better. Here's a simple analogy to illustrate: Imagine that you are in a long line at a Wal-Mart checkout counter, and you notice a woman in a Wal-Mart uniform with a key and a cashier bank in hand, walking down to the far end of the line of closed cashier booths. Don't you take the calculated risk and jump out of line and follow her? I sure would. With a stock, the evidence is good enough to take an initial position. This "shoot now and ask questions later" strategy actually creates opportunity *and* mitigates risk. One word of caution: Utilize a tight stop until you see some follow-through with price and volume.

During this move in the industry group, sentiment is usually apathetic or outright negative. The faulty logic maintains that the move should be discounted as an aberration since the fundamental conditions do not warrant a change in valuations. As the move continues in the face of doubt, add to a position to make it larger. The stocks are discounting future change, and as long as the relative strength improves and there are other factors displayed in their trading patterns, an initial position should be increased.

Figures 11.5 through 11.7 show stock charts that are from the same industry group, gold and silver mining. In the spring of 2001, the entire group was trading in a neglected state, and trading for a total of $10 billion in market capitalization, less than one NASDAQ 100 technology company.

Notice the relative strength and weekly volume change coming into the shares. These conditions rang every bell in our system, and our positions were initiated. Now, what if the money manager had been following

FIGURE 11.5 Royal Gold—Weekly Price, Volume, and Relative Strength Chart (*Source:* Chart provided by MetaStock.)

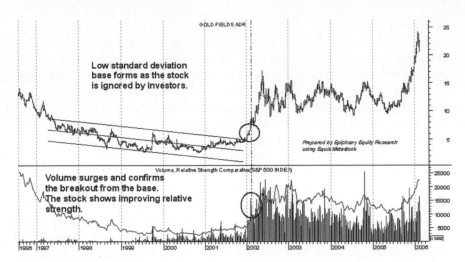

FIGURE 11.6 Gold Fields—Weekly Price, Volume, and Relative Strength Chart (*Source:* Chart provided by MetaStock.)

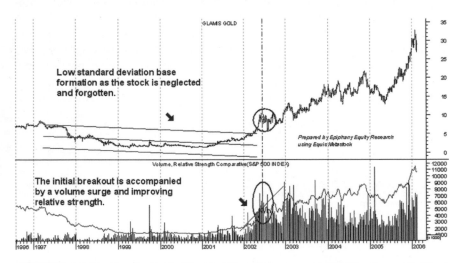

FIGURE 11.7 Glamis Gold—Weekly Price, Volume, and Relative Strength Chart (*Source:* Chart provided by MetaStock.)

the sector and bought these stocks based on value? There is a risk that the position would have been held for many months, even years before the new uptrend started. By stalking the group and allowing the stocks to show you when to buy, that opportunity risk is eliminated. If the new trend has any durability, waiting for the signal and missing the first 5 percent of a new uptrend is exercising proper risk control.

HOW TO DIG

The real work is in the digging. But doing this work, looking for investment ideas, is the most satisfying part of my profession. Finding stocks in great positions to buy or short is what I love to do.

There are two main research systems that I use to look for stocks. With these, I will normally look at a minimum of 4,000 names using computer programs and manually one by one. This list does not include other chart work on nonequity and global markets. I start very early in the morning—no phone, no TV, no colleagues. Looking at the data on your own, with no other input, sets the stage for your best trading. By 9:30, I need to oversee trading portfolio and prospective investment price action.

Depending on the time frame, about 30 proprietary scans with varying technical and fundamental criteria are performed, sifting through and generating pools of investment prospects. Although I cannot give away the formulas or even the screen descriptions, the scans are quite deft at isolating opportunities. For my purpose here, I will give one thing away: A high-quality input within the initial base is insider buying. My screen for this is a stock trading within 20 percent of its five-year low and that two separate insiders have bought the stock over the past six months. These have to be qualified purchases, in some size, and without a related option exercise. As mentioned before, my clientele used to include officers and insiders. They will sell stock for a variety of reasons—a new house, a divorce, diversification, and so on and many of them don't want to do the sale but must for liquidity reasons. However, they buy their stock for only one reason. Insider buying is usually a characteristic seen in the initial base structures. Figures 11.8 and 11.9 represent examples of stocks that begin their moves from quiet bases. Lions Gate, in Figure 11.9, had six separate insider buy transactions before the stock displayed any significant strength.

Normally my manual list matches well with the computer scans. I prefer to do both so as not to miss any prospects from either method, and to have an innate sense of the process. I imagine that I am flying a plane, but even if I put it on autopilot, I want to keep my hands on the controls and get a sense of what is going on.

Most traders will focus on daily, hourly, or some type of minute chart. Even though the holding period is short, a study of the weekly and monthly charts will allow for extending holding periods to prevent exiting winners too early. Another reason for going with the weekly time frame is to increase your winning trade ratio. Day-trading or making trades that last only a few days requires perfect execution, which is an unreal expectation. Too often, profit is left on the table because a trader or investor is operating on a short time frame.

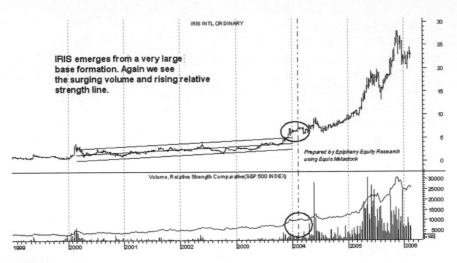

FIGURE 11.8 IRIS International—Weekly Price, Volume, and Relative Strength Chart (*Source:* Chart provided by MetaStock.)

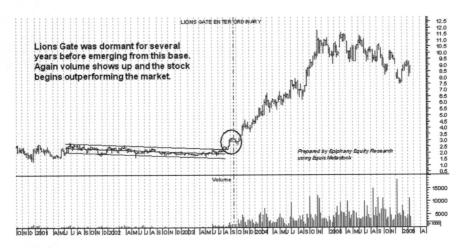

FIGURE 11.9 Lions Gate Entertainment—Weekly Price, Volume, and Relative Strength Chart (*Source:* Chart provided by MetaStock.)

Another reason for working with weekly charts is the time it takes to properly do the work—before the list is eventually honed down to do more fundamental research, which is conducted later in the process. For purposes of this chapter, and the fact that my investment prospecting discipline is primarily technical analysis driven, I do not cover the fundamental analysis in detail. Rather, I believe the key for trades is to find investment prospects using technical analysis, without trying to decipher stories and getting bogged down early in circled arguments about what might happen to a certain market, economy, commodity, industry, or stock.

One more reason to consider an intermediate-term time frame is that it is much easier to call a longer-term trend change than it is to call a shorter one. The scarcest commodity in the marketplace is patience. For those who have been used to trading on a short-term basis, try to utilize a weekly time frame on a few positions in the manner discussed here. The result may be less work versus monitoring every tick—and the potential to make more money.

FOCUS ON STOCKS, NOT INDEXES

Although industry group charts may shorten the time needed to isolate areas for investment, the underlying index members may be skewing the data. For instance, the restaurant group's largest weighting is McDonald's. Although the group is full of great performers, such as PF Chang's and Starbucks, recent performance shows that the industry group chart did poorly. Because of that, great stocks can get missed. To generate alpha, you have to dig and look at individual stocks' price action and their relative strength.

For instance, while the wireless communication services group chart was moving to new lows during 2002, two stocks were separate from the pack because of their large weekly base structures and positive changes in their relative strength versus the market and their industry group. That these companies were distinctive and had great fundamental prospects was a plus. It would have been easy to pass over the industry group due to the industry chart and sentiment. However, the scans we perform and our manual efforts to analyze stocks identified these names early in their new uptrends. Figure 11.10 shows the stocks of two Russian telecom providers, Vimpelcom and Mobile Telesystems, moving up well ahead of the entire telecom sector, signaling their continued outperformance of the group.

For those who lack either the commitment or the time to do this type of work, remember the 80/20 rule. Conducting scans with the correct criteria will eventually put you in front of the best prospective stocks. These candidates can still be installed on your watch list and monitored for best entry. My goal is to acquire positions in stocks before they make it to many popular scans or lists.

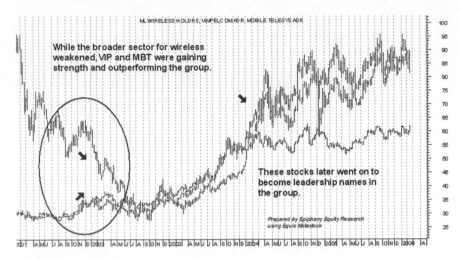

FIGURE 11.10 Weekly Price Chart of Wireless Telecom HOLDRs with Overlay of Vimpelcom and Mobile Telesystems (*Source:* Chart provided by MetaStock.)

BUYING FURTHER ALONG THE TREND

It's not always possible to catch the very beginning of a trend change when it happens, or when you miss the initial base breakout. There will still be opportunities to enter a trade. An effective buy point is what I refer to as an *ABC pullback* or *undercut low.* My preference would be to execute this method on a weekly or even monthly chart basis, but it works on the daily charts as well. One of the hardest things for a portfolio manager to do is to step up and buy a deeper pullback in a stock. This method should allow some confidence.

No matter what your candidate list consists of—stocks, indexes, commodities, and so on—the ABC pullback occurs during most uptrends, effectively offering an investor a sale price with a level of risk that I perceive as being quite acceptable. The optimal conditions for such a trade are:

- The stock should have signs of high accumulation before the pullback. Preferably, the 200-day and 30-week moving averages are sloping upward or in relatively steep uptrends.
- The current base is not past a fifth stage, meaning over the course of the last three years this is not the sixth (or a higher number) weekly pullback.

- The industry group maintains a respectable breadth reading, meaning the advance/decline line of the sector is in an uptrend, or related industry stocks are acting well.
- The pullback in the stock should not be earnings related. Earnings-related breakdowns in price are not the optimal conditions.
- Sentiment in the group that has shifted to a more negative stance during the pullback is a plus.
- The pullback contains no downside gaps on huge volume. In fact, be sure that the largest weekly volume bar in the pullback is not a down bar, especially when it closes near the low portion of the bar. It may still work, but it is not optimal.
- The weekly bars have closes that are either near the mid- to high point of the bar, and/or the next weekly bar is supportive and negates some of the damage of the previous weekly bar.
- Short interest continues to be prevalent, or better yet is rising.
- Be sure the base is not too deep. Too much weakness in a stock with too many higher weekly down bars is not acceptable.

Figure 11.11 gives an example of a weekly price and volume chart on the stock, Newmont Mining, that has moved out of a large, initial base. The undercut lows are good short- and intermediate-term buy points.

As you are setting up the position, be aware that occasionally a high-volume shakeout may occur near the buy point, pushing the stock under a supporting moving average. Be on the lookout for the weekly bar to have

FIGURE 11.11 Newmont Mining—Weekly Price and Volume Chart (*Source:* Chart provided by MetaStock.)

a close preferably above the shakeout area. A tail on the weekly bar, with positive price action to follow, is about as good as it gets.

Look for better support to come near the 30-week moving average. Watch out when utilizing moving averages, however. I consider them poor areas for stops and better for buys or shorts. Allow the daily price action to play out as long as volume readings don't go against you. Stop-loss areas are usually price-bar-defined and coincide more with former base structures and retracement levels.

Most technical traders get hung up on patterns. From our trading, we have found that relative strength is a higher-quality input. As long as your buy points are coming in at undercut lows and/or key moving averages, fish from a pool of stocks that are displaying improvements in relative strength.

Additional positions can be put on as the stock is clearing the base. *Open skies* is a term often used to describe stocks moving to new highs. If you see a stock, which you bought deep within a base, move to a new high, you know you are executing perfectly. Additional positions can be put on at supportive moving averages. I would prefer something near the 10-week. At our firm, we do not price-average down on positions. If the stock is not acting within the range that you predicted, it is best to be out of the trade. Stocks don't get cheaper and more attractive to us if we are long—they get punted.

Your target on the trade should be a move to at least the top of a newly defined uptrend channel, but that is determined by market conditions and group strength. Moves above the trend channel, especially on an upgrade, are normally sell points.

Now that we have covered an effective area for stock buys, let us move to the short side.

SHORT SETUPS

I utilize several short setups. The one that I demonstrate here relies on a weekly chart to initiate. I prefer to see most of the following criteria:

- The stock is moving out of a sixth-stage base or older.
- The short interest reading is near its historical low.
- The stock has recently experienced an earnings-related price break and is recovering in a weak manner. A plus would be if the stock was recently defended by an analyst, and has trouble holding that upgrade price that day.
- The aforementioned recovery had low daily or weekly volume bars.

- The stock has a flattening or downward-trending 30-week moving average.
- The stock has a wide and loose price structure. This means that the stock is displaying larger weekly price swings later in its trend.
- Sector breadth is poor, and other stocks in the group are struggling

Shorting at the initial break is one method I found to work well for quick holding periods, but it carries more risk than another method I also use. This method allows the stock to recover from a massive hit, usually from an earnings-related adjustment. The stock will usually recover a good portion, at least a 0.618 retracement of the price break, comparing the high point and the recent low. This could take several weeks, even months after the first high.

A nuance that I would look for is a recent negative *outside weekly* bar. This means that the current price bar opened above the top of the range of the previous weekly price bar, and closed below the low point of the previous weekly price bar, usually on above-average volume. This typically occurs near the end of the recovery.

Like all the illustrations in this chapter, I have included actual trade setups. Figures 11.12 and 11.13 represent short sales based on the concepts explained.

My preference is to short above the 30- and 10-week moving averages. We utilize a momentum divergence, along with a market and sector breadth divergence reading to supplement our timing of the trade. Usually

FIGURE 11.12 Apollo Group—Weekly Japanese Candlestick Chart with Volume (*Source:* Chart provided by MetaStock.)

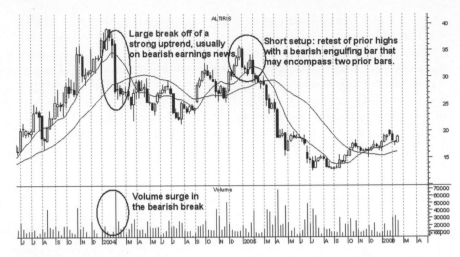

FIGURE 11.13 Altiris—Weekly Japanese Candlestick Chart with Volume (*Source:* Chart provided by MetaStock.)

another day or two of recovery to retrace about half of the negative outside weekly price bar will yield the optimal point to lay out the first short on the stock. However, I would not risk being out of the trade for that optimal scenario to fully develop.

Shorts are not like longs in that during the initial part of the topping process in a market, industry, or stock, one should cover the short on a move to the bottom part of a range or top of a previous base point, or on a break caused by fundamental news. Once you are in the latter stages of the topping process, and more stocks are moving in downtrends, it is less important to cover as quickly or as often. Just let prices drip away.

CONCLUSION

Traders and investors may consider themselves 100 percent technical or they may have a bias toward fundamental analysis. Putting these disciplines together, however, one can sift through a myriad of potential opportunities to identify stocks that may be poised to make a move—and then conduct the fundamental analysis to make the case. Technical analysis will not provide reasons for a move, up or down. Rather, it alerts you to the potential of something happening in a likely direction. For the "why," you will have to rely on fundamental analysis, but usually this can be confirmed only after a trend has changed and been established.

Given the cyclical nature of markets and the irrational behavior in the investment environment, the best way to proceed is with a combined approach. Let technical analysis identify those stocks—and in particular those stocks within industry groups and sectors—that appear favorable for a long or short position. Then, by scaling into a position and waiting for the story to unfold, you can take advantage of a market move by getting in before everyone else piles on.

CHAPTER 12

New World Trading of Old World Markets: European Derivatives

Timothy Corliss

For professional traders and investors in the United States, there is another world to consider: European derivatives. Although these markets can be idiosyncratic, particularly compared with U.S. trading that is dominated by exchange-based activity, they also present unique opportunities to diversify holdings, hedge positions, gain leverage, or benefit from investment exposure to a particular industry segment or geographic region.

The markets for European derivatives and in particular options, which are the focus of much of this chapter, are not as deep and liquid as their U.S. counterparts. In the United States, options are traded on six exchanges. In addition to the transparency and liquidity of having multiple exchange listings for options, this also makes the U.S. market more competitive. With a computer keystroke, a professional trader or broker in the United States can route an order to any exchange or even execute large block trades on more than one exchange.

By contrast, the majority of European options are traded off-exchange, particularly for the size of trades involved in institutional activity as discussed in this chapter. To put this in perspective, of the European options on individual stocks that are traded by institutions, 75 percent of that volume is over the counter or traded off-exchange, while 25 percent is listed. For options on indexes, institutional transactions conducted over the counter account for about two-thirds of the volume, while one-third is listed.

This added complexity should not be avoided, however. By nature, complexity creates more opportunity. But before going further, we just consider the essential question when trading any market: How does one profit? The desired end result for trading any market is to make a profit. With any investment or trade, execution is based on a snapshot of that market, which assumes efficient pricing at the time the transaction is completed. All information is theoretically known and priced into the security at the time of the trade. News, fundamentals, and valuations are all taken into consideration. How then can one make a profit in efficient markets?

One way to profit with European derivatives is to understand the various market participants and their rationale style of trading. By becoming familiar with these players and their rationale for trading, we understand the counterparties of our own trades, and thus obtain a trading edge through this knowledge.

UNDERSTANDING MARKET PARTICIPANTS

One of the first things to understand about European derivatives trading is that most of this activity is not retail; it is institution to institution, involving trading liquidity of between $1 million and $15 million for a single stock and $5 million to $25 million for an index. As an aside, given the idiosyncrasies of European option markets—with different multipliers per contract (you may think one contract represents 100 shares when it's really 1,000 shares), different settlement dates, and so forth—it's best to quote the transaction in *shares* of the underlying stock.

To trade European options, one needs to know the market participants. In other words, if a U.S.-based trading or investment firm is buying European options, it needs to know why the counterparty is likely selling. For example, the other party could be selling to take a profit, to hedge a position, or as part of a more complex transaction. It could also be that the other party is speculating but from the opposite point of view. If this is the case, the U.S. firm is now head-to-head with a large European brokerage or investment firm that has the opposite opinion on a particular stock or index, which means one party is going to be right (and profitable) and the other one is going to be wrong (with losses on the trade).

As a speculator or directional trader, understanding what motivates other market participants and how they operate provides valuable insight. This market knowledge helps to explain why, for example, a particular market maker has a wider bid/ask spread than another brokerage firm, or why a broker is "bid only" for a particular option. Being aware of market dynamics, such as when option liquidity might increase because a company has issued convertible bonds, can also help with trade execution. With that in mind, let's take a look at the market participants and how they operate.

Market Makers

Although European options can be traded on exchanges, liquidity and depth are generally poor. Institutional market makers provide liquidity and are willing to show bids and offers on options for various trading sizes. Market makers at large bulge bracket investment banks and broker dealers are well-capitalized institutions. They will quote prices depending on how much they can hedge their trading book and the trading style of the end customer. The market maker can usually turn order flow into a profit. Unlike liquidity in the United States that can be accessed instantaneously, European options generally take 10 to 15 minutes for liquid large-cap stocks to be priced. Mid-cap and small-cap stocks can take up to an hour, even when trading delta-neutral.

Market makers at large investment banks and broker dealers are usually most efficient at quoting prices for options on large-cap stocks or European indexes. For mid-cap and small-cap issues, local traders are most familiar with the underlying stock and the volatility at which it should trade. Unless a U.S.-based trader has established a relationship with several local options brokers, it is most likely that trader will end up paying the local broker's market *plus* the bulge bracket broker's markup.

An important distinction from the U.S. market is that European market makers are *not* obliged to make a market in options on a particular stock. By comparison, U.S. market makers quote bids and offers on put and call options at numerous strike prices. Because they are not obligated, European market makers can set very wide bid/offer spreads. The trader needs to be cagey and call only the market makers he thinks can provide the best pricing; otherwise the trader may find market makers moving the market. There may be a time that a market maker is bid only and won't make an offer because the firm's consolidated book is short too much of this particular volatility (or vice versa—the market maker is offer only because the book is too long a particular volatility). The alternative is then to find another market maker who is willing to offer the volatility that you're willing to buy. Be careful not to call too many market makers as that would let on to the broader market that you are a buyer or a seller. Traders need to guard their positions in thin markets.

Market makers are usually well informed about company fundamentals and from customer order flow. Since the option market is over-the-counter (OTC), the market maker can bid below and offer above current market prices. A broker may only be willing to make a market in one direction because the firm does not want to be a buyer (or a seller) regardless of the price. Market makers' volatility curves and dividend assumptions in their pricing models give them the best edge to trade bid and offer and still make a profit for their trading books.

Given these dynamics, Europe options trading is less competitive than in the United States. Therefore, the directional trader or speculator needs to find the market maker with the best bid/offer prices. This usually involves finding the market maker who is the most familiar with the security. To illustrate the variation in bid/offers at any given time—and depending upon the prevailing conditions, fundamentals, and dynamics of the market—I was recently quoted a range of prices on a Volkswagen option. Clearly a large-cap DAX constituent should have good liquidity, but upon calling three large broker dealers, I received three separate markets. One market maker bid 72 and offered at 85. Another was 70 bid at 80 offered, and a third was 70 at 77.

Unlike in the United States, with a wide variety of avenues to access liquidity, Europe is a smaller market with only a handful of large bulge bracket brokers, large investment banks, and broker dealers. Unless a large trader or institution in the United States has a relationship with a European market maker, it's unlikely someone will be able to buy at the bid and sell at the offer. In fact, that rarely happens. It's more likely that the U.S.-based directional trader will have to pay the offer and sell on the bid.

Directional traders are most likely to trade with a market maker rather than on an exchange. When directional traders ask for a price, market makers have to assess their risk on an individual trade basis, especially when a transaction is taking place ahead of a news event or other special situation. Because European options markets are generally thin, the market makers are aware that they won't be able to unload their positions and, therefore, must decide whether to hedge or take a position based on the firm's view of the stock.

Once the trade is executed, the market maker may end up wearing the long or short position resulting from buying or selling options. To offset that risk, market makers may hedge with a position in another calendar month or with underlying stock to reduce their delta exposure. Or market makers may use a comparable stock to hedge the sector exposure. For example, a market maker who is long Nokia volatility may sell Ericsson volatility so that the consolidated book is hedged within that sector.

One important factor to keep in mind is that because market makers are so well informed and amply capitalized, it is difficult to gain an edge when trading against them. Also, because of the time it takes for market makers to quote prices, be sure of the strategy you plan on implementing before you execute. Do not wait for the last minute of the trading day.

Convertible Arbitrageurs

A convertible arbitrageur (or *arb*) is generally a trader who supplies volatility. For review, a convertible arbitrage strategy is usually long bonds and short equity. However, by owning the convertible bond, the holder is effectively an owner of an option to convert the bond to stock, or basically a long-dated option. In order to both finance the bond purchase and hedge volatility, the bondholder usually sells short-dated volatility. As a rule of thumb, short-term volatility is usually higher than long-term volatility. However, this is not a hard-and-fast rule. At times, convertible arbs may find the credit default swap market a better hedge for their positions. In this instance, they would sell the long-dated option and buy a credit default swap.

This convertible arb activity does affect the options market. When convertible bonds are issued, all markets—corporate bond, equity, stock loan, credit default swap, and volatility—need to adjust to the new supply of paper. Because of the sheer size of convertible bond offerings, there is a period of price adjustments, usually a day or two.

Understanding how and when convertible arbs are active, the directional trader can take advantage of trading opportunities. As the convertible arbs sell front or short-dated volatility to finance the purchase of a convertible bond, there is a commensurate increase in the supply of volatility. This, in turn, puts pressure on both price and volatility, but only for a short period of time, providing a window for a directional trader to buy options before volatility returns to its normal levels.

Volatility Traders

Traders of volatility attempt to take positions when they see situations in which volatility is either over- or undervalued. Using quantitative models they screen the stock market universe for discrepancies, arbitraging a stock's implied volatility and its historic volatility. These traders (and their black-box proprietary trading programs) have a keen sense of where implied and historic volatility should be. As a result, it is difficult to gain an edge against them. They also position themselves in variance swaps, which arbitrage index volatility versus the volatility of the individual index constituents. While this does supply the market with volatility, prices are usually tight, making it difficult to capitalize on these opportunities. Market makers generally are the other side of volatility traders.

Overwriters

This group also supplies the market with volatility. It consists mainly of institutions that attempt to enhance returns by selling premiums on holdings to receive additional income. What typically happens with an over-writer is they are long stock and sell out-of-the money calls to collect pre-mium. They often sell to market makers who, in turn, are left long volatility (usually through calls) and then try to sell them at a profit before the option expires. Through this activity, overwriters are suppliers of volatility.

The overwriter sells the volatility (by being a seller of out-of-the money calls) to a market maker. Through that transaction, the market maker has those calls in inventory. Now, when I, as a directional trader, approach the market maker to buy calls, I am more likely to get a good price because the market maker is long calls and wants to sell. Only through calling various market makers will price discovery show who is long volatility and wants to make an attractive offer.

Directional Traders

These participants are trading the direction of the underlying stock or in-dex, using options as the vehicle for its inherent leverage and the ability to manage capital exposure through the premium at risk. Directional traders may be the best or worst informed on news, fundamentals, events, and special situations that influence a stock. In general, these traders are buy-ers of volatility.

Better-informed directional traders try to gather information that the market does not yet know, through their own valuations, industry con-tacts, upcoming events, and so forth, and then assess whether the option market prices are correct, given their expectations of how specific stocks or sectors will likely perform. Poorly informed traders either have low-quality information or they trade on emotion. These traders may buy op-tion premium only to have it erode over time. Or they implement positions poorly without reviewing pending events that could dramatically alter the volatility picture. (As one can imagine, market makers love these poorly informed players because they are a source of profit.)

Within the universe of directional traders are hedge funds, proprietary traders, banks, pension funds, and so forth. The group nature of this type of participant is difficult to determine, given the variation of investment style, philosophy, knowledge, and experience on the individual level.

TRADING VOLATILITY

When trading European options, what one is really speculating on is volatility and whether it will expand or contract, thus making an option more or less valuable. The rationale for buying or selling volatility is grounded in the directional trader's opinion about a particular stock. It may be based on an upcoming shareholder's meeting, earnings announcement, a road show, new product launch, or other event that would likely move the stock. In addition to having a particular outlook, the directional trader must also be convinced that the stock will move more than the amount that is already reflected in the price of the option without suffering too much from time decay. In other words, based on the directional trader's analysis of a particular issue and/or sector, the option would be undervalued in the case of buying options or overvalued in the case of selling.

When the directional trader approaches a market maker for a price of an option, the market maker must also analyze whether the option is overvalued or undervalued in light of current and future events and circumstances. The market maker does not want to end up selling an option for too low a price or buying for too high a price. Nor does the market maker want to get stuck with a position going into a potentially volatile event. Given that the entire transaction is over the counter and negotiated by two parties, the market maker may not have a price quote at the ready. Rather, the market maker may have to consult with the firm's analysts, look at the calendar of events that could affect the stock over the next several weeks, and so forth. Given the lack of liquidity of European options, the market maker also has to determine whether a special situation—such as an earnings release or a conference at which a company's management is speaking—will adversely impact the ability to unload a position ahead of that event. With all these dynamics in mind, including whether the market maker will try to hedge or hold a position on the books, bids and offers are quoted.

If the market maker thinks that the directional trader is right in the assessment that, for example, an option is undervalued, the bid/offer spread will likely be very wide. The wider spread will allow the market maker to do an offsetting transaction. Or, if the market maker does not want the exposure, there may be no offer to sell the option; the market maker remains bid only.

Let's walk through a hypothetical transaction using a stock such as Volkswagen. As a directional trader, I would focus on near-term events and whether the volatility of the options on the stock was currently overvalued or undervalued given what I believe will happen with volatility in the future. Both price direction and volatility are determining factors in whether the trade will be profitable. Once the reference price of the underlying stock is fixed, then the only remaining variable is volatility. Obtaining the best option price is a two-step transaction.

European options trade much like the foreign exchange market, in which the forward contracts are traded based on a known spot price and then the forward points are negotiated. With European options, the spot price, or delta, of the underlying stock is fixed through an outright transaction. The first step, therefore, is to trade the underlying options' delta-adjusted amount. Once that price is known, the delta (reflecting the underlying price of the stock) is locked in. Now, it's time to find a market maker who is quoting bid/offer prices on volatility that best fit the directional trader's needs. Once the transaction is completed, there is no need to worry about the impact of the stock price, as it is fixed in the transaction. The directional trader stands to make or lose money only as the premium on the option (reflecting the volatility) expands or contracts.

Using our Volkswagen example, let's say I analyze various risk/reward structures, and I have determined the best fit using historical returns and implied volatility. (See Figures 12.1 and 12.2).

I want to be a buyer of 100,000 shares of Volkswagen February call options with a strike price of 51 euros a share (Feb 51 call options). The delta at this time is 41. The first thing I would have to do is buy the Volkswagen stock outright, in this case 41,000 shares, which would lock in the spot price (or delta) of the stock. These shares will later be exchanged with an option market maker or broker dealer for call options at the

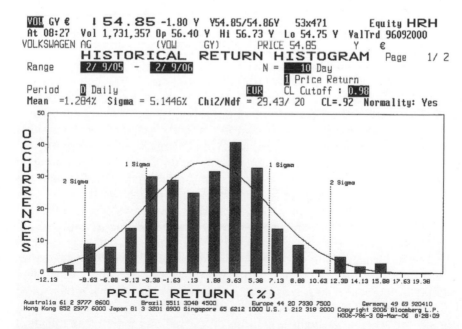

FIGURE 12.1 Historical Return Histogram for Volkswagen (*Source:* © 2006 Bloomberg L.P. All rights reserved. Reprinted with permission.)

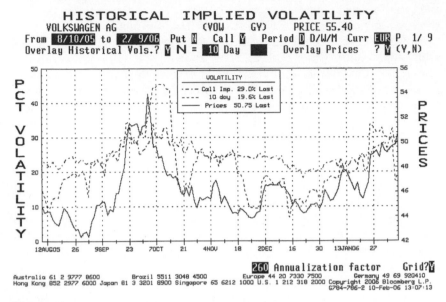

agreed-on price. With the price of the stock locked in through this transaction, it does not matter now if Volkswagen shares rise or fall.

The second step is to obtain the best volatility of the call option. I would call a select number of brokers for a market on the call options. If the prices quoted are satisfactory, as a buyer I would commit to buying 100,000 shares of Volkswagen call options. Now that I have bought the call options, I anticipate that both volatility and the price of the underlying stock will increase, which in turn will make my position more profitable.

As Figure 12.3 shows, within 24 hours of initiating this trade, implied volatility moved 14 percentage points, increasing more than 50 percent since the trade was initiated—showing that it pays to be early.

Here's another example of option trading, but with a slightly different strategy. With the German retailing environment seeming to improve, going long a retailing stock seemed like a good theme. I had bought stock in Metro, a German retailer, with good fundamentals. I looked at the historical return over a 20-day period within the past year. Probability was calculated to be about a 66 percent chance the stock could move either up or down 5 percent. In the middle of February, Metro's trading pattern suggested to me that it might break out of its trading range to the upside. I could stay long the stock if it did break out, but in addition to the long stock position I bought the March 44 call option for .50 with the notional

<HELP> for explanation, <MENU> for similar functions.   P110 Equity **CALL**

CALL SUMMARY PAGE

VOW GY   VOLKSWAGEN AG   06:13   Hedge:M   Hit 99 <go> for option model defaults

50.50 +.82 Bid 50.50 Ask 50.53   Days 8 Fin Rate 2.50 Volat: 23.97

| € E Euro | LAST TRADE INFO | | | IMPL.VOLAT | | HEDGE | | | *THEORETICAL |
VOW Feb 06	Bid	Ask	Last Chnge	Bid	Ask	Del	Gam	Vega	Price Diff
1) 2 C40	9.93	10.92	9.71 unch	b.int	122.6	1000*			10.52 +.10
2) 2 C41	8.98	9.87	8.72 unch	b.int	108.5	1000*			9.52 +.10
3) 2 C42	8.08	8.88	7.72 unch	b.int	99.67	1000*			8.52 +.04
4) 2 C43	7.18	7.89	6.72 unch	b.int	90.80	991	007		7.52 -.01
5) 2 C44	6.23	6.85	5.73 unch	b.int	78.42	987	011		6.52 -.02
6) 2 C45	5.24	5.72	4.74 unch	b.int	59.59	999*	001*		5.53 +.05
7) 2 C46	4.40	4.62	3.78 unch	b.int	42.38	996*	007*		4.53 +.02
8) 2 C47	3.46	3.67	2.82 unch	b.int	38.71	957	042	.01	3.54 -.02
9) 2 C48	2.55	2.71	1.98 unch	19.53	32.68	898	086	.01	2.59 -.04
10) 2 C49	1.72	1.83	1.56 +.31	23.86	28.88	787	145	.02	1.72 -.05
11) 2 C50	1.05	1.12	1.00 +.30	25.20	27.61	612	192	.03	1.01 -.07
12) 2 C51	.54	.60	.51 +.14	24.80	26.84	413	199	.03	.52 -.05
13) 2 C52	.23	.29	.21 +.01	24.35	26.94	234	158	.02	.22 -.04
14) 2 C54	.03	.09	.05 unch	25.02	31.60	064	058	.01	.02 -.04
15) 2 C56			.01 unch	b.int	b.int	002*	004*		.00

<HELP> for explanation, <MENU> for similar functions.   P110 Equity **CALL**

CALL SUMMARY PAGE

VOW GY   VOLKSWAGEN AG   06:05   Hedge:M   Hit 99 <go> for option model defaults

51.63 +1.0 Bid 51.61 Ask 51.63   Days 7 Fin Rate 2.51 Volat: 24.05

| € E Euro | LAST TRADE INFO | | | IMPL.VOLAT | | HEDGE | | | *THEORETICAL |
VOW Feb 06	Bid	Ask	Last Chnge	Bid	Ask	Del	Gam	Vega	Price Diff
1) 2 C40	11.18	12.29	10.64 unch	b.int	159.4	971	009		11.65 -.09
2) 2 C41	10.22	11.24	9.64 unch	b.int	144.3	970	010	.01	10.65 -.08
3) 2 C42	9.23	10.08	8.65 unch	b.int	121.1	997	003		9.65 unch
4) 2 C43	8.38	9.04	7.65 unch	b.int	107.7	971	013		8.65 -.06
5) 2 C44	7.58	7.72	6.66 unch	b.int	64.83	1000*			7.65 unch
6) 2 C45	6.60	6.73	5.67 unch	b.int	58.72	989	009		6.65 -.01
7) 2 C46	5.63	5.74	4.70 unch	b.int	52.26	974	019		5.65 -.03
8) 2 C47	4.67	4.77	3.75 unch	32.77	47.53	949	035	.01	4.65 -.07
9) 2 C48	3.74	3.84	3.31 +.46	36.39	44.66	904	057	.01	3.66 -.13
10) 2 C49	2.87	2.96	2.58 +.56	37.25	42.25	834	086	.02	2.70 -.22
11) 2 C50	2.11	2.18	1.93 +.60	38.23	41.15	730	115	.02	1.81 -.34
12) 2 C51	1.46	1.51	1.50 +.68	38.31	40.10	602	136	.03	1.07 -.42
13) 2 C52	.92	.98	.96 +.48	37.32	39.40	462	143	.03	.54 -.41
14) 2 C54	.29	.36	.30 +.13	36.53	39.86	212	105	.02	.08 -.25
15) 2 C56			.10 +.01	b.int	b.int	009*	014*		.01

FIGURE 12.3 Quote Screen Showing Gain in Implied Volatility for Volkswagen Call Options (*Source:* © 2006 Bloomberg L.P. All rights reserved. Reprinted with permission.)

amount equal to the long position. (See Figure 12.4.) The strategy employed here was stock substitution.

As the stock traded at the strike of 44, I sold half my stock, creating a delta-neutral position on the call. At the price of 45, I sold the second half, leaving me my original long position through call exposure only (see Figure 12.5). Effectively, even though momentum indicators such as RSI show Metro to be overbought, I will continue to participate in the upside potential of the shares based on the larger theme. If Metro drops below the 44 strike of the call, I can revisit buying back my long sale of stock. By selling stock at an average of 44.5, I have taken out the cost of the call option and limited my downside exposure.

In addition to buying options on a single stock, directional traders can also buy options on European indexes, such as the German stock index the DAX, France's CAC, or the United Kingdom's FTSE. The corollary for making such a trade in the United States would be to buy calls on the Standard & Poor's 500 Index (S&P 500). In the U.S. market, this can be as simple as getting a quote from the Chicago Board Options Exchange (CBOE), where S&P Index options trade, or calling a broker and finding out the current bid and ask, which will no doubt be a narrow spread. Thanks to the liquidity and price transparency of the exchange-traded

<HELP> for explanation.   P110 Equity **CALL**

CALL SUMMARY PAGE

MEO GY   METRO AG   09:38   Hedge:N
    42.15 -.58 Bid 42.09 Ask 42.10   Days 31 Fin Rate 2.52 Volat: 20.85

		LAST TRADE INFO			IMPL.VOLAT		HEDGE			*THEORETICAL	
MEO Mar 06	Bid	Ask	Last	Chnge	Bid	Ask	Del	Gam	Vega	Price	Diff
1) 3 C30	11.34	13.04	12.74	unch	b.int	109.9	1000*			12.21	+.02
2) 3 C32	9.50	10.92	10.75	unch	b.int	89.46	1000*			10.22	+.01
3) 3 C34	7.77	8.59	8.77	unch	b.int	61.26	1000*			8.22	+.04
4) 3 C35	6.83	7.54	7.78	unch	b.int	52.70	999*	001*		7.23	+.04
5) 3 C36	6.11	6.31	6.79	unch	b.int	33.64	996*	005*		6.23	+.02
6) 3 C37	5.14	5.34	5.82	unch	b.int	30.84	988	012		5.24	unch
7) 3 C38	4.19	4.37	4.86	unch	b.int	27.41	956	035	.01	4.27	-.01
8) 3 C39	3.29	3.45	3.94	unch	17.78	25.44	898	066	.02	3.34	-.03
9) 3 C40	2.46	2.60	3.05	unch	19.96	24.17	810	100	.03	2.49	-.04
10) 3 C41	1.74	1.86	2.24	unch	20.73	23.50	689	130	.04	1.75	-.05
11) 3 C42	1.16	1.25	1.22	-.33	21.17	23.02	548	146	.05	1.14	-.06
12) 3 C43	.72	.80	1.01	unch	21.34	23.02	404	142	.05	.70	-.06
13) 3 C44	.42	.50	.64	unch	21.53	23.47	278	121	.04	.39	-.07
14) 3 C45	.24	.31	.40	unch	22.04	24.19	183	093	.03	.20	-.07
15) 3 C46	.14	.20	.25	unch	22.87	25.32	120	067	.03	.10	-.07
16) 3 C47	.08	.17	.18	unch	23.62	28.33	087	049	.02	.04	-.08
17) 3 C48	.05	.20	.12	unch	24.76	33.66	078	040	.02	.02	-.11
18) 3 C50	.01	.16	.07	unch	24.48	39.06	050	025	.01	.00	-.08

Australia 61 2 9777 8600   Brazil 5511 3048 4500   Europe 44 20 7330 7500   Germany 49 69 920410
Hong Kong 852 2977 6000 Japan 81 3 3201 8900 Singapore 65 6212 1000 U.S. 1 212 318 2000 Copyright 2006 Bloomberg L.P.
G784-786-3 14-Feb-06 9:38:18

FIGURE 12.4 Metro Call Option Quote Screen(*Source:* © 2006 Bloomberg L.P. All rights reserved. Reprinted with permission.)

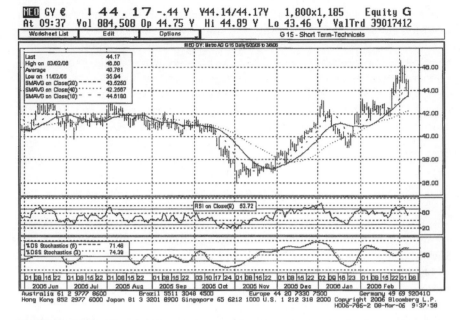

FIGURE 12.5 Chart Showing Metro Call Option Performance (*Source:* © 2006 Bloomberg L.P. All rights reserved. Reprinted with permission.)

S&P Index options, the broker knows the price to quote you and the price at which he is likely to get filled on the floor of the exchange.

In Europe, once again, the game is played very differently. Even with index options, when it comes to larger institutional quantities, the trades are negotiated with a market maker. The first step would be to negotiate a spot trade to establish the delta. Since there is no real depth for institutional trades, the broker dealer would have to execute a DAX futures trade first to establish the delta on behalf of the customer. Then, as a second step, the broker and the customer would negotiate the volatility for the call option on the DAX futures.

Here is the language that would be used to negotiate such a transaction. The directional trader would call a large bulge bracket investment bank or broker dealer and inquire about DAX call options. The market maker would then respond with the current price and conditions for such a trade. For example, a market maker might say, "My market for February DAX 5800 calls is 10 at 11, but only if my trader executes his delta at this reference price." At this point the directional trader has two options. A trader who is anxious and needs to transact a large volume may request prices outside the parameters of the current market, just to get the trade done. The trader would ask the market maker what their risk price is. This risk price would shift delta exposure to the market maker, but resulting in a wider bid/offer for the option. A trader who can afford to be patient, however, can trade at the current market in increments, in effect spoon-feeding the market in smaller sizes. Any trader who has to "pay up" because of impatience usually has a very good reason.

Heading into the end of February, momentum indicators seemed to indicate we had moved too far too fast. The near-term trigger for a pullback would be March 1 as asset managers typically buy stock at the beginning of each month to keep asset allocations in balance between cash and stock. When analyzing historical volatility for the Euro Stoxx index (see Figure 12.6), it seemed fairly valued between 14 and 15, neither cheap nor rich. Therefore, buying put options was purely a directional opinion on price of the index.

I bought March 3700 puts on both Feb 27 and Feb 28, ahead of March 1 (see Figure 12.7). On March 3, European markets did correct slightly. The RSI moved from 70 to 49, so I sold half my put position into the sell-off of the index. As I had taken the cost out of the put position, I let the balance run through the release of the U.S. February monthly employment data at the end of that week.

To examine this trade more closely, the reason I entered the trade

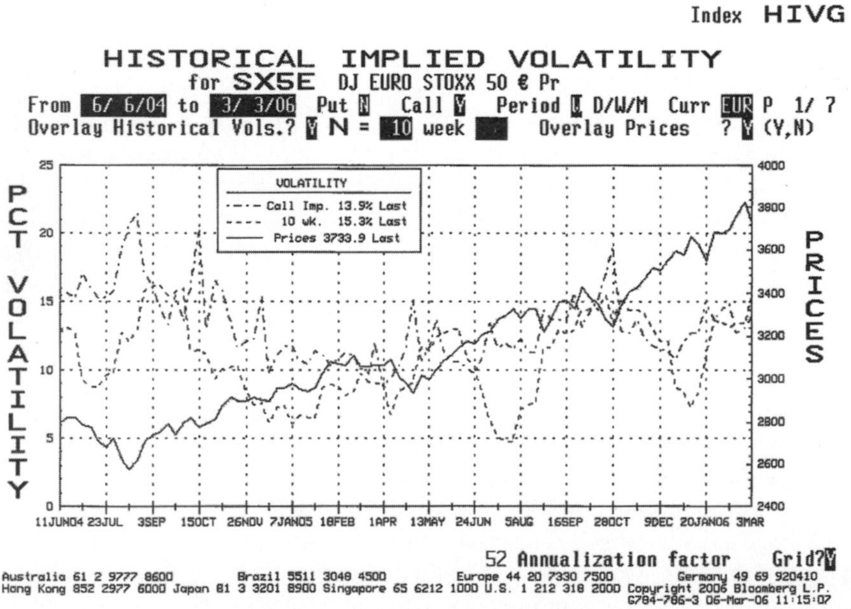

FIGURE 12.6 Historical Volatility for the Euro Stoxx Index (*Source:* © 2006 Bloomberg L.P. All rights reserved. Reprinted with permission.)

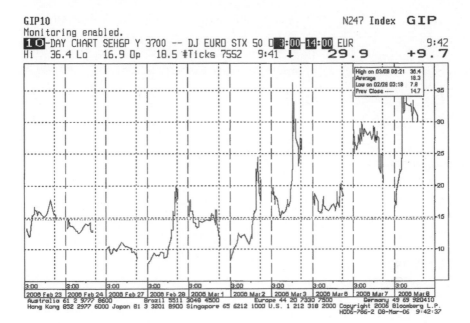

FIGURE 12.7 Graph of Euro Stoxx Intraday Call Prices (*Source:* © 2006 Bloomberg L.P. All rights reserved. Reprinted with permission.)

over two days was because of a 10 percent differential between the bids and offers at the time (see Figure 12.7). By being patient, I was trying to enter the trade ahead of the catalyst. As Figure 12.8 shows, momentum indicators revealed that the index was overbought, confirming the rationale for making the trade.

As these examples illustrate, because the European market is less competitive than the U.S. market, relationships are all the more important. If someone were to call up a European market maker out of the blue, the conversation would probably not result in an instantaneous quotation of prices. The market maker doesn't know what type of customer the person is, how much information they might have, or whether the person has an edge on news or fundamentals. In other words, the market maker needs to know who is on the other side of the trade before quoting a price. Once a relationship has been established, and the market maker knows there is nothing nefarious about the pricing request, then the bid/offer conversation is far more straightforward. The market maker knows that when someone is asking for a quote, that individual is looking to buy or sell an option and not just trying to take advantage of an uninformed trader.

Relationships, of course, are built over time. When a U.S. trader or

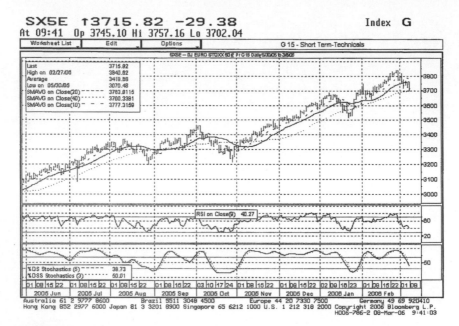

FIGURE 12.8 Momentum Indicators on Euro Stoxx Daily Chart (*Source:* © 2006 Bloomberg L.P. All rights reserved. Reprinted with permission.)

investor is entering the European market, an introduction is needed. If someone is looking to establish a relationship in Europe, it's best to have a referral from or through an existing U.S. relationship.

ADVANTAGES OF TRADING EUROPEAN OPTIONS

Despite what may look like disadvantages of trading in Europe, including the rituals of negotiating off-exchange transactions and the frictional points along the way that increase the costs of trading, there are distinct advantages in this market. The obvious one is that European exposure provides diversification. A more subtle reason stems from the off-exchange nature of trading European options. Because the market makers and other participants are used to trading over-the-counter products, the need to negotiate a customized product is not a barrier to doing business. In fact, large bulge bracket investment banks and broker dealers are well-versed and experienced in quoting customized options and derivatives.

Thus, a directional trader can have a plain vanilla option on a European stock or index that looks much like its U.S. exchange-traded counterpart. A highly customized option transaction can be negotiated, such as an option on stocks that don't have listed options. The basis for this flexibility is European traders are more familiar with new products and they are more focused on volatility than price. This also means that European traders are more aware of near-term triggers and events that will likely result in increased or decreased volatility. Granted, it's difficult to gain an advantage against a market maker with the large capitalization, analyst resources, and the breadth of market activity of a large investment bank or brokerage. However, a trader who sees the picture from the volatility perspective will be able to find someone to quote bids and offers on options. The question isn't whether the trader will be able to get a price, but rather what the price will end up being.

Furthermore, the European mentality in the marketplace reflects an indifference to whether a customer is a buyer or a seller. Since the market maker's job is to provide liquidity, these European players want to make money on making a market within the bid/offer spread. Because the market is thin, these market makers are also more accustomed to taking on risk. A U.S. market maker, by contrast, is typically more concerned about the direction of the market, whether the counterparty was a buyer or a seller, and how quickly an order could be executed and hedged with an offsetting position. In other words, the U.S. market maker is trying to lay off that risk as quickly as possible.

The European market maker, however, is willing to hold a position, at least for a short time, knowing that it will take longer to hedge or offset it. As a result, when someone approaches a European market maker with a larger size trade to execute than normal, the bid/offer spread will reflect the market maker's need to accommodate the liquidity of the trade. It will no doubt cost more to buy a large number of options, but the reason is that the market maker is taking on more risk by holding the other side of that position.

HOW TO TRADE EUROPE

When the directional trader implements a trading strategy, it's essential to have an exit strategy already in place for both timing and price. While this is a truism of trading in any market, it's even more important in Europe where the options market is not as liquid as in the U.S. The basic questions that the directional trader must continually be asking are: Why am I placing this trade, where do I think the market is going, what is the timing, and what is the price target? As part of the exit strategy—and assuming that all goes according to plan—the trader must know whether he wants to unwind the option, sell a different option, or delta hedge with underlying stock. A trader may also opt to close one position as the option expires and initiate a new one, going through the same exercise of establishing the delta and then negotiating the volatility. A trader who has transactions with two different market makers must go through cross-settlement to exit both positions.

Establishing positions with more than one market maker has strategic advantages. Consider the following scenario. As a directional trader, you typically buy calls. Thus, a market maker becomes accustomed to your activity as a call buyer. If you trade with more than one market maker, however, there may be a time when you are going back to a broker from whom you've typically bought calls, only this time you are a seller to take a profit or unwind a position. When you ask for the market maker's two-way price, he may be better bid than offered, thinking that as usual you are a buyer. Referring back to the Volkswagen trade, once volatility has exploded close to the earnings release, you would need to decide whether the more favorable risk/reward would be to hedge volatility by selling a higher call, shorting stock to hedge delta, or unwinding the option.

Let's say you unwind the Volkswagen 51 call and the screen market is 1.46 at 1.51. Now it's time to play this like a poker game. The market maker is someone from whom you've usually bought options. But this time when you are calling, you are a seller. However, the market maker assumes you are a buyer—although you haven't said anything to mislead him, because you have only asked for a market in the option. The market maker gives you a bid of 1.5 and, assuming you are a buyer, 1.65 offered. This time, however, you hit him on the 1.5 bid to sell your options, essentially executing your trade in the middle of the screen spread at a more favorable price—or at least not at the price he was expecting. By selling the call, you have now sold higher volatility than you bought. You have also accepted your delta back, so you are now long stock, which is also currently higher with the move in price to a delta of 60—or 60,000 shares. Since the volatility increased ahead of the event playing out, you now need to determine your risk appetite into numbers and trade accordingly.

As with any option, these instruments are used as a substitute for stock. Options offer the inherent advantages of leverage (one option contract is equivalent to some multiple of shares) and lower capital at risk. When buying a call option, all the capital that is at risk is the premium paid. Beyond these advantages, European options offer further incentives for trading because these instruments can be customized. A trader can specify, for example, an American-style option that can be exercised at any time, or a European-style option that trades at a slightly lower premium, which can only be exercised at expiration.

Trading European options also carries advantages for stocks that are dual listed in the United States as American Depositary Receipts (ADRs) and as shares in a local market. Examples of dual listed stocks are Nokia,

Vodafone, and Ericsson. When dealing in these issues, make sure you are trading the best market for what you are looking to execute. There may be times when the Nokia ADR has better pricing than the Nokia ordinary share traded in Finland. Depending on market discrepancies, currency fluctuations, or other factors, it may be better to buy Nokia ADRs here versus Nokia options in Finland.

To find the best price, traders also have to take into account volatility differences. For example, coming into an event that is likely to move a stock, I've taken advantage of the fact that the ADRs have not yet reflected the volatility that is already present in the locally traded shares, and as a result managed to buy cheaper volatility in the United States. There isn't a pure arbitrage between ADRs and local markets, but you'll get a better execution by looking at all markets.

NEW TRENDS IN EUROPEAN DERIVATIVES

The customization that is possible with European options allows a segue into a new trend in European derivatives, which I believe will create exciting opportunities for directional traders and speculators. Trading of equity baskets has emerged in Europe and is being offered by a few large banks and brokerage firms. These new equity baskets can be traded as an exchange-traded fund (ETF), which behaves like a stock with your account debited if you sell short and credited if you are long. Or the equity baskets can be traded like a swap, which makes them more like futures. The equity baskets are useful in leveraging, hedging, and substitution for shares. They are also a one-delta product, meaning they move tick-for-tick with the underlying shares.

Equity baskets are not listed on any exchange; market markers are willing to customize them. This is unlike ETFs such as the QQQQ, which tracks the NASDAQ-100; SPDRs (Spiders), which track the S&P 500; and DIA (Diamonds), which tracks the Dow. For example, you could buy an equity basket to provide exposure to a certain sector, such as European telecom stocks. Equity baskets have equal weighting among the shares, which is far superior for portfolio correlation than buying an existing index such as the DJ Telecom Index that is very heavily weighted toward Vodafone and Telefonica. In fact, those two shares represent about 40 percent of the index, as of this writing. The equal weighting of the equity baskets increases their appeal as hedging instruments, as well as for a means of providing exposure to a certain sector.

The equity baskets trade on the basis point spread of the net asset value (NAV) of these baskets. Liquidity is predetermined by the bank or broker offering the basket. For example, let's assume a trader wants to be long a pan-European telecom basket. Pulling up a screen showing a broker's offerings, the trader can see the NAV of the basket. The trader then contacts the broker and references the basket she wants to trade. A trader doesn't need to indicate whether she is a buyer or a seller, but may simply ask the broker for the last price on the telecom basket. Based on the current NAV of that basket, the broker will quote a bid and an offer, depending on the size of the trade, which might range from $5 million to $25 million. Although most of these products are not fungible between brokers—they can only be traded with one particular broker or investment bank—they do provide great liquidity and exposure within a specific sector or subsector.

For the directional trader, the appeal of the equity baskets is clear, but these new products do beg the question: Why would a broker decide to make a market in all these baskets, given the increase in its capital commitment? The reason goes back to the nature of derivatives trading in Europe. When a directional trader buys or sells these baskets, the market maker by default becomes long or short these stocks. When this happens, the market maker has a few choices. He can keep the trade on his own book and hope to reduce his exposure in time at a profit, or he can internalize the flow within the brokerage firm. To explain, assume that I am a seller of the telecom basket to the broker. The broker, by default, is long that basket, which breaks down to specific constituent stocks. The broker can be long those stocks and assume the risk, or the brokerage firm can market each of those individual shares to other customers who want to trade these issues. Now consider that the broker may make 10 basis points on the bid/offer for the basket, 20 basis points on commission, and then make additional basis points on the trading of the shares. It's a profitable enterprise for the broker.

For the directional trader, the equity baskets provide a good opportunity to gain exposure across a sector or subsector in advance of news or an event that may affect more than one stock, or one stock more than another within a particular sector or subsector. For example, let's assume a trader sees a macro event that is likely to influence a subsector: in this instance, Italian banks. The hypothetical event is that the Bank of Italy is expected to lay off a governor who has been unpopular. Because of this expected development, the trader wants to have long exposure to Italian banks. Instead of executing a dozen different orders to buy Italian bank stocks, the trader gains instant exposure by buying a basket. Or a trader may have long exposure in the oil service sector. However, the trader fears that a pending Department of Energy inventory report will be negative. Rather than sell stocks, the trader might decide to short the oil services basket to provide a hedge. Once that fear passes, the hedge can be covered, and the trader can retain oil service exposure.

Another strategy using the equity baskets (see Figure 12.9) would be

Backpage P122 **Index** **GSSR**

200<Go> to view in Launchpad

12:56 **GS Europe Subsector Baskets** PAGE 1 / 5

	Description	Ticker	Bid	Last	Ask	Size	% Chg	Time
1)	GS BANK IRELAN	GSSBBKID	1104.93	1107.70	1110.46	5000	0.09	11:24
2)	GS BANK ITALY	GSSBBKIM	1133.03	1134.17	1135.30	5000	-1.05	11:24
3)	GS BANK IT POP	GSSBBKIP	1227.11	1230.19	1233.27	2000	-1.99	11:25
4)	GS BANK NORDIC	GSSBBKNO	1123.21	1124.94	1126.58	10000	0.18	9:55
5)	GS BANK UK-GBP	GSSBBKUK	1129.75	1130.60	1131.45	2500	0.09	11:24
6)	GS SOFTWARE	GSSBSFTW	1026.38	1027.92	1029.46	5000	-0.10	11:25
7)	GS SEMI	GSSBSEMI	1096.96	1098.06	1099.15	5000	-1.17	11:25
8)	GS MED TECH	GSSBMEDT	1098.02	1099.67	1101.32	5000	0.36	11:25
9)	GS BIOTECH	GSSBBIOT	1056.25	1059.43	1062.61	5000	0.57	11:25
10)	GS PHARMA	GSSBPHAR	1033.73	1034.24	1034.76	10000	-0.77	11:25
11)	GS OIL SERVICE	GSSBOILS	1288.32	1290.26	1292.19	5000	-0.62	9:55
12)	GS ITG OIL GAS	GSSBOILI	1077.46	1078.00	1078.54	10000	-1.01	11:25
13)	GS REAL ESTATE	GSSBREAL	1098.58	1100.23	1101.88	5000	1.01	11:25
14)	GS TELCO MEZZO	GSSBTELM	1052.03	1053.61	1055.19	5000	-1.31	11:25
15)	GS TELCO WIREL	GSSBTELW	1001.21	1002.71	1004.22	5000	0.35	11:25
16)	GS MEDIA AGENT	GSSBMEAG	1076.70	1078.31	1079.93	5000	-1.01	11:25
17)	GS AERO&DEF	GSSBAERO	1094.57	1095.66	1096.76	5000	-0.18	11:25
18)	GS UK ENGINEER	GSSBUKEN	1183.71	1186.67	1189.64	2500	-0.08	11:24
19)	GS MACHINERY	GSSBMACH	1197.73	1200.13	1202.53	5000	-0.08	11:25
20)	GS TRANS-INFRA	GSSBTINF	1123.90	1126.15	1128.40	5000	-0.44	11:25

Australia 61 2 9777 8600 Brazil 5511 3048 4500 Europe 44 20 7330 7500 Germany 49 69 920410
Hong Kong 852 2977 6000 Japan 81 3 3201 8900 Singapore 65 6212 1000 U.S. 1 212 318 2000
G784-786-2 10-Feb-06 12:56:54

Page P122 **Index** **GSSR**

200<Go> to view in Launchpad

12:57 **GS Europe Subsector Baskets** PAGE 2 / 5

	Description	Ticker	Bid	Last	Ask	Size	% Chg	Time
1)	GS PAPER &FORE	GSSBPAPE	1160.11	1161.85	1163.59	5000	0.00	11:25
2)	GS LUX GOODS	GSSBLUXG	1110.28	1111.94	1113.61	5000	0.63	11:25
3)	GS TOBACCO	GSSBTOBA	1043.09	1044.14	1045.18	5000	0.68	11:25
4)	GS UK HOMEBUIL	GSSBUKHO	1238.18	1239.42	1240.66	2500	-0.40	11:25
5)	GS GEN RET HAR	GSSBGRHL	1084.87	1087.04	1089.21	5000	1.59	11:25
6)	GS GEN RET SOF	GSSBGRSL	1116.34	1118.58	1120.82	5000	-0.09	11:25
7)	GS TRANS AIR	GSSBTRAA	1155.01	1157.32	1159.63	5000	-0.77	11:25
8)	GS TRAN RD &RR	GSSBTRAR	1100.81	1103.57	1106.33	5000	1.01	11:25
9)	GS MINING(GBP)	GSSBMINE	1282.00	1284.57	1287.14	2500	-2.58	11:25
10)	GS STEEL	GSSBSTEL	1333.91	1336.58	1339.26	2500	-1.62	11:25
11)	GS BEVERAGES	GSSBBEVS	1042.96	1044.52	1046.09	5000	0.10	11:25
12)	GS FOOD	GSSBFOOP	1098.04	1099.14	1100.24	5000	0.09	11:25
13)	GS AUTOS	GSSBAUTO	1108.75	1109.31	1109.86	10000	2.97	11:25
14)	GS AUTO COMPTS	GSSBAUCO	1173.76	1174.94	1176.11	5000	0.77	11:25
15)	GS UTIL ELEC	GSSBUTIE	1134.54	1135.68	1136.82	10000	0.09	11:24
16)	GS UTIL GAS	GSSBUTIG	1006.46	1007.47	1008.48	5000	-0.30	11:25
17)	GS SEK ENGINE	GSSBSWEN	1111.58	1113.25	1114.92	50000	-1.59	11:14
18)	GS FOOD RETAIL	GSSBFORE	1075.58	1076.66	1077.73	5000	-0.09	11:20
19)	GS CHEMHYBRID	GSSBCHYB	1130.44	1131.00	1131.57	5000	0.62	11:24
20)	GS INDUS GASES	GSSBCGAS	1181.63	1182.23	1182.82	5000	-0.34	11:25

Australia 61 2 9777 8600 Brazil 5511 3048 4500 Europe 44 20 7330 7500 Germany 49 69 920410
Hong Kong 852 2977 6000 Japan 81 3 3201 8900 Singapore 65 6212 1000 U.S. 1 212 318 2000
G784-786-2 10-Feb-06 12:57:13

FIGURE 12.9 Equity Basket Screen Shot (*Source:* © 2006 Bloomberg L.P. All rights reserved. Reprinted with permission.)

to acquire or hedge against exposure that runs along a certain theme: for example, German stocks, or mid-cap high-beta stocks. If someone is a growth manager in Europe and is worried about an event that could change the landscape for European investment—such as the German election in 2005—one way to reduce risk without the manager needing to eliminate the names in his portfolio would be to establish a short position in equity baskets as a hedge.

SUMMARY

Equity baskets are the latest in the customizable derivatives being traded in the European market. Over time, I believe these equity baskets will proliferate and trade more frequently. They also reflect the nature of derivative trading in Europe, especially that of options. While European options lack the liquidity and price transparency of their U.S. exchange-traded counterparts, they do offer unique opportunities for the professional trader or investor who is focused on volatility.

These transactions are more complex and involve negotiating with a broker to determine the price at which a particular trade will be executed. But with time and experience, a U.S.-based directional trader can establish relationships with European brokers and banks to facilitate these transactions. Just because a market is complex doesn't mean it should not be traded. Rather, the complexity needs to be studied and understood, and the inherent opportunities capitalized on.

CHAPTER 13

Options Applications to Pairs Trading

Dennis Leontyev

In their search for increased stability, and accepting that the triple-digit gains of the Internet boom are gone, many investors have turned to fixed income securities, cash instruments, and to increasingly popular market-neutral strategies. One specific market-neutral strategy, which has not been widely publicized but has endured for years as a successful approach among many institutional money managers and hedge fund experts, is explored in this chapter. The strategy is called *pairs trading*. Although this strategy can be applied to stocks, bonds, currencies, futures, or to any securities or markets that exhibit the characteristics that are discussed here, the focus of this discussion is primarily on equities to illustrate, and then on options.

The first consideration is the nature of market-neutral investing. This establishes the framework to discuss pairs trading. Once this foundation is in place, the addition of options theory to the strategy will be both less complex and more accessible to the reader. It is important to note that the discussion in each of these three sections is not meant to be exhaustive on its respective subject; countless books have been written on market neutrality, pairs trading, and options theory.* The goal of each section is to

---

*One book that is highly recommended as a more exhaustive study on this topic, and which is referred to briefly in this chapter, is *The Handbook of Pairs Trading* (Hoboken, NJ: John Wiley & Sons, 2006), written by my colleague Douglas Ehrman. In it he goes into a detailed, step-by-step discussion of these theories, which will give those interested in a greater understanding of this strategy a solid foundation.

provide the reader with the minimum context necessary to understand the overriding focus of the strategy discussion.

MARKET NEUTRALITY

The term *market-neutral* can be applied to a wide range of investment products and has become an increasingly popular label in recent years, as investors have sought shelter from the vagaries of market fluctuations. It is often mistakenly equated with *risk-free*. This misconception has been narrowly focused on in the marketing of these types of products, often applying the label to anything than could be considered, even loosely, to reduce market exposure or systematic risk. In spite of this confusion, market neutrality is a powerful investment tool.

It will be useful at this point to provide a formal definition of market neutrality that can be applied to all market-neutral strategies:

A market-neutral strategy derives its returns from the relationship between the performance of its long positions and the performance of its short positions, regardless of whether this relationship functions on the security or portfolio level.

A portfolio's performance is driven by relative performance rather than by absolute performance, as is the case in traditional long-only portfolios; a trader is not concerned with the performance of the individual securities, but rather with performance relationships. The return on a market-neutral portfolio is a function of the return differential between the positions that are held long and those that are held short. This relationship may be between a long and a short portfolio, each consisting of a large number of securities, or may be between two individual securities, as is the case with pairs trading. As the market rises, the independent value of both the long and short securities appreciates, so the overall portfolio value remains constant. Similarly, if the market declines, both the long and short securities will decline in value. If the change in value of the long positions equals that of the short positions, the value added from equity selection will be zero, and the investor will earn close to the prevailing risk-free rate. The trader's objective, however, is to design a portfolio in which the long portfolio outperforms the short portfolio so that a profit may be earned.

When following a traditional long-only strategy, a trader is limited by the client-specified benchmark, and cannot maintain short positions. This long-only constraint reduces the trader's ability to efficiently utilize his forecasts of the relative attractiveness of all the securities in his investment universe. Suppose, for example, that a trader expects a large performance differential between two stocks in the same industry—the first is expected to have a higher-than-average return and the second to have a lower-than-average return. In a traditional strategy, the trader would incorporate this information by buying the stock with the higher expected alpha. However, he could not effectively utilize the information about the stock with the lower expected alpha. In a market-neutral strategy, the trader can take both a long position in a high alpha security and a short position in a low alpha security, thereby using all the available information. This ability to transfer this information to the portfolio enhances the return for a given level of risk. Simply put, the ability to use more information translates into a higher information ratio for market-neutral strategies.

THE HISTORY OF PAIRS TRADING

Before continuing the investigation into pairs trading, putting the strategy into a historical context may be of some interest. Pairs trading and market-neutral strategies are not new. They have been around in one form or another since the beginning of listed markets and have been studied and used by some of history's most notable traders. Prior to the hedge fund boom, these strategies were found folded into the portfolios of high-net-worth individuals and institutional traders who had the ability and resources needed to make them work. They were rarely differentiated by their specific characteristics, but rather represented collections of trades within a larger framework. The explosive growth of the hedge fund industry, however, has both brought these strategies to the mainstream and provided a vehicle by which their efficacy could be understood.

Jesse Livermore, perhaps the most famous trader of all time, is considered to have been the first pairs trader and, in fact, used certain principles of pairs trading in all of his analysis:

> *Tandem Trading, the use of sister stocks, was one of the great secrets of Livermore's trading techniques and remains just as valid today as it did in years gone by. This technique is an essential element in both Top Down Trading and in the maintenance of the trade after it has been completed. Livermore never looked at a single stock in a vacuum—rather, he looked at the two top stocks in an Industry Group and did his analysis on both stocks.**

---

*From *Trade Like Jesse Livermore*, by Richard Smitten (Hoboken, NJ: John Wiley & Sons, 2004), pp. 42–43.

In this explanation of Livermore's trading style, monitoring *sister stocks*, or two similar stocks in the same industry, was done to help confirm the analysis of either. Livermore traded under the assumption that trends within an industry would hold for the few largest issues within that industry; if he determined that the two largest stocks within an industry were moving in tandem, he was comfortable deciding that a legitimate trend had been identified. Within this context, he was using tandem trading to construct directional trades that tended to be longer-term. Livermore was famous for his ability to spot a long-term trend and ride it for significant profits.

Over the course of hundreds or thousands of tandem trades, it is not difficult to see how Livermore would have developed a feel for the regular fluctuations that occur between pairs of stocks. While primarily interested in the study of long-term trends, the inclusion of sister stock considerations in his analysis led to Livermore's reputation as the original pairs trader. If we accept this as the origin of pairs trading, the strategy on which the remainder of this discussion focuses has roughly 100 years of history upon which to build. While the tools and technology that support the strategy have advanced immeasurably in that period, the principles at the core of the theory have, in fact, changed very little.

MARKET NEUTRALITY IN PAIRS TRADING

Certain specialized types of market-neutral trading—of which pairs trading is one—approach the market from a different perspective. As distinguished from long/short trading, which is simply trying to ensure that the long portfolio as a whole outperforms the short portfolio, some traders, mainly statistically arbitragers and pairs traders, try to capitalize on perceived price anomalies within a defined group of related stocks. This type of trader operates on the assumption that while these anomalies may persist in the short term, over the long term they will disappear through natural market forces in a process known as *mean reversion*. In essence, they believe that over time the relationship between these stocks will revert back to its historical average or mean.

If one considers a group of stocks all within the same industry, historically, the group will trade at an average price relationship to one another, as well as to the index of that specific industry. The long-term stability of this relationship is intuitive because the index, comprised of the stocks in that industry, is directly affected by the performance of its individual components. However, when one considers the price relationship between one of the components and the index in the short term, the relative price of the stock will tend to fluctuate both above and below its average relationship; at times a given stock will outperform the index, while at others it will underperform. The same average price relationship and fluctuations around that average exists between two stocks within the industry.

A mean reversion trader will try to buy the stocks or securities that are underpriced relative to the historical average and sell those that are overpriced. In effect this type of trader will break his investment universe down into several small subsets, ranking each subset separately. The combination of longs from each subset comprises his long portfolio and the combination of shorts from each subset comprises his short portfolio. This type of trading may use a different model for each group of stocks or may apply the same model to each subset individually, but in all cases the objective is to take an appropriate position in securities that will revert back to an expected historical price relationship.

The specific rules by which the mean reversion trader may choose to add and remove securities from either his long or short portfolio will vary from trader to trader and are largely a matter of individual style. Some traders will remove a stock when its price reverts back to the mean as expected. Others will hold the stock until it has moved back through the mean and begun to diverge in the opposite direction to some extent. Again, there are no correct ways to formulate these rules, but their creation and execution likely will have a significant effect on portfolio performance.

PAIRS TRADING: A MARKET NEUTRAL STRATEGY

Now that the basics of market-neutral strategies have been explored, it will be useful to turn the discussion to pairs trading and how it fits into the overall market-neutral framework. A useful place to begin is to provide a formal definition of pairs trading:

> *A nondirectional, relative-value investment strategy that seeks to identify two companies with similar characteristics whose equity securities are currently trading at a price relationship that is out of their historical trading range. This investment strategy will entail buying the undervalued security while short-selling the overvalued security, thereby maintaining market neutrality.*

This definition is useful in highlighting both how the strategy relates to market neutrality and how it differs from other strategies in that category. *Pairs trading* is a mean reversion trading approach that uses dollar neutrality to mitigate systematic risk. It goes beyond other similar strategies, however, because rather than building baskets of securities in both the long and short portfolio, pairs trading limits its analysis to the relationship between two stocks whose relationship forms the basis of a trade. Where other mean reversion traders may consider the relationships between individual stocks within the context of adding a stock to either the long or short portfolio, the pairs trader either buys a pair as a unit or skips the trade completely.

This specialized approach to trading analysis both differentiates the strategy from others and makes stock selection the most critical step in the trading process. During the stock selection process, traders are looking for quantifiable metrics that have strong predictive ability across a wide range of stocks. For most traders, this involves the creation of a multifactor model that can be used to rank all of the stocks in the trading universe. Pairs trading models can be fundamentally or technically driven. However, they not only fall under the special case of mean reversion models, but they go a step further by only considering mean reversion between two securities rather than mean reversion of a single security to its peers.

Under a technical approach to pairs trading, the bulk of the analysis is performed on the pair as a whole rather than to the individual stocks; the pair is created as a price ratio, the new trading entity, and then individual indicators are applied. The implication here is that stocks must be paired before the analysis is undertaken. This feature of pairs trading illustrates the importance of correlation analysis to the trading process, as it is the primary vehicle by which stocks are paired. The higher the correlation between a pair of stocks, the more likely the pair is to follow the expected mean reversion pattern. Some traders may wish to include other factors in the matching process that they believe strengthen the underlying relationship that they are trying to exploit. Regardless of the specific factors selected, the goal of the matching process within the equity universe is to ensure that the resulting pairs are highly related to one another and are likely candidates to revert to the historical relationship in cases where they have temporarily diverged.

In pairs trading, portfolio optimization requires that each pair be analyzed and determined justifiable before it is included in the portfolio. During the stock selection process, the investment model is applied to pairs that have been matched based on statistical criteria that judge the pair to be both correlated and experiencing enough divergence away from the historical mean relationship to warrant the trade. Before the trade is included, a fundamental and technical overlay should be performed to assure that the pair could be justified as sound.

The fundamental overlay involves examining each stock in the pair from a fundamental analysis perspective. The trader is not trying to become an expert on the fundamentals of each company, but rather checking to be sure that the fundamentals do not contradict his statistical and model pairing. This step does not require the trader to determine that the fundamentals of the stock he intends to buy are superior to those of the stock he intends to short, although this is an added confirmation that the trade is sound. Rather, the trader is checking to ensure that the fundamentals of the two stocks under consideration are not such that proceeding with the trade would go squarely against a clear fundamental bias in the opposite direction.

The other check that the trader performs during the fundamental overlay is on the recent and anticipated news on each stock. This check first ensures that a news-driven price shock is not responsible for a justified divergence that may persist. It also ensures that there is not a company announcement pending that may cause a price shock that could be detrimental to the trade. Some examples of the type of announcements that might lead a trader to reject a trade are current or pending earnings information, the results of potentially costly litigation or regulatory investigation, and major management shifts. In these cases, the trader would reject the pair because despite the historical price relationship between the two stocks, the trader believes that this relationship may have changed in a fundamental and permanent way; in essence, he does not believe that mean reversion will occur.

Similar to the fundamental overlay, the trader will also conduct technical and sentiment analysis on each of the stocks in his intended pair. He is again looking for arguments against the trade that would cause it to be rejected. A simple example of this would be a case in which the intended long stock appears to be under significant downward pressure and the intended short is under significant upward pressure. The technical review suggests that rather than mean reversion, the trader can expect the trade to continue its divergence. In this case, the trader would reject the trade but continue to monitor it for a reversal in technical factors that would make the trade justifiable in the near future.

In each of these cases, the trader is attempting to optimize his portfolio by excluding pairs that have strong external arguments against their success. The inclusion of this step should not suggest that the trader is second-guessing his trading model, but rather that he is assimilating useful information into the process that the model may not be designed to account for. The inclusion of these steps can have a significant positive impact on portfolio performance by eliminating some trades that would otherwise cancel the success of several other profitable trades.

THE GRAPHICS OF PAIRS TRADING

In cases when the technical trader is dealing with highly correlated pairs of stocks, before the application of technical indicators that are applicable to pairs trading, he must chart and analyze each prospective pair. By looking at the ratio between two equities, a trader can see the intervals between convergence and mean reversions, and thereby he can intelligently project the time it is likely to take a trade to achieve a desired profit objective. If a correlation analysis is done on a relatively long period of time, it is not prudent to engage in short-term trading based on this analysis. Obviously, short-term traders should apply more weight toward short-term correlation computations in order not to create a disconnect between their analysis and their expectations.

The simplest way to visualize a relationship between two equities is to chart the ratio between those two equities. A chart should be constructed by dividing one stock by the other. By doing this, a new trading vehicle is created, and from a technical viewpoint considering it as one trading unit rather than a relationship between two stocks is preferable.

Figure 13.1 shows the charts of the Diamonds Trust (DIA), the Dow Jones Industrial Average ETF, and the S&P Depositary Receipts (SPY), the S&P 500 ETF, respectively over the same time period. A cursory examination of the two charts reveals a great deal of similarity; this is not unexpected given the tendency of the major averages to move in the same direction on any given day. From the graph alone, however, it is impossible to determine how closely these price movements mirror one another.

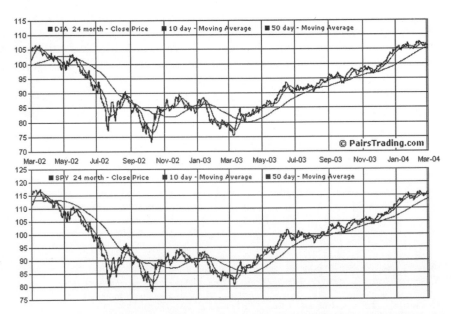

FIGURE 13.1   DIA and SPY Daily Charts with 10-Day and 50-Day Moving Averages

Without further analysis, a trader might decide that these stocks are likely to have a high statistical correlation to each other, but he has no basis on which to turn this assumption into a potentially profitable trading opportunity. A simple correlation analysis will provide support for this assumption, but it provides little additional information about the pair.

In Figure 13.2, the relative performance for the two ETFs for the same time period are plotted on the same graph. This information is more useful because it makes clear that the prices of these two instruments go through periods of relative over- or underperformance, but this information still does not provide a concrete rule by which a trader can construct profitable trades. The analysis required falls outside the scope of the skills of most directional traders; what is required is a means by which a directional trader can relate to a pairs trade in a familiar way.

In order to gain useful information about the likely behavior of the price relationship, the trader must consider the pair from a market-neutral point of view. By graphing the price ratio between the two ETFs (DIA/SPY), the trader is considering the price action of the relationship from a dollar-neutral perspective. Figure 13.3 represents the chart of the dollar-neutral price action over a specified period of time. Once the relationship is considered from this perspective, one sees quickly that employing this type of market neutrality makes trading this pair a far easier proposition. Figure 13.3 displays a price relationship that moves in a definite range over the period of time being considered. This is useful for the trader because he can now predict not only the likely direction that the pair will move, but also the degree to which the relationship is likely to change. Now that the pair has become the unified trading vehicle that is more familiar to a directional trader, he can apply the same types of analytic tools to the pair that were previously applied to single stocks or indexes.

Clearly, not every pair will produce as obvious a graphical representation as does this one, but from this example the power and importance of considering a pair from this perspective is obvious.

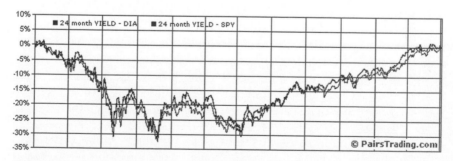

FIGURE 13.2 DIA and SPY Daily Yield Chart

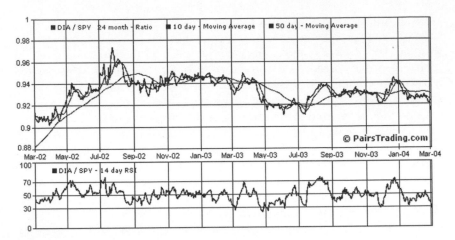

FIGURE 13.3 DIA Divided by SPY (Ratio Chart) with 14-Day RSI

THE TECHNICALS OF PAIRS TRADING

The most common indicators used in this approach can be broken into three groups: moving average indicators, market strength indicators, and volume as an indicator. Moving average indicators center on a stock's moving average for the development of the indicator and alert the trader as to whether a pair is currently above or below its historical average. These numbers can be helpful because they give a smoothed picture of the stock's price action over a given period of time. Market strength indicators are centered on the concepts of overbought and oversold. They consider how the number of buyers apparent in the market compares with the number of sellers apparent in the market. When this relationship becomes distorted, the market for a given stock is said to be either overbought or oversold. Volume as an indicator is used primarily to confirm a trader's view of other information; it is used to gauge the intensity of the underlying stock move.

While there are literally hundreds of indicators that may be applied to a pair, this chapter will only consider one to illustrate its application to a pair rather than an individual stock or security. The Relative Strength Index (RSI) is an interesting indicator because it does not measure relative strength in the classic sense. Usually, when a trader refers to the relative strength of a position, he is referring to its strength relative to the strength of an index or benchmark. In the case of RSI, the indicator is measuring the internal strength of the position relative to itself. While this seems counterintuitive, consideration of the equation and the appropriate use of its output should clarify this problem.

The RSI formula is as follows:

$$RSI = 100 - (100/[1 + RS])$$

where:

RS = Average of net up closing changes for N days/
       Average of net down closing changes for N days

The trader selects the number of days to be used; 5, 9, and 14 are standards used by most traders and are included in most commercially available software programs.

The RSI will range from just above 0 to just under 100, but it is extremely rare to see a number close to either of these extremes. Most commonly, RSI values will fluctuate between readings of 30 and 70. At extremes, it will move under 30 or above 70. Many traders prefer to use 20 and 80 to indicate oversold and overbought conditions, but the level selected is an individual preference.

An RSI value that is approaching an extreme theoretically indicates that a reversal can be expected to occur in the immediate future. Figure 13.4 depicts the chart of a stock's price action and the corresponding RSI reading. Considering the chart, one can see that extreme RSI readings (at or above 70 and at or below 30) often are associated with price reversals in the security or pair under consideration. These reversals tend to occur at or shortly after the extreme reading is taken, so the trader should not consider such a reading to be an immediate trading catalyst.

RSI measurements can be a useful tool in analyzing pairs of stocks

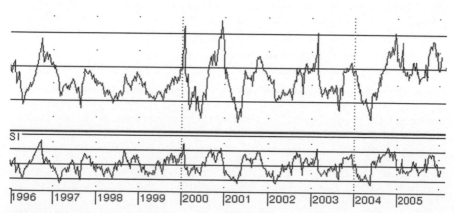

FIGURE 13.4 Oscillating Chart Pattern with RSI

and can give the technical trader a significant edge. The specifics of RSI for a price relationship of paired stocks are similar to those for an individual stock, but they may be even more pronounced. One of the ways to use RSI is to look for a divergence between the chart of the stock and RSI readings. When a divergence is detected, it may indicate a major trend reversal rather than a regular fluctuation.

No single indicator is either without flaws or sufficient as a rule for all trading decisions, and none are appropriate for all traders. Each individual must achieve a certain level of comfort with a series of indicators for them to be successful.

OPTIONS APPLICATIONS TO PAIRS TRADING

Now that the basic foundation of the theory has been discussed, the discussion of more complex applications is appropriate. To reduce risk and maximize profit potential, it is natural to apply options to an attractive strategy such as pairs trading. Options provide at least four major advantages:

1. Options can be used as a hedging instrument to reduce risk.
2. Options can be used as a speculative instrument to maximize returns.
3. Options provide leverage (less capital is needed to achieve the desired results).
4. Combinations of options open up new trading opportunities.

The majority of options strategies can be applied to pairs trading, but regardless of the specific approach chosen, the goal is to increase the probability that any given trade will be successful. A combination of pairs trading and options trading, despite its apparent complexity, is an excellent way to increase the probability of success.

The single most important factor that separates profitable traders from those who lose money is the careful application of risk management techniques. All traders would like to use a system with a perfect success rate, the holy grail of trading techniques, but this is not realistic. A prudent trader does not merely consider how much money he can make on a trade or on a portfolio, but focuses his analysis on risk management characteristics. The main questions become: How much can a trader lose if he is wrong, and what can be done to avoid or minimize those inevitable losses?

It is in this pursuit that options play an essential role.

Long Options

The first and most straightforward approach is to substitute stocks with options. Instead of buying one stock and shorting the other, one may buy calls on the long stock and buy puts on the short stock. Keep in mind that this strategy should be treated as one trade (not two different bets). The trader should open and close the two sides simultaneously. In the majority of cases, one side will be a winner and one a loser.

Recall that the goal of a market-neutral strategy is for the long portfolio to outperform the short portfolio and for profitable trades to outperform those that lose money. In the case of a simple option substitution, the trader essentially strangles a pair of stocks. It is advisable to use in-the-money or at-the-money options to avoid fighting theta decay; in case of long options strategy, time is the enemy of a trader. Options are wasting assets, meaning that time erodes the value of an option.

If the pair performs as expected (the long stock outperforms short stock, regardless of the absolute direction), it is a winning trade. Additionally, if there is a significant move up or down for both stocks (remember that these are correlated stocks expected to move in the same direction), this also produces a winning trade, regardless of which stock outperforms. Just as in a straddle or strangle strategy in a pure options trade, if there is a large enough move in one direction, one side can appreciate indefinitely, while the other can only decline to zero. Because the simple substitution of options into the pairs trading framework creates a profit not only if the underlying stocks perform as expected, but also if there is a significant directional move in both (assume relative performance is near zero), the probability that the trade will be profitable has been increased.

Selecting the appropriate expiration month is a direct function of the expected duration of the trade. The trader should select options that are sufficiently far from expiration to both allow the mean reversion process to occur and to keep time decay at a minimum. Longer-term options are more expensive because they allow more time for the option to move in favor of the owner. The goal of the pairs trader is to select options that are sufficiently far from expiration to allow the trade to work, and yet minimize the overpayment of premiums.

An additional risk management advantage of the use of an options substitution is that the trader has a maximum downside risk exposure that is equal to the premium paid for the options involved in the trade. There is, therefore, no need to place stops, be exposed to whipsaws, or be open to losses resulting from gap-opens that render stops ineffective. The maximum risk is predetermined, regardless of the price action of the underlying stocks.

A Long Option Example   From a profit potential standpoint, there are two factors working for a trader: relative performance of underlying stocks and a potential of a large move in any direction by these two correlated stocks.

For example, ABC is trading at 50, and XYZ is trading at 75. A pairs trading strategy would be to buy three shares of ABC and simultaneously sell short two shares of XYZ in order to be dollar-neutral. The long options substitution pairs trading strategy would be (at-the-money) to buy three ABC 50 calls and to buy two XYZ 75 puts.

Options Spreads

In order to be hedged on both sides of a pairs trade, the trader may wish to construct vertical spreads on both securities. The advantage of spreading a pair is that risk management parameters are embedded in a trade; the trader, therefore, does not have to be concerned about either determining the proper level for stops or that he will be unable to execute them if needed. In a typical equity pairs trade, the trader sets stops at levels he wishes to represent as the worst case scenario for that pair. When using vertical spreads, these levels are built into the trade and are literal rather than estimated levels. Vertical spreads can be done with in-the-money or out-of-the-money options with the condition that each spread is consistent with the other.

To illustrate this strategy, let's consider a bull call spread as a proxy for the long security and a bear put spread as a proxy for the short security. Once again, ABC is trading at 50 and XYZ is trading at 75.

Bull Call Spread: Long three ABC 50 calls and short three ABC 55 calls

Bear Put Spread: Long three XYZ 80 puts and short three XYZ 75 puts.

The trader needs to be cognizant of implied volatilities of options on both securities in order not to overpay for spreads. Another important factor to consider when employing this approach is that spreads have limited gain potential. In practice, therefore, the trader needs to make sure that, in case of a large move in the same direction by both securities, the maximum potential gain of one spread is larger than a maximum potential loss of the other.

Long and Short Options

Another interesting approach to applying options to pairs trading is to compare implied volatilities of the two stocks in a pair. If there is a divergence in implied volatilities of the two analyzed securities, this presents another arbitrage opportunity.

Assume that options on ABC are more expensive than XYZ. Rather than buying ABC and selling short XYZ, as an equity pairs trade, the trader might consider selling expensive options and buying relatively cheap options while still preserving a pairs trading approach. One would sell ABC puts (a neutral or bullish bet on ABC) and buy puts on XYZ (a bearish bet on XYZ).

If the underlying stocks appreciate, the options will expire worthless, and the trader will have captured the difference in the premium on the puts. The same outcome holds true if both stocks remain at the same price by expiration. If both stocks go down and ABC outperforms XYZ as expected (XYZ declines more than ABC), there is a potentially unlimited profit potential. This strategy can lose money only if a trader's pairs trading analysis is wrong and the underlying stock on the short side of the trade outperforms the one on the long side.

As an example, with ABC trading at 50 and XYZ trading at 75, a pairs trading strategy would be to buy three shares of ABC and simultaneously sell short two shares of XYZ in order to be dollar-neutral.

A long/short options strategy would be to sell three ABC 50 puts (more expensive options) and to buy two XYZ 75 puts. The trader must make sure that the premium received for ABC puts is larger that the premium paid for XYZ puts.

IMPLIED VOLATILITY

Implied volatility (IV) is a measure of a theoretical value designed to represent the expected future volatility of the security underlying the option. The factors that affect implied volatility are the exercise price, the risk-free rate of return, maturity date of the option, and the premium (price of the option). Implied volatility appears in several option pricing models, including the Black-Scholes model, and can be a valuable tool to the pairs trader.

It is important to distinguish between the implied volatility of a security and the corresponding *real volatility* (RV) on that same security. Although IV is highly correlated to RV, IV levels incorporate the anticipation of future price movements of a security into the calculation. For example, IV can increase dramatically before an earnings announcement or a government report that is expected to affect the price of the stock. Options become more expensive in anticipation of a potential move of a stock. Options also become more expensive during price declines due to the expected rising demand for hedging activity and increase in real volatility. It is interesting to note that changes in IV have very little predictive value of future RV of a security, but serve as a solid measure of sentiment within the market regarding the security in question.

From a market-neutral perspective, the most important observation that can be made from analyzing IV is the fact that correlated securities show consistently correlated IVs. To an even greater extent than other measures, IVs tend to show mean-reverting patterns. The difference in IV of two or more correlated securities also shows very stable mean-reverting characteristics. This phenomenon is explained by the fact that the IVs of two option contracts with the same maturity must mean-revert at expiration. This feature does not imply the possibility of constructing a risk-free trade, however, because future prices of securities remain unknown. What is significant is that certainty of a single component of a trade can shift the probability of a successful outcome rather dramatically.

This implied volatility discussion opens up a considerably different approach to pairs trading. Instead of arbitraging prices of correlated securities, the trader may choose to arbitrage implied volatilities of two securities—in other words, selling IV on one stock and buying IV of another stock. Since there are no direct instruments that allow trading implied volatility, a trader needs to construct options strategies on both stocks that can create an IV arbitrage situation.

Trade Construction Examples

Each of the following examples is based on the assumption that stock ABC is trading at 50, and each includes a graph that illustrates possible outcomes of the trade.

Buying Implied Volatility   A trader can buy implied volatility by buying a straddle or a strangle. Buying a *straddle* involves the purchase of an equal number of puts and calls of the same strike price and the same maturity. Buying a *strangle* involves a purchase of an equal number of puts and calls of *different strike prices* and the same maturity. Increasing implied volatility means that purchased options (both puts and calls) become more expensive. Furthermore, a large price move can produce potentially unlimited gains. The risk is limited to the premium paid for options. Time decay (theta), however, represents a disadvantage.

Example of straddle:
Long 10 December 50 calls
Long 10 December 50 puts

Example of strangle:

Long 10 December 55 calls

Long 10 December 45 puts

Figure 13.5 illustrates the four possible outcomes of this trade:

1. The bold solid line shows what happens at expiration.
2. The lower dashed line shows what happens if IV declines by 30 percent today.
3. The upper dashed line shows what happens if IV advances by 30 percent today.
4. The bold dashed line shows what happens if IV remains the same today.

Neutralizing Gamma and Delta This is a more elegant way to be long IV. The best way to construct this strategy is to create a calendar ratio spread. This means that the trader buys a larger number of calls of longer maturity and sells a smaller number of calls of shorter maturity at the same strike price, in order to neutralize gamma. The correct number of contracts needed to properly construct the trade can be determined through the use of any commercially available options software.

The next step is to sell short an appropriate number of shares of the underlying stock in order to neutralize delta. The beauty of this strategy is that theta is relatively neutral; therefore time decay does not play an important role. The worst-case scenario is a limited loss, while the

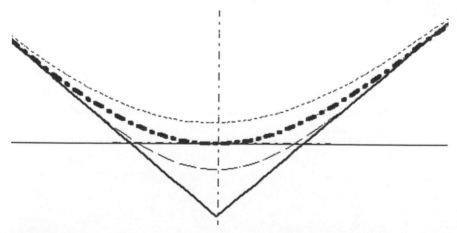

FIGURE 13.5 Profit/Loss Scenarios of Long Straddle Options Strategy

theoretical gain is unlimited, just as it was when using a straddle or strangle strategy.

For example, with ABC is trading at 50, this strategy could contain the following components:

> Example of calendar ratio spread:
>> Long 10 February 50 calls
>> Short 6 January 50 calls
>> Short 300 shares of ABC stock

Figure 13.6 illustrates the four possible outcomes of this trade:

1. The bold solid line shows what happens at expiration.
2. The lower dashed line shows what happens if IV declines by 30 percent today.
3. The upper dashed line shows what happens if IV advances by 30 percent today.
4. The bold dashed line shows what happens if IV remains the same today.

Selling Implied Volatility   Selling IV can be accomplished by two strategies: selling a straddle or selling a strangle. Selling a straddle involves a sale of an equal number of puts and calls of the same strike price and of the same maturity. Selling a strangle involves a sale of an equal

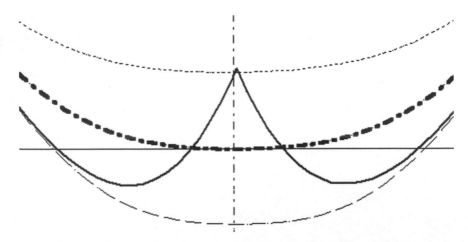

FIGURE 13.6 Profit/Loss Scenarios of Delta and Gamma Neutral Options Strategy

number of puts and calls of different strike prices and the same maturity. Decreasing implied volatility means that sold options (both puts and calls) become less expensive. The disadvantage of shorting options is potentially unlimited loss in case of a large price move of the underlying security. Time decay (theta) represents a major advantage of shorting options due to the fact that options lose premium as they approach expiration.

Example of straddle:

> Short 10 December 50 calls
>
> Short 10 December 50 puts

Example of strangle:

> Short 10 December 55 calls
>
> Short 10 December 45 puts

Figure 13.7 illustrates the four possible outcomes of this trade:

1. The bold solid line shows what happens at expiration.
2. The upper dashed line shows what happens if IV declines by 30 percent today.
3. The lower dashed line shows what happens if IV advances by 30 percent today.
4. The bold dashed line shows what happens if IV remains the same today.

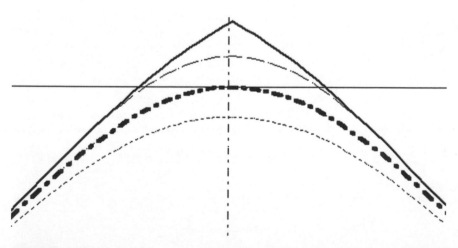

FIGURE 13.7 Profit/Loss Scenarios of Short Straddle or Strangle Options Strategy

Reverse Calendar Spread   A reverse calendar spread involves buying shorter-maturity options and selling longer-maturity options of the
same strike price. A trader may choose this strategy in order to avoid a potentially large loss, just as in a case of selling straddles or strangles. A reverse calendar spread has a limited loss, which is an advantage, but time
decay represents a negative factor.

Example of reverse calendar spread:
   Long 10 January 50 calls
   Short 10 February 50 calls

Figure 13.8 illustrates the four possible outcomes of this trade:

1. The bold solid line shows what happens at expiration.
2. The upper dashed line shows what happens if IV declines by 30 percent today.
3. The lower dashed line shows what happens if IV advances by 30 percent today.
4. The bold dashed line shows what happens if IV remains the same
   today.

There are numerous other ways to trade implied volatility in a context
of pairs trading. The preceding examples are the most common and the
most effective ones. Implied volatility arbitrage strategy has a high proba-

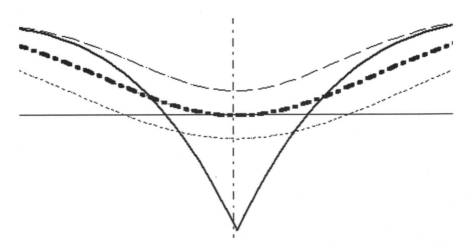

FIGURE 13.8   Profit/Loss Scenarios of Reverse Calendar Spread Options Strategy

bility of a successful outcome if executed correctly, but a trader needs to be aware of execution costs and liquidity issues.

CONCLUSION

This chapter illustrates that there are alternative methods to trading. There are numerous instruments, underutilized by traders, which if used properly can substantially increase the probability and consistency of success in this difficult endeavor. Adding these tools and methodologies to one's arsenal creates an advantage in terms of risk management and probabilities as well as opening up new possibilities. Hopefully this discussion has helped broaden your horizons as a trader.

Beyond the Horizon

Fari Hamzei

It's the unconquerable soul of man, not the nature
of the weapons he uses, that insures victory.
—General George S. Patton

Throughout history, the ability to see over the horizon has brought the warrior a strategic advantage. Those who can detect what lies ahead gain an unprecedented superiority in the battle space. In the U.S. Air Force, that role is tasked to the Boeing E-3 Sentry, the Airborne Warning and Control System (AWACS), integrating sophisticated airborne radar with a high-altitude platform full of supercomputers and exotic sensors to continuously sweep the battle space several hundred miles away, looking for friendly or for aircraft. In our increasingly complex financial market conditions, with geopolitical and economic uncertainties, traders and investors need to equip themselves with the same kind of beyond-the-horizon view.

Although some technical models and sophisticated structural tools can be deployed to predict the likelihood of a particular event occurring in the nearby time slice, the longer the time frame, the less accurate technical and structural analyses become. When perspective shifts from the coming days and weeks to months and multiyear time frames, traders and investors must employ a different kind of radar for the market. They must shift from the technical and structural analyses to fundamental analysis.

The fundamental view is grounded in company and sector-specific operational and financial data, enabling projections and probabilities to be formed from that vantage point. For example, looking at the events of today and the forces and trends that are emerging, one can project such things as the potential for supply/demand imbalances, geopolitical scenarios, and the likelihood of a worsening or an improving economy. The technical view, on the other hand, is based on price, volume, moving averages, relative strength, and other indicators that are constantly changing. The structural analysis gets even fuzzier. The farther out one looks, the less accurate the purely technical and structural views become. For these reasons, when looking beyond the horizon for economic, geopolitical, and market-based factors that will likely influence our world and our markets in the next 2, 5, 10, or more years, we must look through a fundamental lens.

The fundamental view of the proverbial macro picture is no different than what long-term investors use when buying a stock. Technical analysis may be utilized to identify a stock that is basing or that has exhibited indications of early buying interest. Once it is on the radar, fundamental factors come into play: Does the trader or investor like the business or sector that the company is in? What about the financials? What is the opinion about management? In the post–Sarbanes-Oxley era, such information is not only more readily available, but even more critical. No matter what the chart indicates right now, for the long-term story one must go to the fundamentals. The industry that a company is in now will likely be the one it is in for at least the next few years. Certainly, companies can change industries, whether through acquisitions, divestitures, or development of new product lines, but these strategic moves tend to happen slowly. The core competencies of a company dictate the industry it is in today and where it will most likely make its profits tomorrow.

Taking a fundamental look at economic and political factors as of this writing, with the first quarter of 2006 coming to a close, we see continued conflict in the Middle East, energy consumption and supplies that could easily be disrupted by geopolitical events, inflation concerns, the weakness of the dollar, questions about the strength of the U.S. economy, the rise of China and India as economic powers, and a world population that has surpassed 6.5 billion and will close in on 8 billion in a few years. With this insight, we can deduce what *may* occur in the years ahead. It goes without saying that there is no way to be absolutely certain about what *will* occur. The best minds in government, economics, and on Wall Street can be and have been wrong before. This long-term fundamental view, however, helps one to be prepared or at least watchful for events as they begin to unfold and break over the horizon.

A BRIEF HISTORY OF THE FUNDAMENTAL VIEW

My introduction to the fundamental view beyond the horizon began back in the mid-1990s when I was a student of Professor Richard Roll of the UCLA Anderson Graduate School of Management. Professor Roll had been a vice president at Goldman, Sachs & Co., and founded and directed its mortgage-backed securities research group.

Back in the mid-1990s, Roll predicted that interest rates would drop to record lows around the turn of the century—levels that had not been seen in 30 or 40 years. I had taken Roll's course because I was trading Treasury bond futures at the time. When he made this pronouncement, my body was shaking: I knew then that the move that had begun with then-Secretary of the Treasury Lloyd Bentsen, in concert with the guidance from his successor, Goldman Sachs' ex-Co-Chairman Robert Rubin, would not just eliminate the issuance of new 30-year Treasury bonds per se, but would also start a deliberate effort to pay down the massive U.S. government debt by first balancing the federal budget.

The term structure of the interest rates is a montage of the future expectations of our global bond market participants. With the perception that the U.S. government will be able to better manage its finances through careful tax increases and shrinking defense spending in the post–Cold War era, the government would be able to decrease its appetite for borrowing. This would in turn create less and less demand for the long end of the yield curve, and someday in the future, with the budget surplus generated, one could pay down the national debt. This made absolute sense to me. The only thing I hadn't counted on was the impact of the upcoming globalization, including the explosion in instant availability of information.

Other events would also influence the interest rate scenario, hastening the actualization of Roll's prediction. In 1998, a hedge fund backed by the brainpower of geniuses—Long Term Capital Management (LTCM)—failed. It was the first salvo of hedge fund and corporate banking malfeasance that would rock both Wall Street and the U.S. banking system, with a potentially negative impact on the overall economy if it was left unattended. Long Term Capital Management had seriously overencumbered its assets to multiple lenders, resulting in a fictitious balance sheet. No one had dared to question the truth and credibility of what LTCM presented. That changed when Russia defaulted on its domestic debt. LTCM could not liquidate its vast holdings, and its supposedly perfect hedging strategy imploded. The rise and fall of LTCM over about a two-year time frame showed how Wall Street was moving at a faster pace—a tempo that would quicken in the years to come. Moreover, the fall of LTCM was an early example of the corporate scandals that continue to shake Wall Street to this day: Enron, WorldCom, Tyco, HealthSouth . . .

Corporate scandals and malfeasance awakened the sleeping watching dogs that had been lulled into complacency by the rising stock market. Who would want to raise a fuss while things were good and everyone—including individual investors—was getting richer? When the NASDAQ bubble burst and the market declined sharply, however, the watchdogs started howling. The horrific terrorist attacks of September 11, 2001, sent shock waves through already weakening markets. The terror attacks slowed down the economy, especially in the transportation and hospitality sectors, and hastened the decline of the stock market. A rapid rise in the defense sector was not nearly adequate to offset the overall decline of the markets. Problems had been fomenting for years on Wall Street, creating some structural issues in the financial world. With the decline in the stock market, these problems were now in the spotlight.

To respond, the Federal Reserve began introducing massive liquidity by printing hard cash to the point that interest rates moved to artificially low levels. Where did the cash go? Real estate. After September 11, individual investors had little interest in stocks. Taking advantage of cheap interest rates and a strong nesting instinct that was overtaking the country, people bought houses: bigger, new, and grander. They pumped their own money into houses that would become their refuges, filling them with expensive creature comforts such as big-screen televisions and gourmet kitchens. Wall Street responded with more exotic mortgage-backed securities that capitalized on this housing trend. All this domestic building in concert with strong demand from the growing economies of China and India, however, sparked a significant rise in demand for basic materials. With the Fed's policy of keeping the economy afloat on ample cheap money, no one seemed to notice the inherent inflationary effects of more expensive materials.

The warning signs of inflation were there and still are, including increased demand for energy and higher gold and silver prices. This is the landscape of mid-2006, as of this writing. Wall Street has largely cleaned up its act. The major corporate scandal lawsuits have been paraded out in the financial media. Interest rates have begun to edge up from artificially low levels, and cheap money is getting tighter and tighter. As we scan the horizon and try to peer beyond the limits of what we can clearly see, inflation and debt are two major issues to watch.

SCANNING THE ECONOMIC HORIZON

Higher energy prices and more expensive basic materials will continue to affect the economic outlook. Exotic mortgages that allowed homeowners to move from 3,000-square-foot homes to 5,000 and 6,000 square feet may become a problem as rates move higher, causing what looked like cheap loans to become unaffordable nightmares. The other scenario is the adjustable rate mortgage (ARM) resets, the impact of which could be felt for years to come.

Energy will become an even more critical issue, not only because of the conflict and geopolitics of the major oil-producing region, but also because of increasing demand. Gasoline prices of $3-plus per gallon have not soured the American appetite for monster-sized SUVs. Add to that the economic development of China—where only a fraction of the population currently has cars—and the new economic powerhouse of India, and the world will face an unprecedented long-term crisis of energy consumption. On the supply side, there are major questions about availability. One uncertainty is Iran, and whether the U.N. Security Council will impose sanctions over its nuclear ambitions and, if so, whether those sanctions would be effective. Of course, in that scenario, available crude oil supplies for the West will be further tightened. Major concerns over the future viability of the Saudi oilfields have also been raised, including by oil expert and author Matthew R. Simmons (author of *Twilight in the Desert*, Hoboken, NJ: John Wiley & Sons, 2005). Gasoline refining capacity, particularly in the United States, is also problematic because virtually no new capacity has been planned. (A refinery being developed in Arizona is the first new refinery construction in the United States in 30 years). Older refineries along the Gulf of Mexico have demonstrated their vulnerability to natural disasters.

Inflation, energy, a potential softening or even collapse of the housing market in pockets where prices rose too fast to unrealistic levels, and burgeoning U.S. government debt are fundamental factors that cannot be ignored. How will it all play out in the market? Some scenarios are worth considering.

The topping of the real estate market, particularly in the frothy areas where those who sell early can make big profits, will result in windfalls of cash for some. These early, savvy investors will then have money to invest, which will not likely go toward a second or even third home. Rather, they will turn once again to the equities market. Investors will likely be drawn to such economic activities as capital expenditures—including technology upgrades by companies—and heavy machine tools. Many infrastructure investments that were put off are now coming due. As companies upgrade, demand for infrastructure, from cell towers to computer networks, will rise.

In energy, an insatiable world appetite for oil, along with higher crude oil prices, will support the development of alternative energy sources. This will also be facilitated through more derivative products for both speculation and hedging. A strange bright spot in an otherwise grim picture of oil is the likelihood that expensive energy and supply concerns could slow down the economy. That will help ease the supply/demand imbalance, but from the view of the equities market it is an obvious negative factor. A slowing economy would exacerbate other problems as well, including consumer solvency and the ability to service mega-mortgages and the U.S. debt levels, which are needed to finance military operations abroad.

Another scarce resource that is gaining increasing notice is water. Growing populations, particularly in areas that have experienced growth beyond the current capacity of the local water resources, raise concerns about water supplies. This will create tension and opportunities, mirroring the energy supply/demand picture.

This is a tumultuous view beyond the horizon, underscoring the challenges that face our national leaders in the age of terror, scarce resources, global warming, and a world population that is headed toward the 7 billion mark. For the investor, speculator, and trader, these scenarios also make for even more challenging market conditions. Yet the role of the markets will be imperative. As most students of the market recall, the stock market was founded to give companies access to capital, and options and futures markets were established to help transfer risk for producers and consumers. In the age of complex derivatives, a truly global marketplace, and instant dissemination of information, the markets will continue to play an important role for risk transfer as well as speculation.

NAVIGATING THE UNCERTAINTIES

To navigate the uncertainties, however, new and more sophisticated strategies will be necessary, many of which have been discussed in this book. The mission of this book has been to provide a series of bright spots in both theme and methods to turn one's hard-earned dollars into bigger nest eggs for the future. Although the future is uncertain, and there is no guarantee that what we experienced in the past will be repeated, history does offer some comfort. We know that every 10 years or so, a particular sector outshines everything else. In the 1980s it was the financial sector, in the wake of deregulation and the advent of tools and vehicles that allowed companies to get more efficient, particularly in merger and acquisition activity. In the 1990s, information technology boomed. Venture-capital tax incentives from the Reagan era began to pay off in the 1990s, which helped incubate the technology sector and such things as the Internet and rapid miniaturization of semiconductors. As technology rose to the forefront, Intel, Cisco, and Microsoft were added to the Dow Jones Industrial Average—certainly companies that would not have been thought of previously as typical Dow components.

The next frontier, I believe, will be biotech. As we approach the end of this decade and enter the next, maturing and retiring baby boomers will be the catalyst for an explosive movement in health care costs. Interestingly, the boom in information technology and the development of faster and more powerful computers along with ever-cheaper memory prices assures the biotech industry of the tools it needs to develop the next generation of fantastic, cutting-edge drugs and medical devices. We project that demand from aging baby boomers who desire quality of life and health beyond that experienced by previous generations will lead to an expanding role of the biotech industry in our economy.

The anticipated boom in biotech will not benefit every pharmaceutical and medical device company to the same degree. Indeed, as we've seen in recent years, what looked like promising therapies—Vioxx, for example—can be fraught with problems. Therefore, investors need to be discerning as they examine the fundamental landscape of this sector. As David Miller suggests in his chapter, one way to approach investment opportunities in this sector is not to chase the big names, but rather to examine the second tier.

Looking ahead, we would expect volatility to remain relatively low. What will be more notable, however, will be the shape of the volatility curve. Given the efficiencies of the markets, increased liquidity, and the magnitude of the players—including the U.S. government—we would expect short periods when volatility will spike. Overall, however, volatility will likely remain in line with current levels. This environment will likely lead to growth in derivatives, including new futures and options products. To capitalize on the low-volatility, high-liquidity environment and the need for greater leverage, option funds will also grow in number and popularity. As Jon Najarian observes in his chapter, the era of the small, individual market maker has ended, and the age of the market taker, including the mammoth trading houses and funds, has already begun.

As a student of the volatility indexes (such as VIX, VXO, and VXN), as designed by Professor Robert Whaley of Duke University and implemented by Alex Jacobson (among others at CBOE), I have come to understand that the absolute levels of volatility are not as meaningful as the changes and patterns in the volatility. In particular, one needs to watch the patterns that immediately *precede* the change in volatility. Astute minds in volatility, such as those at Lehman Brothers, in their research are emphasizing the shape of the VIX curve before a sudden change in volatility. This underscores that the overriding factor is not the absolute value, but the shape of the volatility pattern and what it reveals about market behavior. This is a critical factor that has been overlooked by the financial media, which continues to focus at the absolute value of the VIX.

The individual trader and investor must also focus on volatility cycles, and not the statistical volatility, which provides a rearview-mirror look at market behavior. Rather, the volatility of each individual stock or index must be derived in accordance with VXO protocols, using these volatility cycles to better time stock and derivative transactions.

The view over the horizon is mixed, with bright spots of opportunity and storm clouds of concerns. The walk down Wall Street could very well be tumultuous at times. I am not bearish, however, about the markets or investment in general. In fact, overall I am positive and upbeat, but with the caveat of caution and discernment. The best rewards will go to those who pick individual stocks and commodities using sophisticated tools. As we see in market sectors such as biotechnology, the higher technology wins. The same holds true in the investment arena.

The investment time frame of this decade and out to 2010–2020 will yield many fundamental themes. Rather than chase opportunities or bet on a trend before it emerges, one has to proceed with caution. Assessing opportunities across the global landscape, India—a democracy with economic expansion in areas such as automobile parts and outsourcing—appears to be a natural. (In its March 6, 2006 issue, *Newsweek* noted that more than 125 of the Fortune 500 companies have research and development bases in India. The country is expected to rank number three among world economies in 2040.) Although China's population and growing consumer appetites are also appealing, its political climate signals caution for investors. Even the prospect of democracy arriving in China raises the question of how peaceful that transition might be. From a political perspective, the European Union is more conservative and stable, sporting the largest consumer market, and its expanding venture capital base will likely yield some opportunities. A larger concern there is the possibility that its economic growth could be slow or even stagnant in the years to come. This might produce a trading range for European markets, which favors derivative players but not the traditional investor.

The conundrum of the Middle East is not easily reconciled, but if one takes a long-term view of the next 25 years or so, more hopeful scenarios emerge. I believe that real peace will come to the Middle East one day, with the emergence of democracy and an end of the hostilities among Israelis and Palestinians. When that occurs, the economic opportunities will be unparalleled. The confluence of cultural wealth, natural resources, and educated people will yield a fertile crescent of economic expansion and investment opportunity. I would go so far as to say a robust and transparent marketplace will one day be established in the Middle East, which would have the potential of outpacing other global indexes. It may be located in Tel Aviv or perhaps Baghdad, which seems fitting for the cradle of civilization.

As the 1980s and 1990s taught us, investors have no fear for their peace and safety. They discover niches and exploit them. This same desire to discover opportunities will drive future investment activity, but with the realization of geopolitical tensions, the constant threat of terrorism, and economic shocks possible from factors such as interest rates, basic material costs, energy supplies, water resources, and population explosion. This reality results in a different world in front of us, a sobering moment that reveals the complexity of this brave new world of investments. The brave, however, continue to march forward into the future, armed with the best early warning tools that provide a strategic advantage.

About the Author

Fari Hamzei is the founder of Hamzei Analytics, LLC (www.Hamzei Analytics.com), which is in its eighth year of providing cutting-edge proprietary analysis and indicators to institutional and professional traders.

Hamzei Analytics tied for first place in stock market timing in a national ranking competition by *Timer Digest* for the last 90 days, 180 days, and 52 weeks, as of May 8, 2006.

Mr. Hamzei is a member of the faculty of the Options Institute of the Chicago Board Options Exchange (CBOE), and presents at its Options Institute Master Session (OIMS) for serious traders and investors in Chicago. He is also a frequent speaker at International Securities Exchange (ISE) educational options conferences. Additionally, he presented in May 2006 at the optionsXpress's "optionsXpo 2006" in Chicago, an educational event for retail investors and traders. Recognized for its in-depth and unique commentary and analysis of the stock market, and in particular options and equity index futures, Hamzei Analytics, is dedicated to providing quantitative market analysis. Hamzei Analytics, features sentiment data in real time for 500 of the most active indexes, equities, sector HOLDRs, and index-tracking stocks.

Frequently quoted by CNBC, Bloomberg and RealMoney.com. Mr. Hamzei is also featured on TradeStation.com and eSignal.com forums. He has spoken at numerous trading and investment forums in the United States and Canada and has written several articles that have been published in *Technical Analysis of Stocks and Commodities* magazine and on the eSignal.com website. He is also the group leader of the Los Angeles eSignal/TradeStation/RealTick/MetaStock Users Group (www.Active-Traders.org).

Mr. Hamzei is a graduate of Princeton University with a BSE degree in financial engineering, and was a director of strategic planning at Northrop Grumman Corporation, Aircraft Group.

About the Contributors

Frank Barbera, CMT, is a co-manager of the Caruso Fund, a multi-million-dollar hedge fund that seeks to make gains trading precious metals, stocks, and currencies. He began his career in the early 1980s working with John Bollinger at Financial News Network in Los Angeles. After FNN, Frank spent 10 years as an on-air market analyst for KWHY-TV in Los Angeles. His first money management position was at the Kavanaugh Fund in Santa Monica, a hedge fund subsidiary of Goldman Sachs. His technical work in gold and gold stocks is considered among the best in the industry.

Greg Collins is the chief operating officer and a portfolio manager of an Orlando-based hedge fund managed by Tuttle Asset Management, LLC. He also serves as chief executive officer of the institutional investment research firm Fountain Hill Investments, LLC. Mr. Collins is the former editor-in-chief of the financial commentary website Minyanville.com. Previously he worked with a Boston-based hedge fund as an analyst and trader. His career began in sales with SG Cowen and later at Lehman Brothers, covering mid-market institutional and bank clients, and he has spent the last eight years analyzing the market via a blended technical and fundamental approach.

Timothy Corliss is a partner and director of trading at Sierra Global Management, a $300 million fund that invests primarily in European equities and derivatives. Sierra Global offers three distinct strategies: a long/short hedge fund strategy, a hedged long strategy, and a concentrated long strategy. Prior to joining Sierra in 2000, he was a senior trader with the State of New Jersey, Division of Investment, where he implemented international equity and fixed income trading strategies for its investment programs. Before that, he was an associate with Bankers Trust for eight years on its Global Markets Proprietary Trading Desk.

Jeff deGraaf, CFA, CMT, is chief technical analyst at Lehman Brothers and a perennially top-ranked technical analyst on Wall Street, having earned *Institutional Investor*'s top honor in the 2005 edition. His 15 years of experience and keen sense of market history provide investors with perspective and clarity, while his CFA charter-holder and economic background provide a valuable link between the fundamental and technical process. A managing director at Lehman Brothers, he is a member of the firm's Investment Policy committee and is continually conducting cutting-edge research to further the investment process and technical discipline.

Phil Erlanger, CMT, is president of Phil Erlanger Research. He was Advest's chief technical analyst in the 1980s, and spent five years as senior technical analyst for Fidelity Management. He is a two-time past president of the Market Technicians Association, and won their Best of the Best Award for Computer Assisted Analysis in 1997. He has lectured at universities such as Rutgers, MIT, Boston University, and Emory, and as an adjunct professor at Bentley College, where he taught technical analysis.

Alex Jacobson is the vice president of education at the International Securities Exchange (ISE). From 1985 to 2000, he was with the Chicago Board Options Exchange (CBOE), most recently as vice president of business development. During his tenure at CBOE, he was instrumental in developing its liaison to the brokerage community. He was also significantly involved in the initial development of the Options Industry Council and is a founding member of the Options Institute. Prior to 1985, he was a top-producing broker and options trainer at Merrill Lynch, Pierce, Fenner and Smith, Inc.

Dennis Leontyev is president and chief investment officer of Experity Group, LLC, a growing hedge fund company. At Experity Group, he is also the portfolio manager of two market-neutral derivatives hedge funds. He has 14 years experience in the financial industry with expertise in trading and hedge fund management, with substantial experience in futures, options, and equity trading. He is also the options strategist and editor of the Hamzei Analytics Options Trading Service (HOTS).

David Miller is the CEO and co-founder of Biotech Stock Research, LLC, publisher of *Biotech Monthly*. Launched in October 2001, Biotech Stock Research (www.BiotechStockResearch.com) combines a monthly newsletter format with alerts on breaking news on more than two dozen development-stage biotechnology companies under coverage. His firm is one of the few independent research firms in that it accepts no money from the companies it covers, does no outside consulting in the biotech space, runs no mutual or hedge fund, and is 100 percent subscription-supported. In addition, David was CEO of a successful technology company and a university professor.

Jon "Doctor J" Najarian is a co-founder and partner of www.Insideoptions.com an online publisher of financial commentary about the derivatives markets and www.OptionMonster.com, an information portal that provides retail investors with access to the easiest and fastest source for news, market research, stock and especially options information. Jon has been a trader since 1981 and through investment trusts still owns seats on the NYSE, CBOE and CBOT. Since 1994 'Doctor J' has been a business correspondent for Fox television and is the host of the CBS radio, "Taking

Care of Business with Doctor J," which airs in Chicago and is available on iTunes. He also appears daily on www.FirstBusiness.us, a business news magazine that airs on CBS, ABC, NBC, Fox, and UPN networks in over 200 cities across the U.S.

Tim Ord is the president, editor and publisher of "The Ord Oracle," established in 1990, which is an electronic advisory newsletter that recommends S&P, NASDAQ, and gold stocks trades. He is frequently listed in the top 10 market timers in the country. *Timer Digest* ranked Tim No. 5 in gains for the S&P and No. 2 for gold timer in 2004. He has more than 25 years of trading experience and placed fourth nationally in the option division in the United States Trading Championship in 1988.

Steve Shobin is the vice chairman at AmeriCap Advisers, LLC. He is a former managing director of Lehman Brothers, where he was an adviser to the Soros Fund and to Stanley Druckenmiller, and a former first vice president of Merrill Lynch. A veteran of more than three decades on Wall Street, he developed unique methodologies for projecting the long-term trends of stocks and industry groups, incorporating various techniques for controlling risk. He has advised some of the world's largest mutual funds, hedge funds, and institutional investment managers on stock selection and portfolio structuring. He has been a member of the *Institutional Investor* All-American Research Team in 1997, 1998, 1999, and received a number one ranking in the year 2000 just as he was leaving Lehman to join AmeriCap.

Jeffrey Spotts, CMT, is a hedge fund manager for Prophecy Funds. He has more than 16 years of experience providing portfolio management to corporations, institutions, and high-net-worth clients. He began his career in 1989 at Merrill Lynch where he was responsible for over $500 million of client assets under management. In May 2001, he launched Prophecy Asset Management, a technically managed hedge fund. Jeff provides technical market commentary to Bloomberg TV and teaches a behavioral finance segment of a graduate studies course for several colleges.

Kai-Teh Tao is the president of Asgard Management, LLC, an institutional money management firm that opportunistically invests utilizing proprietary fundamental research derived from its broad network of contacts. He was formerly chief investment officer and principal managing director of Watson Asset Management, which subsequently became Watchpoint Asset Management. Prior to that, he had been a portfolio manager working with the flagship Watson Investment Partners Fund, as well as launching its sister fund, the Watson Offshore Fund. In 1999, he began the Watson Small-Cap Fund.

Kevin Tuttle is the president and chief equity strategist of Tuttle Asset Management. He is also the co-founder of the Orlando-based investment firm Church Street Capital, LLC, and currently runs a managed growth portfolio for high-net-worth clientele. Prior to Church Street Capital, he worked at Wachovia Securities Financial Network, First Union Securities, JW Genesis, and a small regional firm where he began his career in 1992.

Index